SPECIAL OPERATIONS
DURING THE
AMERICAN REVOLUTION

SPECIAL OPERATIONS
DURING THE
AMERICAN REVOLUTION

ROBERT L. TONSETIC

CASEMATE

Philadelphia & Oxford

Published in the United States of America and Great Britain in 2013 by
CASEMATE PUBLISHERS
908 Darby Road, Havertown, PA 19083
and
10 Hythe Bridge Street, Oxford, OX1 2EW

ISBN 978-1-61200-165-4
Digital Edition: ISBN 978-1-61200-166-1

Cataloging-in-publication data is available from the Library of Congress
and the British Library.

10 9 8 7 6 5 4 3 2 1

Printed and bound in the United States of America.

For a complete list of Casemate titles please contact:

CASEMATE PUBLISHERS (US)
Telephone (610) 853-9131, Fax (610) 853-9146
E-mail: casemate@casematepublishing.com

CASEMATE PUBLISHERS (UK)
Telephone (01865) 241249, Fax (01865) 794449
E-mail: casemate-uk@casematepublishing.co.uk

CONTENTS

MAPS

For
Polly Ingram Tonsetic

PROLOGUE

To understand the origins of special operations during the American Revolutionary War, one must have a clear view of warfare on the North American continent during the preceding 168 years. From the founding of first English settlement at Jamestown, Virginia in 1607, English colonists and explorers were in contact with Native Americans. Native Americans lived in tribal societies; the lifestyle, culture, and method of warfare of the various tribes varied greatly, and was closely connected to the natural environment in which they lived.

Along the Atlantic seaboard, where the first settlers landed, the land was forested with fresh, flowing rivers and streams, and an abundance of game and fish. While there were disputes, and inter-tribal wars, the level of violence never escalated to the level of total war and annihilation. Tactics were heavily dependent on speed, mobility, and surprise, and warriors would skillfully exploit the terrain to quickly approach within striking distance of their enemies. Typical operations included raids against enemy villages, and ambushes of small groups of enemy warriors in heavily forested areas. Hunting and scouting were integral to the lifestyle of Native Americans, and warriors used the same skills in warfare—stealth and concealment were routinely employed when closing in and surrounding an enemy. Weapons proficiency was also a highly prized attribute in a warrior. For long-range combat warriors relied on the bow and arrow, and for close-in fighting, clubs, the stone hatchet and the tomahawk were the weapons of choice. Casualties among combatants were usually limited in number, and the warriors usually spared the women and children of their adversaries, preferring to take them captive and integrate them into the tribe. There was, however, one practice inherent in native warfare that was abhorrent by European standards—male captives, including wounded prisoners, were subjected to ritual torture and execution. Some historians and anthropologists suggest that these practices acted as emotional compensation to the participants for practicing some level of restraint in combat.[1]

Native Americans also went to great lengths to protect their villages and families from enemy raiding parties. Defensive measures included the use of log palisades around their villages, within which their wives and children could take refuge. Sentries were also posted on avenues of approach to the village on a 24-hour basis to provide early warning of an enemy raid. If marauding war parties could not gain entry to the fort through stealth, a siege was sometimes mounted, however, these sieges were usually short since supplies and provisions were stockpiled within the stockade. Native Americans did not burn fortified enemy villages due to the risk posed to noncombatants.

In the early 1600s, the English began to arrive in North America and establish colonies along the eastern seaboard, first at Jamestown on Virginia's tidewater peninsula, and then in New England, establishing the Plymouth Colony, and later the Connecticut and Rhode Island colonies. At first, the Native Americans did not perceive the small numbers of Englishmen as a threat to their culture or way of life. Rather they viewed the curious new arrivals as trading partners and potential allies against rival tribes. When colonists began to arrive in ever-increasing numbers and began to expand their holdings, clearing forests and planting crops, it became apparent to the tribes and their leaders that their way of life was under threat by the new arrivals. Conflict was inevitable.

Seventeenth-century Europeans arriving in North America brought with them a completely different theory and practice of warfare to that of the Native American tribes. Seventeenth and eighteenth European wars were fought between armies, not entire populations. Battles were fought in open fields with tight regimental formations marching in step and obeying the commands of their sergeants and officers as they closed on similarly organized enemy formations. Halting within a few yards of the enemy ranks, in line formation, the musketeers would halt, load their weapons, and then fire a volley into the enemy formation. The matchlock muskets were notoriously inaccurate—only effective when fired at close range at a compact formation of enemy soldiers. During the lengthy reloading sequence the musketeers were protected by infantrymen armed with pikes, and cavalry armed with Wheelock pistols and sabers. The objective was to completely destroy the enemy force, and casualty rates in battle were extremely high. In about 1680, the ring or socket bayonet was invented. With bayonet fixed a musket could be used as a weapon even after it had been fired. The bayonet did away with the need for pikemen, and led to the adoption of the bayonet charge during the final assault on the enemy formation. It was quite natural that the colonists would rely on their traditional way of war to protect their settlements in the New World, however, they soon learned that Native American warriors did not make war in the same manner.

The first English colonists were not accompanied by regular troops when they first sailed to North America, and they resisted bringing in English troops to subdue the Native Americans, fearing they would never leave. Instead they relied on individual professional soldiers and soldiers of fortune—men like Captain John Smith, Miles Standish, and John Underhill—to organize the defense of their settlements. Understandably, these men relied on a system based on a model developed in their own country. The shortage of manpower, and the substantial expense of maintaining full-time military organizations, necessitated a reliance on local militias to protect the settlements. All able-bodied men were required to serve in the militia company of their town. The companies were mustered on a regular basis to receive training and drill, and were mobilized when the security of the settlement was under threat. The professional soldiers and appointed officers attempted to instill discipline and basic military skills into the men. The men had an assortment of military equipment and weapons. Sometimes this included body armor, such as short-waisted breast-and-back plates, or metal helmets. Until the 1630s, the most common firearm was the heavy (20-lb) matchlock musket with firing rest. Matchlocks were very inaccurate, took a long time to reload, and required a lit match to fire them, making them almost impossible to use in rainy or damp weather. From the 1630s, the matchlock was gradually replaced with the lighter and more reliable flintlock musket. The militia was also armed with broad-bladed swords, cutlasses, halberds, and pikes. The first militia companies would soon learn that their heavy awkward weapons and cumbersome equipment were ill-suited for the dense forests and swamps of New England and the Virginia lowlands.

The militia companies were drilled in tight formations on open parade grounds with a drummer beating a marching cadence. While the martial air of the drills may have impressed onlookers, the drill fields bore no resemblance to the terrain on which they would most often face their enemies. While the Native Americans were at first terrified of musket fire, they quickly overcame their fear and were soon attempting to trade food, furs, tobacco, and other goods for the weapons.

On March 22, 1622, the first major clash between English settlers and Native Americans occurred at the Jamestown settlement. Attempts by the Virginia Company to integrate the Native Americans living in the Jamestown area into the English settlements, in order to Christianize and civilize them, angered the powerful Powhatan nation. By 1622, it was apparent that the English intended to expand their settlements, threatening the Native American way of life. The powerful Chief Opechancanough's response was to stage a massive surprise attack on the settlements to annihilate the settlers and drive them from the region. The attack would target the outlying settlements as well as the Jamestown fort. As a ruse, the warriors came to the settlements the day before the attack, bringing gifts of food to share in a feast with the English. The following morning the warriors mingled and socialized with settlers before suddenly seizing the Englishmen's own tools and weapons to kill them indiscriminately. First they attacked the families occupying the plantation houses, and then they turned their attention to the workers in the fields. They also burned the dwellings, barns, and destroyed the livestock and crops. In total, around 347 men, women, and children were slaughtered in the surprise attack—nearly one-quarter of the English settlers in Virginia.[2] Survivors from the outlying plantations fled to the Jamestown fort, which had been warned of the impending attack by an Indian boy who had been Christianized by the English. In addition to the casualties, the loss in crops and supplies left the English in a precarious situation, facing the prospect of starvation during the upcoming winter.

When news of the massacre reached England later that summer, the

Virginia Company and the king responded by shipping supplies and weapons to Jamestown. Realizing that the Powhatan fully intended to destroy them, the English settlers undertook their own campaign of annihilation during the late summer and fall of 1622. The Englishmen took their revenge in a ruthless manner, attacking and killing the Powhatan wherever they found them; burning crops before they could be harvested; launching raids to destroy Powhatan towns, and hunting down survivors with dogs. As a final act of retribution, the Jamestown leaders arranged a peace parley with the Powhatan during which they poisoned the Indians' share of the wine for a ceremonial toast. Some two hundred Native Americans died from the poison, and the settlers killed another 50.[3] The climax of the war came in 1624, after the English won a large-scale battle at the town of Pamunkey, and a peace treaty was finally negotiated in 1632. By that time, the English had avenged their 347 deaths several times over, and a precedent for future frontier warfare between the European settlers and the Native Americans had been set.

Fifteen years after the Jamestown massacre, the relations between the Puritans and Native Americans in New England reached boiling point. The trouble began in the lower part of the Connecticut River valley, where the Pequot had established themselves as the dominant tribe, mainly due to their lucrative trade with the Dutch colonists. Other tribes were forced to become tributaries to the Pequot. The arrival of English traders and settlers in the early 1630s changed the balance of power in the area, and threatened the Pequot's economic and political dominance in the region. The murder of an English trader on Block Island in 1636 resulted in a military response by the Massachusetts Bay Colony that in turn led directly to the Pequot War. During an expedition to punish the murderers, who were not Pequot, a native guide and interpreter who accompanied the English killed a Pequot. The Pequot viewed this action as an unprovoked attack, and immediately undertook military action against English settlements in the region. During the winter of 1636–37, the Pequot laid siege to Saybrook fort. The following spring Pequot warriors attacked English settlers at Wethersfield, leading Connecticut and Massachusetts to declare war on the Pequot.

The Pequot War of 1637 saw the birth of a new way of war for the English in North America. It was total war, during which offensive campaigns were launched into Native American territory to wage war not only against warriors, but noncombatants as well. Moreover, the war provided the first severe test of the militia's tactical expertise and weaponry in the rugged forested New England terrain. One episode in particular serves as an example of how a militia force and its Indian allies carried out a daring and brutal "special operation" against the Pequot.

On May 18, 1637 a mixed ninety-man force of militia from Massachusetts Bay and Connecticut Colony sailed in three ships to Narragansett, where they were able to recruit a force of 60 Mohegan and two hundred Narragansett warriors for an expedition against the Pequot fortified village at Mystic. Captain John Mason of Connecticut was in overall command of the expedition, and Captain John Underhill of Massachusetts Bay was the deputy commander—both men had previous military experience in Europe. In unseasonably hot weather, the mixed force of militia and their Indian allies made a 30-mile forced march through rugged terrain to approach the village. The attackers forded the Mystic River at dusk on May 25, and made camp at Porter's Rocks, a short distance from the Pequot village, where they made their final plans for the attack. It was agreed that the English would assault the village while the Indians encircled the village to prevent any Pequot from escaping. Mason reassured his Indian allies that noncombatants, women and children, would not be deliberately killed. The attack was to commence at dawn.

At the base of the hill upon which the fortified village sat, Mason made final preparations, deciding to split his militia force. After creeping up the wooded slope, Mason and Underhill each took a 20-man squad and simultaneously assaulted the two entrances to the fort. After fighting their way inside, the Englishmen found the interior of the fort densely packed with wigwams, the narrow lanes between them providing no room to maneuver, or effectively employ their cumbersome muskets. During the first few minutes, the English force suffered two men killed and 20 men wounded including Captain Mason. Realizing that his men would never prevail in the fighting inside the village, Mason decided to set fire to the wigwams, and withdrew back outside the palisade. His men formed a tight inner cordon around the village while his Indian allies formed the outside ring. Fanned by a swift wind, the entire village was on fire in a few minutes. As the Pequot attempted to escape the inferno, the militia kept up a heavy volume of fire, killing dozens. It was all over in about an hour. In all the Pequots lost 100–150 warriors.[4] In addition, the tribe lost between 200 and 250 women, children, and elderly tribe members.[5] The English reported only seven captured, another seven escaped their captors. Mason's Indian allies were shocked and horrified at the carnage. They had never deliberately used fire to destroy their enemies, and rarely slaughtered noncombatants indiscriminately.

As Mason's column withdrew with its wounded toward Pequot harbor, where English ships were waiting to evacuate them, it was attacked repeatedly from the rear, front, and flanks by Pequot warriors from other villages. The English countered by firing into any swamp or thicket which might harbor an ambush until their ammunition was almost expended. Upon reaching the harbor, Captain Underhill boarded the ships with the wounded soldiers and warriors, while Captain Mason led the remaining English and natives on a 20-mile march overland to Fort Saybrook. The wanton destruction at Mystic broke the back of the Pequot nation. It is estimated that the massacre killed one-quarter of its population.[6] The English victory also resulted in the Pequot being abandoned by their allies. Forced to leave their villages, the Pequot broke down into smaller bands and sought refuge with other friendly tribes. Many were hunted down and killed by Mohegan and Narragansett warriors.

The expedition to attack and destroy the Pequot fortified village at Mystic demonstrated the ability of the militia to engage in unconventional warfare. They traveled light, carrying only their weapons, ammunition, and a few supplies; maneuvered at night; and fought side by side with native warriors. Their raid against Mystic, deep in Pequot territory, had a profound psychological effect on the Pequot's willingness to continue the war. Militia firepower also proved overwhelming throughout the war. Most of the Connecticut militiamen were most likely armed with matchlock muskets however—based on records of arms shipments to the Massachusetts Bay Colony—it is likely that some of the Massachusetts men were armed with the newer and more reliable flintlock muskets, or shorter-barreled carbines. Although the English were able to win their war with the Pequot, the next generation of New Englanders would face a much stronger and better-armed foe.

King Philip's War was a bloody armed conflict between English colonists and several Native American tribes in southern New England between September 1675 and August 1676. By second half of the 17th century, the English population of the New England colonies had grown to around eighty thousand settlers, dispersed in 110 towns, most of which were in Massachusetts and Connecticut. The rapid growth of the white population continued to put pressure on the native tribes, threatening their way of life and culture. Loss of hunting territory, starvation, and disease including epidemics of smallpox, typhoid, and measles had significantly reduced the Native American population in the northeast. It has been estimated that by 1675, the Native American population in the region was around ten thousand, of which four thousand were members of the powerful Narragansett tribe, spread across western Rhode Island and eastern Connecticut. Although the various tribes often warred against each other, spoke different linguistic dialects, and had no long-standing alliances, they all felt the increasing pressure by the whites on their societies. Tensions reached boiling point when a Plymouth Colony court convicted and hanged three members of the Wampanoag tribe for the murder of another member of the tribe for allegedly warning the English that the Wampanoag chief—King Philip—intended to sanction Native American attacks on widely dispersed white settlements. Viewing the court's action as a violation of their sovereignty, warriors of the Wampanoag tribe attacked a number of isolated homesteads in the vicinity of the small settlement of Swansea. The English retaliated and destroyed a Native American town at Mount Hope. During the summer of 1675, the war spread rapidly, with other tribes joining the war under the leadership of King Philip. The towns of Middleborough, Dartmouth, Brookfield, Deerfield, and Northfield were attacked by the Native Americans, leading the New England Confederation to formally declare war on them. The violence continued to escalate throughout the fall and winter of 1775–76, with both sides launching attacks and retaliatory attacks. Although the number of native warriors never approached the numbers of militia, many warriors were now armed with muzzle-loaded flintlock muskets as well as steel tomahawks and knives, and they continued to excel in forest warfare. When the local militias proved unable to prevail against the tribes and crush the uprising, the governor of the Plymouth Colony, Josiah Winslow, recognized the need for a special full-time force that would model its composition and tactics on the Native American way of war. Winslow selected Captain Benjamin Church, his aide, to form an experimental company of men who would train and operate using Native American tactics to attack Indian war parties, and raid their camps in the dense forests and swamps.[6] Today, Church is considered the father of the modern US Army Rangers.

Church eventually received authorization to recruit friendly, neutral, and formerly hostile Native American warriors into his company. The warriors taught Church's men forest warfare tactics, including how to track hostile war parties through forests and swamps, how to set deadly ambushes, and how to conduct raids on enemy camps. Church's company played a decisive role in the Great Swamp Fight of November 1675 when Josiah Winslow led a combined militia and Indian force against the Narragansett tribe. Winslow's men moved at night over frozen swampy terrain to attack a Narragansett fort. In the attack, the militia and their native allies killed some three hundred Narragansett, and destroyed the tribe's winter stores of food. Although he was wounded in the fight, Church recovered and continued to lead his ranger company until August 1676, when the Native American chieftain, King Philip, was cornered in Rhode Island's Assowamset Swamp. One of Church's elite ranger teams tracked down the chief, and he was shot and killed by one of Church's Indian scouts effectively ending the costly war.[7] Benjamin Church continued his service during King William's War (1689–97), and Queen Anne's War (1702–13), leading a total of five expeditions against the French and their Indian allies in Maine and New Brunswick, Canada. Before his death in 1718, Benjamin Church compiled and published the notes he had taken during his service. The notes provided the foundation for an evolving Ranger tactical doctrine for irregular and special warfare operations.

During the French and Indian War (1754–63), the American colonists continued to build on the lessons learned during previous colonial wars. Throughout the war, irregular warfare raged along the vast frontier that stretched from northern Georgia to New England. Perhaps it was George Washington's prescience that led him to seek a role in that conflict that would provide him with first-hand knowledge of irregular warfare. In fact, it was Washington's personal involvement in an expedition on the frontier that helped spark full-scale war between France and Britain. On

May 28, 1754, Washington led a small force of Virginia militia and Mingo warriors in an attack on the camp of a small party of French Canadians and Indians near Uniontown in southwestern Pennsylvania. The French were led by Joseph Coulon de Villiers de Jumonville. Several of the Canadians were killed in the surprise attack, including Jumonville. The death of Jumonville remains controversial, however some evidence suggests that he was killed after he was taken prisoner by the Mingo chief known as Half King.[8]

The incident sparked outrage among the Canadians and in the French government since war between Britain and France had not yet been declared. When Jumonville's half-brother, who was in command of Fort Duquesne, was informed of the incident, he attacked Washington and his men at Fort Necessity, forcing them to surrender on July 3, 1754. The surrender document, written in French, described Jumonville's death as an assassination, which caused uproar when the news reached Paris and London. Washington was forced to withdraw to Virginia after the incident, and was heavily criticized in Britain and France.

A year later, at the age of 23, Washington volunteered to serve as an aide-de-camp to Major General Edward Braddock on an expedition to capture Fort Duquesne at the confluence of the Allegheny, Monongahela, and Ohio Rivers, the site of present-day Pittsburgh. The lead elements of Braddock's force—some 1,300 men with eight cannon, four howitzers, and about 34 wagons—crossed the Monongahela on July 8, 1754, some 10 miles from Fort Duquesne. Continuing their march on July 9, the British encountered a force of up to 800 French, Canadians, and Indians led by French Captain Daniel Beujeu. The war party's mission was to delay Braddock's advance on Fort Duquesne. The French and Indians managed to envelop the head and both flanks of the British column. The British attempted to counterattack using conventional British tactics with tight formations to mass their firepower. The volley fire proved ineffective against their enemies who remained hidden by trees and powder smoke. Taking fire from three sides, discipline soon collapsed in the British ranks and confusion and panic spread throughout the column. Numerous British officers were killed or wounded, including General Braddock who received a mortal wound. Those officers who survived, including Washington, were unable to restore order. Finally, the breakdown became complete and the survivors retreated in panic. It was a total defeat for the British. Only 460 soldiers from Braddock's 1,300-man advance column escaped unscathed, and only a third of the officers in the advance column survived the battle. The British and Americans suffered over nine hundred casualties, while the French and Indians lost 23 killed and 16 wounded.[9] Braddock died of his wound during the retreat and was buried beneath the road at Great Meadows near where Fort Necessity had stood. After burning most of their wagons, the British force retreated to Cumberland, Maryland. What remained of Braddock's army then marched to Philadelphia, leaving the defense of the frontier to a handful of militia troops. It was a hard lesson for Washington, and one he would not soon forget. The tactics of conventional war as practiced by British Regulars would not prevail over irregulars in the densely forested terrain of the North American frontier. The British still had much to learn about fighting in North America. The militias, on the other hand, were well adapted to irregular warfare.

The most famous irregular force of the French and Indian War was Rogers' Rangers. Organized and trained by its enigmatic and controversial namesake, Robert Rogers, the Rangers were most noted for their conduct of deep reconnaissance, and special-operation raids against distant targets behind enemy lines. Rogers organized the first 60-man Ranger company during the harsh winter of 1755, and by 1757 the force had grown to five companies, including one company of Stockbridge Indians under their leader, Captain Jacobs.[10] Roger's men were rugged self-reliant frontiersmen and adventurers who often eschewed traditional strict military discipline and standards of conduct. However, the Rangers proved capable of operating under difficult conditions in the densely forested mountainous terrain of upstate New York around lakes George and Champlain, and southern Quebec Province. The Rangers also possessed the survival skills required for conducting winter warfare operations, often traveling cross-country on snowshoes to attack French towns and Indian villages on the frontier. The First Battle on Snowshoes occurred on January 21, 1757 when Roger's force of 74 rangers clashed with a much larger force of French, Canadian militia, and Indians near Fort Carillon (later Ticonderoga) at the southern end of Lake Champlain. After suffering 20 casualties, the Rangers were forced to withdraw, but the French and Indians, who also suffered heavy casualties, were unable to mount an effective pursuit due to a lack of snowshoes. On March 13, 1758, the Rangers fought a Second Battle of the Snowshoes when Rogers' men ambushed a much larger French and Indian force.[11] The Rangers suffered heavy losses, and were in turn ambushed as they attempted to break contact and retreat. Rogers reported losing 125 men killed.[12] Only 52 of Rogers' men were able to escape and evade capture in the fight. It was a serious setback for the Rangers. Although Rogers estimated that he had inflicted some 150 casualties on the French-Indian force, the French reported only about 30 men killed and wounded.

Perhaps the most notable of Roger's exploits was his 1759 raid on the Abenaki village of St. Francis, which was located on the south side of the St. Lawrence River some 30 miles southwest of Trois-Rivieres. The village was targeted because it was reputed to be the launching point for a number of raids against settlements and military installations in New York and New England. Under the cover of darkness, Rogers and his men departed Crown Point in whaleboats on September 13. The Rangers rowed north on Lake Champlain for 10 days before reaching Missisquoi Bay on September 23. After hiding their boats and supplies for the return trip, the Rangers moved north through difficult swampy terrain, reaching the south bank of the St. Francis River on October 3. Just before dawn on October 4, the Rangers attacked and burned the village, killing an undetermined number of Abenakis, including women and children. Rogers lost only a few men in the attack, but when he learned that a large force of French and Indians were only a short distance away he ordered a hasty withdrawal.

After learning that his boats and supplies hidden near Missisquoi Bay had been discovered and destroyed, Rogers opted to march south some two hundred miles through uncharted wilderness to reach the British Fort at Number 4. With the French and Indians in hot pursuit, Rogers decided to split his force into groups of 10–20 men, so that they could make better time, and hunt and forage for food more effectively. Their pursuers tracked some of the ranger parties down, and the men were either killed or captured, but other groups managed to evade and escape their pursuers. All of the survivors were near starvation by the time they rendezvoused at the Connecticut River on October 20. Finding that most of his men were unfit to continue the journey, Rogers took three men and descended the Connecticut River by raft, reaching Fort Number 4 on the last day of October.[13] Supplies were then sent upriver to his starving men, enabling them to complete their journey. The four-hundred-mile raid was declared a success by the British, despite the fact that Rogers lost three of his officers, and 46 enlisted, killed or captured. Although Rogers grossly exaggerated the number of casualties and damage he inflicted on the French and Abenaki, it was a psychological victory. The French and their Indian allies soon realized that there were no safe sanctuaries, even in their own territories. The six-week raid demonstrated the capabilities of the Rangers to march undetected in enemy-controlled territory to strike distant enemy targets without warning and then withdraw before the enemy could respond.

Several veterans of Roger's Rangers went on to play prominent roles in the Revolutionary War, including Captain John Stark, the hero of the battles of Bunker Hill and Bennington; Moses Hazen, who achieved the rank of brigadier general in the Continental Army, and Israel Putnam, who distinguished himself at Bunker Hill and was promoted to the rank of major general, among others.

While most of the aforementioned discussion of the evolution of irregular warfare in Colonial America focused on the northeastern colonies, similar examples can be found in the Carolinas and Georgia. Revolutionary War partisan leaders, Francis Marion, Andrew Pickens, and Thomas Sumter, all had experience of irregular warfare on the frontiers of Virginia, the Carolinas, and northeast Georgia during the French and Indian War, and Anglo-Cherokee War of the 1760s. Americans who fought in the French and Indian War and other conflicts along the frontier, including George Washington, did not forget their experiences in irregular warfare, and it is not surprising that special operations would play in important role during the American Revolutionary War.

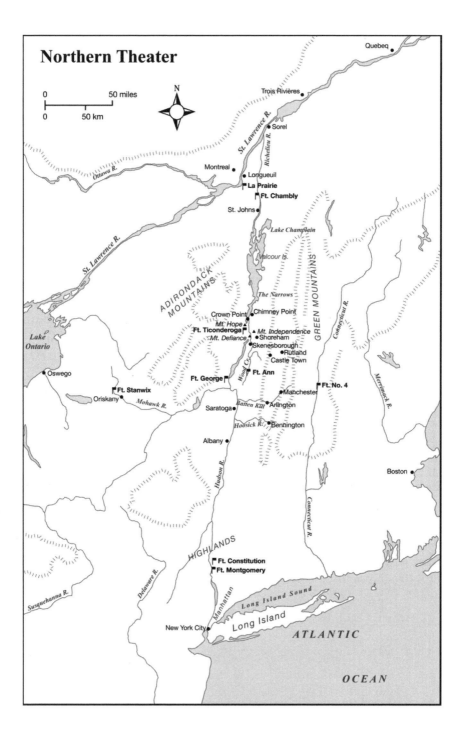

Northern Theater

0   50 miles

0   50 km

N

Quebec

Trois Rivières

St. Lawrence R.

Sorel

Richelieu R.

Ottawa R.

Montreal

Longueuil

La Prairie

Ft. Chambly

St. Johns

Lake Champlain

St. Lawrence R.

Valcour Is.

ADIRONDACK MOUNTAINS

The Narrows

GREEN MOUNTAINS

Connecticut R.

Lake Ontario

Crown Point

Chimney Point

Mt. Hope

Ft. Ticonderoga

Mt. Independence

Mt. Defiance

Shoreham

Skenesborough

Rutland

Castle Town

Oswego

Wood Cr.

Ft. George

Ft. Ann

Ft. No. 4

Merrimack R.

Ft. Stanwix

Manchester

Oriskany

Mohawk R.

Saratoga

Batten Kill

Arlington

Hoosick R.

Bennington

Albany

Hudson R.

Boston

HIGHLANDS

Ft. Constitution

Ft. Montgomery

Susquehanna R.

Delaware R.

Manhattan

Long Island Sound

New York City

Long Island

ATLANTIC

OCEAN

1

THE CAPTURE OF FORT TICONDEROGA

At 5:00 a.m. on May 10, 1775, with only a portion of his assault force in place on the western side of the wind-whipped southern neck of Lake Champlain, Ethan Allen made a decision to launch his assault on Fort Ticonderoga. Only eighty-three of Allen's Green Mountain Boys had made it ashore in two leaky scows after the perilous two-mile crossing of the storm-tossed lake. Darkness was giving way to an early morning fog that would soon burn off under the rays of the rising sun, exposing Allen's assault force. Soon thereafter the fort's slumbering garrison would turn out for their first formation of the day. It was now or never for Allen and his men.

JUST THREE WEEKS AFTER THE FIRST SHOTS WERE FIRED AT LEXINGTON and Concord on April 19, 1775, a small force of American irregulars launched the first special operation of the Revolutionary War. In a daring night assault, Ethan Allen's Green Mountain Boys—supported by Connecticut and Massachusetts militiamen—seized the strategic Fortress Ticonderoga, capturing its entire garrison along with more than one hundred cannon. It gave the Americans their first victory of their War of Independence, and the captured cannon were put to good use during the later part of the siege of Boston. Allen's seizure of Fort Ticonderoga adhered to many of the principles of modern-day special operations, but violated other principles, which could have led to the failure of the mission.

The story begins just after dawn on May 2, 1775, when an exhausted mud-splattered horseman galloped up to the Catamount Tavern in Bennington in present-day southwestern Vermont. The rambling two-story wooden tavern served as headquarters for Ethan Allen's Green Mountain Boys. In the yard of the tavern, stood a 25-foot pole on top of which was a huge stuffed catamount with bared fangs snarling in the direction of New York. The display symbolized the dispute between the settlers in the region, who held New Hampshire land grants issued by Connecticut, and New York authorities, which claimed title to the same territory.

Prior to 1775, the Green Mountain Boys had conducted a five-year campaign to expel New York land claimants and surveyors. When New York authorities sent sheriffs, magistrates and judges to enforce the New York land claims with writs of ejection, Allen conducted a campaign against the New Yorkers. Allen and his men used fear, threats, intimidation, arson, and at times violence to protect the New Hampshire grant settlers. The New York legislative assembly in turn declared many of Greene's men "outlaws" and put prices on their heads. In the violence that followed, New York officials were severely beaten, and New York settlers were forced off their lands. Most of Allen's men were farmers, hunters and trappers, but there were also tavern owners, lawyers, clerks, storekeepers, and at least two doctors. A few were Yale and Harvard graduates.

Many of the officers, non-commissioned officers and older enlisted men were former rangers, who had fought under Robert Rogers, Israel Putnam and John Stark during the French and Indian War.

Although Allen organized his the Green Mountain Boys into a regimental formation with five companies with himself as colonel/commandant, Allen's force can best be described as a paramilitary, or auxiliary military force at best. They did not drill on a regular basis, wore no standardized uniform (most wore farm work clothes, or buckskin hunting shirts), and were lightly armed with muskets, hunting rifles, fowling pieces, and tomahawks. Allen's Green Mountain Boys refused to fight under anyone other than their elected officers.

Ten days after the outbreak of hostilities at Lexington and Concord, Allen and his officers gathered at the Catamount Tavern to meet with members of committees of safety from nearby frontier settlements to exchange views on the revolution. Since the British Crown refused to recognize the New Hampshire Grants, and gave New York legal control over most of modern-day Vermont, a majority of the settlers in the region favored the cause of independence from Great Britain, but it was uncertain how the outbreak of hostilities in Massachusetts would affect the future of the area. A minority favored continued loyalty to the Crown, and others preferred a "wait and see" policy, but there was no doubt in Ethan Allen's mind. He and his men were unequivocally in favor of independence from Great Britain.

The horseman who arrived at the Catamount Tavern on the morning of May 2 was Heman Allen, who had ridden all night from Pittsfield to bring important news for his brother Ethan. Inside the tavern's taproom, Ethan Allen was just finishing breakfast. He gave his brother a hearty welcome, after which Heman briefed him on the latest news—the Revolutionary Committee of Correspondence in Harford, Connecticut wanted Allen and his Green Mountain Boys to capture Fort Ticonderoga as soon as possible.

At 37, Ethan Allen was a tall, dark-haired frontiersman with chiseled facial features. Standing well over six feet tall, Allen's muscular frame was hardened by years of grueling work as farmer, ironworker, and professional hunter. He spent most winters hunting alone in the Green Mountains, and exploring the wilderness along Lakes George and Champlain, sometimes ranging as far north as the St. Lawrence River. He was known to use physical and profane verbal intimidation to impose his way when he thought it was necessary. Although he could quote scripture to his advantage in an argument, most clergymen shunned Allen for his uninhibited use of profanity. Consequently, he had no use for organized religion. Allen was also extremely intelligent and well read. He was also a prolific writer who authored newspaper articles and pamphlets defending the rights of small farmers and landholders on the frontier, who were at the mercy of a legal system that favored the large landowning aristocracy.

Born and raised in rural Connecticut, he was just 17, and preparing to enter Yale, when his father died suddenly. Due to his family's economic circumstances, he was forced to cancel his admission. At the age of 19, Allen volunteered for militia service during the French and Indian War. His company was en route to the besieged Fort William Henry when the commander received word that the fort had fallen. Allen's company turned back, and Allen experienced no further service during the war.

After his brief service in the militia, Allen became a farmer, land speculator, iron foundry and tannery owner before becoming involved in the New Hampshire Grants dispute. His propensity to rebel against tyrannical authority, as well as his love of freedom and his adventurous spirit made him a natural candidate for command of the unruly Green Mountain Boys. While he liked to drink, at times heavily, he was a superb organizer, and his gregarious nature helped insure his election as colonel and commandant of the Green Mountain Boys. His election was recognized and endorsed by the authorities in Connecticut. Because of his demonstrated honesty and trustworthiness, Connecticut's Revolutionary Committee of Correspondence selected Allen to lead a "secret" expedition to capture the British fort at Ticonderoga.

Fort Ticonderoga was strategically located on the western shore of Lake Champlain, on a high promontory that commanded the waterway between Lake Champlain and Lake George to the south. The fort was completed by the French in 1755, and christened Fort Carillon. The fort was star-shaped, based upon the classic 17th-century fortress designs of Marquis de Vauban, the French military engineer. The fort's walls were 7 foot high and 14 foot thick, and the entire works were surrounded by a glacis and a dry moat. Firing ports were arranged so as to be mutually supporting. Within the wall were numerous bombproof shelters, barracks, storehouses, and a powder magazine. Between the southern wall and the lakeshore, the outside of the fort was protected by a wooden palisade. Another redoubt was constructed to the east of the fort to cover the lake's narrows.

The fort was defended by some 3,600 French troops. In 1758, during the French and Indian War, fifteen thousand British and American troops attempted to capture Fort Carillon. Despite their overwhelming numbers, the British and Americans were defeated, suffering more than two thousand casualties, while the French lost around three hundred men. A year later forces led by Lord Amherst occupied Ticonderoga after the French significantly reduced the size of the fort's garrison. Before they withdrew, the French troops blew up the fort's magazine, significantly damaging to the fortifications. After the French and Indian War the British continued to occupy the fort, but only with a small garrison.

There were several reasons why the Americans put a high priority on capturing Fort Ticonderoga. Fort Ticonderoga controlled the primary invasion route to and from Canada. When hostilities broke between the Americans and British in April 1775, a large portion of the British troops in North America were stationed in Canada, and it was feared that the British would launch an invasion using Lake Champlain, Lake George, and the Hudson to sever communications between the New England and the Middle Atlantic states. Conversely, many Americans believed that a majority of French-speaking Canadians would join the rebellion against the British, if American troops launched an invasion of Canada. Fort Ticonderoga could be used as a staging area for such an invasion of Canada. In March 1775, the Massachusetts Committee of Correspondence sent one of its members, John Brown, to Montreal to open communications with its French-speaking citizens to determine their level of support and interest in joining the rebellion against the British. Brown wrote to his Committee to tell them that, "The Fort at Ticonderoga must be seized as soon as possible should hostilities be committed by the King's Troops. The People on the N. Hampshire Grants have ingaged to do this Business and in my opinion they are the most proper Persons for this Jobb."[1]

The capture of Ticonderoga was also a high priority because there were known to be more than one hundred cannon and other artillery pieces at the fort, along with a supply of munitions. The American troops that had encircled Boston since the outbreak of hostilities lacked sufficient artillery to destroy the British fortifications and force the British to evacuate the city. The seizure of Fort Ticonderoga therefore became an imperative for the Americans.

The British were also well aware of the strategic importance of Fort Ticonderoga in controlling the route between Canada and New York. As early as 1767, Guy Carleton, governor general of British North America, wrote that, "It is not only expedient, but indispensable necessary, to keep the lake posts in repair."[2]

Despite Carleton's warning, major repairs were not made. The problem was financial. The French and Indian War had brought the British treasury to the brink of bankruptcy, and measures to force the colonies to assume a portion of the costs of the war were fanning the flames of rebellion. As a result, the defenses at Fort Ticonderoga, Crown Point, and other forts continued to deteriorate. In 1774, the Earl of Dartmouth, Secretary of State for the Colonies, saw that something had to be done, and sent the senior engineer stationed at New York to Lake Champlain to make plans for either repairing the forts, or building new fortifications. During the same year, Sir Frederick Haldimand, acting commander-in-chief of North America, proposed to General Thomas Gage that a couple of regiments be stationed at Crown Point, about 11 miles north of Fort Ticonderoga, "under the pretense of rebuilding that fort, which from its situation . . . not only secures the communication with Canada, but also opens an easy access to the back Settlements of the Northern Colonies and may keep them in awe, shou'd any of them be rash enough to incline to acts of open force and violence . . ."[3]

In November of the same year, Lord Dartmouth ordered General Gage to have both Fort Ticonderoga and Crown Point put "put in a proper state of Defence."[4] The letter did not reach Gage until the day after Christmas, and apparently Gage made no immediate efforts to carry out his instructions. However, very soon after the outbreak of hostilities in Massachusetts in April 1775, General Gage wrote from Boston to General Carleton in Quebec ordering him to send the 7th Regiment, augmented with a force of Canadians and Indians, to Crown Point. However, the orders were sent by sea, and did not reach Carleton until May 19, 1775, nine days after Allen's men seized the fort. In the interim, the commander at Fort Ticonderoga had been warned as early as March to prepare for trouble in the form of, "disorderly People in Arms coming to the Fort and making Enquirys of the situation, and strength of the Garrison."[5]

The Connecticut treasury agreed to release £300 to finance Allen's expedition to capture Fort Ticonderoga. Concurrently, additional men were being recruited in Connecticut and Massachusetts to augment Allen's Green Mountain Boys. On May 3, 14 men from Connecticut led by Captain Edward Mott arrived in Bennington. Among the men were Captain Noah Phelps and Bernard Romans, who were entrusted with the allocated funds. Another of Ethan Allen's brothers, Levi, was also one of the new arrivals. On the following day, Colonel James Easton of Pittsfield Massachusetts arrived with 39 men recruited in Massachusetts.

The leaders then convened in a preliminary council of war, with Colonel James Easton as chairman, to begin planning the expedition. Based on his five years of experience as commandant of the Green Mountain Boys, and his knowledge of the area, Allen was confirmed as the leader of the expedition. Allen had already sent riders out to instruct his Green Mountain Boys to rendezvous at Shoreham near the southeastern end of Lake Champlain, almost directly opposite Fort Ticonderoga. Allen also ordered his men to secure the roads leading to and from Ticonderoga including the Fort Edward, Lake George, Skenesborough, and Crown Point roads. Those guarding the roads were instructed to seize and interrogate anyone traveling the roads leading from the fort, and to turn back all persons attempting to reach the fort. Allen wanted to insure the operation was not compromised, and he recognized the need for timely intelligence, including information on any attempts by the British to reinforce Ticonderoga. He also wanted to prevent any news of the events at Lexington and Concord from reaching the fort's commander. All of the officers on the council concurred that speed, security, and up-to-date intelligence were essential to the success of expedition.

Although it was essential that Allen's men move at speed in order to reach the fort before the garrison was reinforced, measures were adopted to insure operational security during the 90-mile march north from Bennington to Shoreham. Since the plan called for additional men to be recruited along the way, the town of Castleton, some 65 miles north of Bennington, was selected as an intermediate rendezvous point. Castleton was a good choice. The small town had only about 175 residents, and was only a day's march from Shoreham, the final rendezvous point. Ethan Allen owned land nearby and knew most of the townspeople in Castleton and in nearby towns. Although the presence of a large number of armed men in town might have raised the suspicions of some inhabitants, it was not an unusual occurrence. Over the past several years, Allen and his Green Mountain Boys had visited the town several times. Allen was also confident that he could recruit additional men for the expedition from the local population.

As there was major concern that known Loyalists in the region would report the movement of the Patriot force as it moved northward, it was essential that their progress go unnoticed. To achieve this, the force would be split into small groups that would move at different intervals and by separate roads wherever possible. Since the men did not wear uniforms or other military accoutrements, they could easily pass for hunting or surveying parties on their way north. Recruiters were instructed to hand-pick men living on remote farms who were known to be loyal and sympathetic to the Patriot cause.

The council also recognized the requirement for up-to-date intelligence on Fort Ticonderoga, including the condition of the works, the size of the garrison, and its state of readiness, as well as the number of serviceable and unserviceable artillery pieces and munitions on hand. The council therefore decided to send Captain Noah Phelps and Ezra Hecock on a clandestine mission to spy on the fort. The pair departed Bennington on May 3.

Two days later, the lead elements of the expedition departed Bennington, Vermont. Allen's men followed the Vermont Valley northward between the Green Mountains on the east and Taconic Range to the west. As they passed through small towns along the way, the groups dispersed into different taverns and inns to take their meals or purchase food without attracting undue attention. After a march of some 23 miles, most of Allen's men reached Manchester, Vermont, where they took a lunch break of an hour and a half. Part of the force departed Manchester around 5:30 p.m. and followed a route that took them northwest through the Taconics toward the town of Dorset, while others remained in Manchester for a time.

After reaching Dorset, Allen's men generally followed the direction of present-day Route 30, which leads north to Castleton. After the uneventful infiltration march, Allen's men began to arrive in Castleton on the evening of May 7. The following day, the leaders of the expedition convened a council of war to decide on how to proceed. The council's first action was to formalize a command structure for the expedition. Appointments were made based on the number of troops each officer recruited for the expedition. Edward Mott of Connecticut was appointed chairman of the Committee of War, and Ethan Allen was designated as the "field commander." James Easton of Massachusetts was selected as

Allen's second-in-command, and Seth Warner was designated as third-in-command.

Another matter discussed by the leaders of the expedition involved the crossing of Lake Champlain. Hands Cove, a remote beach just west of Shoreham on the southern tip of Lake Champlain, was selected as the departure point for the two-mile crossing. Located in a deep hollow between heavily wooded hills, and therefore hidden from view from Fort Ticonderoga on the opposite shore of the lake, it was an ideal site for embarking. However, Allen's scouts reported that there were no boats in the vicinity.

Allen was informed by local inhabitants that there were boats anchored at Skenesborough, which was located about 25 miles south of Hands Cove at the southernmost tip of Lake Champlain. However, most of the town's residents were fervent Loyalists. Captain Philip Skene of the British Army had settled the town in 1759, and afterwards became a wealthy merchant. By 1775, Skenesborough was an important center of maritime trade between New York and Canada. At the time of Allen's raid, Philip Skene was traveling home from a trip to England, where he had petitioned the Crown for funds to reinforce forts Ticonderoga and Crown Point. Philip Skene's son, Major Andrew Skene, was the Loyalist leader in the Skensborough area, and would resist any attempt by Allen's men to seize boats at Skensborough. A 15-year-old local boy named Noah Lee informed the council that Skene's schooner was tied up at the landing at his nearby estate. The council directed Lieutenant Samuel Herrick to proceed to Skenesborough with a force of 30 men on the afternoon of May 9, capture Major Skene, and seize his boats. Herrick was also instructed to prevent anyone in Skenesborough from leaving the area. After commandeering the boats, Herrick was instructed to sail to Hands Cove under cover of darkness.

As a backup plan, the council ordered Captain Asa Douglass to travel north to Crown Point, Bridport and Panton to search for boats. Large boats of the size required to ferry Allen's men across Lake Champlain were in short supply on the eastern shore, and although Allen had men with boatbuilding skills, there was insufficient time to undertake such a task. Allen knew that without boats the expedition would end in failure.

Allen was also concerned that he had too few troops to capture the

fort even in a surprise attack. With time running out, he sent Samuel
Beach to mobilize additional Green Mountain Boys who lived on the eastern shore of the lake. The recruits were directed to rendezvous with the
main force at Hands Cove on the night of May 9–10. Samuel Beach galloped off on a 24-hour recruiting ride covering some 64 miles, ending at
Shoreham near Hands Cove.

On the morning of May 9, Noah Phelps arrived back in Castleton
from his clandestine reconnaissance of Fort Ticonderoga. After crossing
Lake Champlain in a small boat, Phelps had spent the night at a farmhouse
near the fort. That evening he had overheard a group of soldiers from the
fort discussing the feeble state of the fort's works at supper. The following
morning Phelps, disguised as a peddler, entered the fort on the pretense
of getting a shave from the fort's barber. A Yale graduate and attorney,
Phelps was well aware of the risk he took by entering the fort—if the
British discovered his true identity, he would be tried as a spy and hanged.
His capture would also alert the British, compromising the entire operation. He therefore exercised extreme caution in his conversation with the
British soldiers, and had to alter his mannerisms and speech to maintain
his disguise as a simple itinerant peddler.

Phelps had no difficulty entering the fort. The guards did not ask for
any proof of his identity. As he made his way through the fort to the barber's quarters Phelps observed that numerous cannon were missing from
the firing ports on the ramparts, and the forts walls and gates were in
need of repair. It was also apparent that the garrison was not on an alert
status. On his way out of the fort, Phelps encountered the fort's commander, British Captain Delaplace. The captain complained that he was
having problems with wet powder in the fort's magazine. After departing
the fort, Phelps and his boatman began to row across the lake to the eastern shore. Realizing that he was under observation by fort's sentries,
Phelps refused to assist the boatman and risk demonstrating his skills as
an oarsman until the boat was out of range of the fort's artillery. After
landing on the eastern shore, Phelps returned to Castleton to report the
intelligence he had gathered.

Phelps estimated that the entire garrison numbered fewer than 50
men, and there was no indication that the fort's commander was prepared
for an attack. He also provided information on the layout of the interior

of the fort, and the poor condition of the walls and defenses. Noah Phelps's spy craft was superb, and was essential to the success of the entire mission.

Based on Phelps's intelligence, the council voted to move forward with the operation, and Allen began to finalize his plans for the assault.[6] Although the exact number of men in Allen's force would not be determined until all the men reached Hands Cove, it was apparent from Phelps's estimate that the attackers would have a significant numerical advantage over the defenders. Nevertheless, Allen wanted even more detailed information on the fort. He therefore queried the local residents who were familiar with the fort. A local farmer told Allen that while he wasn't personally familiar with the fort, his teenage son, Nathan Beman, had played in the fort while growing up, and could provide precise details of the fort's defenses. Allen promptly recruited the boy as a guide for the expedition.

_____

About 4:00 p.m. on Monday May 8, an unexpected event occurred at Castleton that threatened to derail the plan to seize Fort Ticonderoga. Benedict Arnold, still dressed in the uniform of a colonel of the Connecticut Foot Guard, charged into Remington's tavern, where he found Captain Mott, who was preparing to join Captain Herrick's force to capture Skenesborough. After identifying himself, Arnold presented his commission and demanded that he be put in charge of the operation. Mott wrote in his journal that, " . . . we could not surrender the command to him, as our people were raised on condition that they would be commanded by their own officers."[7] Several of Allen's men scoffed at Arnold's claim, asking whether he had any troops to back up his claim. He had brought with him only one personal aide. Arnold replied that he intended to assume command of the entire expedition based on his commission granted by the Massachusetts Committee of Safety, and that his captains were actively recruiting men for the expedition in western Massachusetts, and would soon be available for duty.[8] Frustrated and angered by Mott's rejection of his claim, Arnold said that he would take the matter up with Allen personally when he arrived at Shoreham.

_____

Thirty-four-year-old Benedict Arnold had been involved in the rebellion from its earliest days. Born in Connecticut in 1741, the son of a successful businessman, Arnold eventually established himself as an apothecary and bookseller in New Haven, Connecticut. Through hard work and ambition, Arnold expanded his business, and purchased three trading ships to gain a portion of the colony's lucrative West Indies trade. He personally traveled on his own ships on trading missions throughout the American colonies, and to Canada and the West Indies. When the Sugar Act of 1764 and the Stamp Act of 1765 had a severely impact on trade in the colonies and threatened to bankrupt his business, Arnold joined the Sons of Liberty. In defiance of the Stamp Act he became a smuggler of trade goods. Based on his personal wealth and staunch defense of American liberties, Arnold was elected to the position of captain in the Connecticut militia in March of 1775, one month prior to the outbreak of hostilities at Lexington and Concord. Despite his almost complete lack of military experience, Arnold began preparing his militia company for war enthusiastically and diligently. When news of Lexington and Concord reached New Haven, Arnold assembled his company of foot guards and demanded that the town leaders release the arms and munitions held in the town's magazine. The town leaders acquiesced, so after arming and equipping his men, Arnold led them off on the road to Cambridge, Massachusetts, where other militia units were assembling.

During the march to Cambridge, Arnold had a chance encounter with Colonel Samuel Parsons, a well-known Connecticut Patriot who was returning from Cambridge to begin recruiting troops at Hartford. During their conversation, Parsons mentioned to Arnold that there was a shortage of cannon and other artillery pieces at the rebel camp outside Boston. Artillery was needed to lay siege to Boston, and prevent British troops from ravaging the surrounding countryside. Arnold mentioned to Parsons that there were a large number of cannon at Fort Ticonderoga on Lake Champlain. He proposed that the fortress should be seized and the cannon appropriated for use by the Patriot militias.[8] Parsons then proceeded to New Haven, where he met with a group of provincial leaders and proposed the idea of taking Ticonderoga as soon as possible. On their own authority, the men appropriated £300 from the provincial treasury to finance the expedition, and named Captain Edward Mott to head the Connecticut contingent of the expedition. They sent Heman Allen off to Bennington to enlist the participation of his brother Ethan Allen and his Green Mountain Boys in the expedition.

Meanwhile, after reaching Cambridge, Arnold continued to pursue his idea of launching an expedition against Ticonderoga, and proposed to the Massachusetts Committee of Safety an action to seize the fort. Impressed with Arnold's knowledge of the fort and its weaponry, and his background, the committee voted on May 2 to appoint Arnold to the rank of colonel and commander of a force not to exceed four hundred men for the "secret" purpose of capturing Ticonderoga.[9] The committee also authorized an expenditure of £100 to finance the expedition, and gave Arnold 10 horses and 200 pounds of gunpowder for the mission. Arnold was expected to recruit his own men for the expedition in western Massachusetts.

After saying goodbye to his foot guards, Arnold selected a group of captains who were charged with recruiting men to fill the ranks of Arnold's new regiment. He then rushed off to the New Hampshire Grants to locate Ethan Allen, and take command of the entire expedition. By the time Arnold arrived in Castleton on May 8, Ethan Allen was already in Shoreham making final preparations for crossing Lake Champlain.

After his confrontation with Captain Mott on the afternoon of May 8, Arnold set out for Shoreham the following morning to find Allen. Allen's rearguard party followed at a distance, leaving all the provisions behind. When Captain Mott learned that Arnold was traveling to Shoreham to press his claim with Allen, he and Captain Phelps left the party that was on its way to Skenesborough to commandeer boats and retuned to Castleton. After loading the provisions that had been left behind on packhorses, Mott and Phelps started off for Shoreham to locate Allen and inform him of Arnold's intent. Mott recorded in his journal that he feared that Arnold "should prevail on Colonel Allen to resign the command."[10] Mott knew that Ethan Allen's Green Mountain Boys would never agree to serve under Benedict Arnold, and feared that expedition would come to an early end.

Arnold's attempt to assume command of the expedition threatened to throw the whole plan to capture Ticonderoga into confusion and disorder. Command and control, particularly of special operations forces, remains a matter of concern even to this present day. Current US Joint Doctrine, published in Joint Publication 3-05, clearly calls for a "clear and unambiguous chain of command." The doctrine also states that frequent transfer of special operation forces between commanders must be avoided.[11] Unity of command is essential during any operation and it can only be achieved by the appointment of a designated commander with the authority to direct assigned and attached forces during the planning and conduct of the operation. Unfortunately, no such doctrine existed in 1775, and wouldn't exist for over 250 years. The sudden crisis brought about by Arnold's arrival had to be worked out on the ground at Shoreham on the eve of the attack.

When Arnold reached Shoreham around noon on May 9, Allen heard him out, and did not reject Arnold's claim, nor did he resign his command in favor of Arnold. Allen's dilemma was that Arnold held a legitimate colonel's commission from the Massachusetts Committee of Safety, while he held no formal commission at that point in time. On the other hand, Arnold's commission only gave him legitimate command authority over Massachusetts's troops.

When Allen's men learned that he was considering the matter, they declared that they would not serve under Arnold, and if Allen yielded they would club their muskets and march for home. By one account, Allen did show signs of yielding, telling his men, "Your pay will be the same if he does command." "Damn the pay!" his men shouted.[12] While there is no written documentation of any formal agreement between the two men, Allen agreed that Arnold could accompany the expedition as a volunteer officer, and travel at his own "left side" during the assault.[13] Determined to at least participate in the attack, Arnold reluctantly accepted Allen's proposal. He had little choice. He was in Allen's territory, and it was clear that the Green Mountain Boys would not serve under his command. Arnold later wrote in a letter to the Continental Congress claiming that he and Allen "agreed we should take a joint command of the troops."[14] However, there is no documentation to support Arnold's interpretation of the command arrangements. In retrospect, Arnold added nothing positive to the expedition, and by putting his own self-interests and ambitions ahead of the mission he endangered its success.

On the evening of May 9, Allen's men began to arrive at the expedition's final rendezvous point at Hands Cove on Lake Champlain. The moon was in its third quarter, but the cove was not visible from Fort Ticonderoga. Allen was among the first to arrive at the cove. He immediately posted sentinels on the point south of the cove to watch for the boats that were expected to arrive from Skenesborough, and for any unusual lights in the fort across the lake. After posting the sentinels, Allen returned to the cove to greet his men as they arrived.

Allen soon had between two hundred and three hundred men assembled at the cove. As soon as all of his officers arrived, Arnold briefed them on the final plan of attack. There was still no sign of the boats that were to ferry Allen's men across the lake. Unbeknownst to Allen, Lieutenant Herrick's mission to Skenesborough to seize the Loyalist Major Skene, and capture his schooner, *Catharine*, had only been partially successful. Herricks had captured Major Skene, after which he learned that the schooner was a hundred miles north delivering grain and iron to the British garrison at Fort St. Johns in Quebec Province. There were no other boats at Skenesborough large enough to ferry the Americans across the lake and it was too late for Lieutenant Herrick to notify Allen at Hands Cove. The expedition's last hope rested with Captain Douglass, who had been sent north to search the areas around Panton, Bridport, and Crown Point for boats.

Tension mounted at Hands Cove as the night wore on. Allen began to weigh his options. Could the attack be postponed until the following night without the large force assembled at the cove being discovered? Was the operation already compromised by the capture of Lieutenant Herrick, or Captain Douglass? Should the operation be abandoned? Around 3:00 a.m., a large scow appeared on the lake, tacking toward the cove from the north, the direction Allen least expected. As the scow approached the shore, two boys and a black man jumped off. The boys informed Allen that the scow belonged to Major Skene, and that it was laying off Bridport earlier that evening. The boys had learned of the expedition from Captain Douglass, and knowing that the scow was anchored off Bridport, they had paddled out to it, and convinced its black captain to sail to Hands Cove. By that time, the moon had set, and squalls were blowing up to the north. Allen quickly ordered his men to begin boarding the workboat. As the men began to clamber aboard, a second boat appeared out the darkness. It was another boat commandeered by Captain Douglass at Bridport. On board were several recruits from the Bridport area. Allen quickly crammed 83 men into the two boats including himself. Seth Warner, Allen's cousin and third-in-command of the expedition, remained behind with the rest of the men to organize a second crossing when the boats returned.

The two overloaded boats shoved off into the choppy frigid waters of Lake Champlain, with water sloshing over the gunwales. Rainsqualls soaked the men to the bone as the oarsmen rowed toward the western shoreline. The winds were too high to risk raising a sail. It took about an hour and a half to make the two-mile crossing. The boats landed on the beach near Willow Point, about a third of a mile from the fort, at 4:30 a.m. on May 10.

As soon as his men disembarked, Allen ordered the boats to return to Hands Cove for a second crossing. Meanwhile he reconsidered his plans for the assault as he only had about one-third of his men on the western side of the lake, and no supplies other than those they carried. It would take at least three hours for the boats to make a second crossing. By that time, the garrison would be fully awake and alert. A daylight attack on Fort Ticonderoga without artillery support offered little chance of success. The gates would be secured, and the British would pour cannon and musket fire down on the attackers from the ramparts. Allen's men had no ropes, grappling hooks, or ladders to scale the walls of the fort. It didn't take Allen long to make a decision.

With the far eastern sky beginning to pale, Allen ordered his men to form in three ranks on the beach and addressed them:

> Friends and fellow soldiers, you have for a number of years past been a scourge and terror to arbitrary power. Your valor has been famed abroad, and acknowledged, as appears by the advice and orders to me, from the General assembly of Connecticut, to surprise and take the garrison now before us. I now propose to advance before you, and in person, conduct you through the wicket gate; for we must this morning either quit our pretensions to valor, or possess ourselves of this fortress in a few minutes; and,

inasmuch as it is a desperate attempt, which none but the bravest of men dare undertake, I do not urge it on any contrary to his will. You that will undertake voluntarily, poise your firelocks.[15]

All 83 men raised their muskets. After issuing last-minute instructions to the officers, Allen moved to the head of the column, raised his sword over his head saying, "Let's go." The column followed an old French road that led to the fort. The attackers soon had the front of the fort in sight. The fort's walls loomed over them in the darkness. As the Americans neared the fort, their teenage guide, Nathan Beman, skirted the east wall, and led the column toward an entrance on the south wall. The large gate on the south wall of the fort was closed, but there was a smaller wicket gate built within the large gate. The wicket gate was open, guarded by a sentry.

Inside the fort, the garrison of 38 men, plus 24 women and children, were still asleep in their quarters. There was only one other sentry awake inside the guardroom. This was surprising given that Captain Delaplace had applied to General Carleton for reinforcement over the course of the winter, as he had reason to suspect an attack based on "some circumstances that happen'd in his neighbourhood."[16] The only reinforcement that Carleton had immediately dispatched in response to Delaplace's request was a subaltern and 20 men. These had departed Canada in two separate groups on about April 12 and only one of the groups—a 10-man detachment led by Lieutenant Jocelyn Feltman—had reached the fort before the attack.[17] The lack of urgency in providing reinforcements for Ticonderoga and Crown Point, and the complacency of the garrison commander can only be explained by the fact that war had not yet been declared, and the overwhelming majority of New Yorkers remained loyal to the Crown. Moreover, in the first session of the Continental Congress in Philadelphia, it was resolved that under no circumstances should the Patriots molest the garrisons of New York's forts. However, this resolution was passed before the outbreak of hostilities at Lexington and Concord in April 1775, news of which had not yet reached Fort Ticonderoga.

Most accounts describing the attack agree that Allen and Arnold were the first two men to enter the fort through the wicket gate, followed closely by the assault force. The startled sentry at the gate saw Allen charging through the darkness toward him with his drawn sword. He managed to cock his musket and pull the trigger, but luck was with Allen that night. The flint on the sentry's musket failed to ignite the damp powder causing a misfire. The terrified sentry turned and ran into the fort yelling at the top of his voice. Allen chased him through the covered passageway and onto the parade ground. As Allen's men swarmed onto the parade ground, he lined them up in firing formation facing the two barracks, and had them give three loud "huzzahs." Suddenly, a second sentry emerged from the guardroom to find out what the disturbance was all about. The soldier charged Allen with a fixed bayonet, but Allen side-stepped and struck the man on the top of the head with the flat of his sword, injuring him only slightly. Surrounded by Allen and his men, the injured soldier asked for quarter, and Allen granted it on the condition that he point the way to the commandant's quarters. Despite the intelligence received prior to the attack, Allen did not know the entire layout of the fort in detail. The terrified soldier agreed to do so, and pointed toward a door on the second floor of the west barracks.

Meanwhile the fort's second-in-command, Lieutenant Feltman, was awakened by the shouting and commotion. He quickly donned his redcoat, and with pants in hand, rushed toward Captain Delaplace's rooms to wake him and receive his orders. By that time, some of Allen's men were on the bastions of the wing of the fort where the back doors of Delaplace's and Feltman's rooms were located. After pounding on his captain's door for several seconds, Feltman finally gained admittance. He informed his commander that the Americans were inside the fort, and asked for his instructions. He also offered to force his way down the stairs in order to reach the barracks room where the men slept. While he hastily donned his uniform and sword, Delaplace told the lieutenant to go to the top of stairway, and attempt to delay the Americans and find out their intentions.

Feltman then opened a side door and started toward the stairs where he came face to face with Allen who was running up the stairs. Trying to stall the Americans in the stairwell as long as possible, Feltman asked who they were and on whose authority they had entered His Majesty's fort. 'en responded to the lieutenant, who he apparently thought was the commander, by menacingly waving his sword over Feltman's head, while announcing his authority thusly, "In the name of the Great Jehovah and the Continental Congress."[18] He then warned Feltman that, if he did not immediately give up the fort, or if a single shot were fired by the British, "neither man, woman, or child should be left alive in the fort."[19] After learning that Feltman was not the fort's commander, Allen put him under guard and proceeded toward Delaplace's room. Delaplace emerged from his room fully dressed and wearing his ceremonial sword to face the leaders of the expedition. Placed under guard, Delaplace was then taken downstairs to complete the surrender.

Ethan Allen's men wasted little time in taking the fort's entire contingent of troops and dependents prisoner. All told there were approximately 68 soldiers and civilians in the British garrison, including 24 women and children. The Americans also seized all the arms and weaponry in the barracks and armory. The actual capture of what was arguably the strongest British fort in North America probably took less than 20 minutes. No one was killed on either side during the fort's capture, and the British only had one man slightly injured by Allen's sword stroke.

Allen's men wanted to celebrate the fort's capture and it didn't take them long to discover a cellar under the officer's quarters where 24 kegs of rum were stored. Most of the men were soon roaring drunk, much to the disgust of Benedict Arnold, who wanted the men to immediately begin inventorying and determining the condition of the cannon. Allen was not one to deprive his men of a celebration, and therefore sided with his men, later writing, "We tossed about the flowing bowl," and toasted success to Congress and to the liberty and freedom of America.[20]

By the following morning, the remainder of Allen's force, led by Captain Seth Warner, had crossed Lake Champlain and marched into the fort. The fort was now held by between three hundred and four hundred Americans. On May 11, Allen sent Warner with one hundred men to seize the British fort at Crown Point, which was located about 12 miles north of Ticonderoga. Strong headwinds drove Warner's boats back toward Ticonderoga, and the entire force returned the same evening. Warner led a second sortie the following day, successfully reaching Crown Point and investing the fort. The Crown Point garrison consisted of one sergeant and eight soldiers. When the sergeant saw the size of Warner's force, he quickly surrendered the fort without firing a shot.

The small size of Crown Point's garrison did not diminish its importance to the Americans—Allen's men captured the strategic fort intact including 111 cannon.[21] Those cannon—together with the more than one hundred cannon plus mortars, howitzers, and other ordnance taken at Ticonderoga—were of tremendous value to the American army, despite the fact that approximately half of the cannon were in need of repair. The following December, Henry Knox, Washington's chief of artillery, led an expedition to Ticonderoga, dismounted and disassembled 57 of the guns, and transported the artillery by boats and sleds back east to Boston where they were emplaced on Dorchester Heights overlooking Boston. The threatening presence of the American artillery convinced General Gage to evacuate the British army from Boston by sea to Nova Scotia in March 1776.

––––––––––

The capture of forts Ticonderoga and Crown Point was America's first victory of the war. The expedition demonstrated the value of paramilitary forces such as Ethan Allen's Green Mountain Boys, and their ability to operate jointly with state militias, and eventually with regular Continental Army forces. Ethan Allen and the other officers on the expedition were excellent planners who effectively employed the principles of speed, security, and surprise.

The expedition was launched with all possible speed. Forts Ticonderoga and Crown Point had to be seized before significant reinforcements were rushed south from Canada. Elements of the 26th Regiment were already on the move, and the remainder of the regiment was preparing to move when the forts were captured. Allen's men were able to move quickly toward their target unencumbered by artillery or wagonloads of supplies. Traveling in small groups, Allen's men could quickly converge at prearranged assembly areas near their targets further enhancing the speed of the operation. Despite the small garrisons and conditions of Forts Ticonderoga and Crown Point, they were by no means completely indefensible against a force the size of Allen's.

Any breach of security by the expedition could have alerted the British, resulting in the attack on the fort being met with a hail of grapeshot, mortar fire, and musket fire. While most of the population between Bennington and Ticonderoga were sympathetic to the Patriot cause, there were also a number of Tories and Loyalists living in the area who would not have hesitated to alert the British of the expedition. By patrolling and securing the roads leading to and from Ticonderoga, Allen was able to isolate the fort before the attack.

By crossing Lake Champlain during the hours of darkness, and attacking the fort just before dawn, Allen had surprise on his side. Had Allen's boats been spotted crossing the lake, they would have been subjected to bombardment by the fort's cannon before reaching the shore, or Allen's force could have been engaged by the British as it attempted to land on the western shore. In that event, the expedition would have ended in disaster with numerous casualties. Sound backup planning, improvisation, and flexibility also helped insure the success of the operation. Had Allen relied completely on seizing the boats at Skenesborough, and not sent Captain Douglass north on the lake to search for boats, the operation would have come to a halt on the eastern shore of Lake Champlain. Finally, if Allen had waited for his entire force to cross the lake rather than attacking with only eight-three men, it is highly likely that he would have lost the element of surprise. Once daylight broke, his force on the western shore would most likely been discovered since it was only one third of a mile from the fort.

The late arrival of Benedict Arnold, and his efforts to take command of the expedition, very nearly led to the termination of the entire operation. Arnold settled for what he interpreted as joint command with Allen during the attack, but Allen never considered Arnold more than a volunteer officer. The dispute did not, however, end with the taking of Fort Ticonderoga. Arnold continued to assert himself, claiming that he was the legitimate commander at Fort Ticonderoga after its seizure. Allen steadfastly claimed his full right to command the entire force. When Arnold attempted to enforce discipline among Allen's Green Mountain Boys, Allen rebuked him in front of his own men, increasing tensions at the fort. On at least two occasions, Allen's men took shots at Arnold, who they considered a pretender. Despite the continuing controversy over command, Allen and Arnold managed to accomplish several follow-up actions after the attacks on Forts Ticonderoga and Crown Point. The captured arms, equipment, and stores were inventoried and inspected to determine serviceability. The prisoners were looked after, and provided with receipts for any personal property plundered or confiscated before being evacuated to Hartford to await exchange. Additionally, Allen dispatched John Brown, with the fort's captured colors, and Allen's letter announcing the capture of the forts to Philadelphia, for delivery to the Continental Congress. After receiving Allen's letter, Congress and state authorities credited Ethan Allen and his Green Mountain Boys for their capture of the forts.

The command controversy at Ticonderoga highlighted the need for the appointment of an overall commander-in-chief of American forces. George Washington was appointed to this position in June 1775, the month after the American victory at Ticonderoga. This appointment gave Washington the authority to establish clear and unambiguous chains of command for future operations.

In the aftermath of the Ticonderoga expedition, Ethan Allen led a failed expedition to capture Montreal, where he was taken prisoner by the British. He spent more than two years as a prisoner in England and on board various prison ships until he was granted a parole at New York in 1777. He returned home where he learned that Vermont had declared independence in 1777. He remained active in Revolutionary affairs until his death in 1789.

Benedict Arnold went on to lead a failed expedition to capture Quebec city in late 1775, and was later defeated at Valcour Island on Lake Champlain in October 1776. He was, however, given credit for delaying the British advance against Fort Ticonderoga until 1777. He later led forces at Saratoga where he received a severe leg wound, but was given credit for turning the tide of the battle. As a result of his valor at Saratoga, Congress restored Arnold's seniority and he was appointed to the rank of major general in the Continental Army. While recovering from his wounds, Arnold was appointed commandant of the city of Philadelphia, and later assumed command of West Point, New York, where he turned traitor, and plotted to turn West Point over to the British. Barely escaping capture by American forces, Arnold then fled to New York City, where he was commissioned a brigadier in the British Army. During January 1781, Arnold led British troops against American forces in Virginia, burning the city of Richmond and ravaging the countryside in central and southern Virginia. In September 1781, Arnold led a raid against New London, Connecticut, burning the town and massacring the American garrison at Fort Griswold on Groton Heights. Two months after the British surrender at Yorktown in October 1781, Arnold moved to England where he died a traitor in 1801.

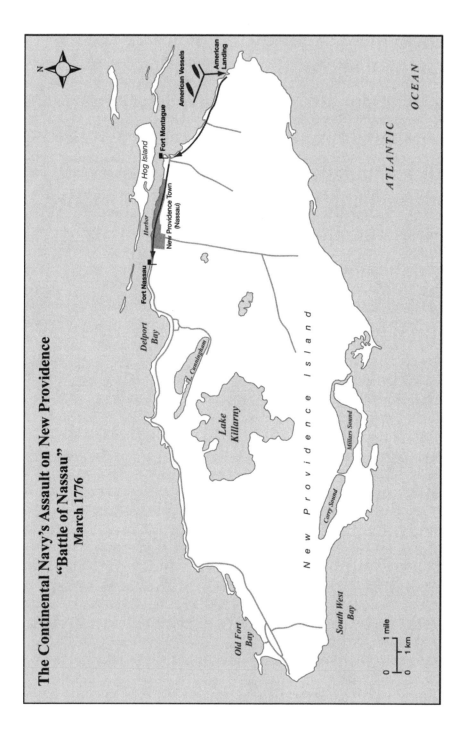

The Continental Navy's Assault on New Providence
"Battle of Nassau"
March 1776

American Vessels

American Landing

Fort Montague

Hog Island

Harbor

New Providence Town
(Nassau)

Fort Nassau

Delport Bay

Lt. Cunningham

Lake Killarny

Old Fort Bay

South West Bay

New Providence Island

Millars Sound

Curry Sound

ATLANTIC OCEAN

N

0   1 mile
0   1 km

THE NEW PROVIDENCE RAID

The 230 marines and forty sailors were crammed below the decks of the American sloop, Providence, and two captured prize sloops. The landing force was ordered to stay out of sight as the ships sailed toward the sheltered port. Although the temperature was a mild 79 degrees, the men were sweat-soaked inside the cramped holds where they could not feel the balmy tropical breezes that swept across the crystal clear-blue waters. The men were more than a little eager to get ashore and strike a blow at their British adversaries. For most of the men, it would be their first taste of combat. Only a handful had been under enemy fire, and more than a few were recovering from a smallpox outbreak that had ravished the ranks of the sailors and marines of the fleet during the two-week voyage from Philadelphia. They were more than ready for a fight. Captain Samuel Nicholas and his lieutenant, John Trevette, both officers in the Continental Marines, were dressed in non-descript clothes with cutlasses and pistols at their sides. The pair remained on deck to keep an eye on the captured crew and pilots as they steered the boats toward the entrance to the harbor. Through his spyglass, Nicholas could make out the silhouette of a small stone fort surrounded by scrub pines guarding the eastern entrance to the harbor. Squinting in the bright morning sunlight, Nicholas could make out the cannon pointing ominously toward sea approaches to the harbor. Suddenly, he saw flames and smoke emerging from the mouths of the cannon followed seconds later by the sounds of the cannon blasts reverberating across the waves.

WHEN WAR BROKE OUT BETWEEN THE COLONIES AND BRITISH IN the spring of 1775, the Americans had only about 80,000 pounds of gunpowder available, which by the end of the year had dwindled to almost nothing. General Washington appealed to the state governments for any quantities that they were capable of producing, but domestic production was virtually non-existent. For a time, it appeared that the future of the American Revolution hinged on finding sources to replenish the Continental Army's supply of gunpowder. Since the Americans had no duly constituted navy, it was difficult to gain access to foreign supplies, and France would not begin clandestinely supplying gunpowder to the Patriots until later in the war. As the struggle entered its second year, the situation was desperate.

During the latter part of 1775, the Continental Congress began serious discussions about creating an American navy. On October 3 and 7, Rhode Island delegates presented resolutions to authorize a fleet of cruisers equipped for the protection of American commerce, but on both occasions the Rhode Island resolutions were tabled. On October 17, the Naval Committee of the Continental Congress presented a plan calling for a fleet of 10 warships, but Congress authorized only four. Six weeks later, Congress authorized the construction of 13 ships for the navy, and on December 22, 1775, Congress unanimously chose Esek Hopkins as commander-in-chief of the new Continental Navy.[1] A month earlier, the Continental Congress authorized, "That two battalions of Marines be raised," and Samuel Nicholas was commissioned a "Captain of Marines."[2] Congress stipulated that men recruited for the Marines should be good seamen, and be acquainted with maritime affairs so that they would be able to serve at sea when required.

Both Hopkins and Nicholas went to work as soon as they received official confirmation of their appointments. Captain Nicholas's first assignment was to enlist the men for service in the Continental Marines, while Hopkins's priority was gathering ships and crews so that he could put a fleet to sea as soon as possible. Both men went about their tasks in an energetic and vigorous manner.

At the outbreak of the Revolution, 57-year-old Esek Hopkins was one of the best-known sea captains in the New England colonies. The Hopkins family was one of the most prominent families in the sea-going colony of Rhode Island. His older brother, Stephen, served as chief justice of the Rhode Island Supreme Court, and nine years as governor of the colony. In 1774, he became one of Rhode Island's two delegates to the First Continental Congress. Stephen's ardent patriotism and political connections served his younger brother's career well, both as a merchant sea captain, and later as a naval officer.

Born in 1718, near Providence, Rhode Island, Esek Hopkins went to sea in 1738, as a common seaman. Hopkins quickly mastered the art of navigation and other sailing skills. After becoming a navigator, he became a merchant, and captained vessels owned and controlled by the Hopkins family. When the Seven Years' War broke out in 1756, Captain Hopkins fitted out one of his ships as a privateer, and took command himself. By capturing several valuable prizes, Hopkins gained fame, notoriety, and personal wealth. Many officers who served under Hopkins during the war with the French later served with distinction as naval officers during the Revolutionary War.

When war between the colonies and Britain appeared imminent, the citizens of Providence turned to Esek Hopkins for assistance to prepare defenses for the town and its harbor. During the summer of 1775, Hopkins directed the construction of earthworks on elevations overlooking Providence Harbor, and a battery of 16-pounders was emplaced at the head of the harbor. When a British fleet stationed at Newport sent two ships to raid the town to capture supplies in August of 1775, Hopkins ordered all the shore batteries to be manned, and a floating battery was built along with fire ships. When the British commanders saw Providence's defenses, they decided not to attack. In October 1775, the Recess Committee of the Rhode Island General Assembly appointed Hopkins brigadier general, and put him in charge of the state's defenses.

After assuming his new billet as commander-in-chief of the Navy, Hopkins moved quickly to assemble a squadron of eight ships, while additional warships were under construction. Those eight ships were merchant vessels, that were hastily converted to armed warships at the ports of Philadelphia and Baltimore. Altogether, the eight ships were armed with a total of 110 guns. Hopkins selected the two-year-old, 440-ton *Alfred* as his flagship. The *Alfred* mounted twenty 9-pounders and ten 6-pounders.[3] Four additional ships soon joined the *Alfred* at the port of Philadelphia. These were the *Columbus* (28 guns), the brig, *Cabot* (14 guns), the brig, *Andrew Doria* (14 guns), and the sloop, *Providence* (twelve 14-pounders). Three additional ships, the schooner, *Wasp* (eight 2-pounders, six swivel guns), the sloop, *Hornet* (ten 9-pounders), and the schooner, *Fly* (eight guns), were outfitted in Baltimore. Those eight vessels, once converted to warships, became the Continental Navy's first fleet.[4] While the ships were under conversion to warships, Hopkins began selecting his captains, recruiting his crews, and drafting signal orders that the fleet would use at sea.[5]

Meanwhile, Samuel Nicholas, captain of marines, recruited the men who would become the first Continental marines. Nicholas had ready access to a pool of tough men who were willing to fight. Thirty-one-year-old Samuel Nicholas ran the Connestogoe Wagon Tavern on Philadelphia's Market Street just three and a half blocks from the waterfront. His wife's family owned the business, and he managed the tavern after his marriage. Nicholas was also acquainted with most of the other tavern owners in the district, including Robert Mullan, who ran the Tun Tavern on the waterfront. After his appointment as captain of marines, Nicholas solicited the assistance of Mullan in recruiting patrons for the marines. Nicholas was looking for tough, strong, adventure-seeking men, who had served as crewmembers on merchant ships and privateers. Taverns along the waterfront were gathering places for seamen and ruffians, but Nicholas had competition in his recruitment efforts. Captains of privateers also prowled the waterfronts seeking crewmembers for their ships. They enticed seamen to sign on as crewmembers by promising them a share of the prize money for any ships and cargoes captured, in lieu of regular pay or other reward. Nicholas and Mullan formulated their own competitive recruiting strategy. First, they appealed to the potential recruits' patriotism and love of country, offering each man the opportunity to serve with honor in the proud new Continental Marines with brave men such as themselves. Along with regular pay and prize money, the recruiters also offered a $17 bounty and "an equal advantage of provisions and clothing." Recruiting posters were posted all over the city advertising the advantages of service in the Continental Marines. Nicholas also promised that anyone who brought a recruit to Tun Tavern, would receive a payment of three dollars. After the arrival of a hundred marine recruits from Rhode Island, Nicholas had no difficulty in filling the ranks of the Continental Marines.

Nicholas was also had strong connections with Philadelphia's rich and powerful. Born in 1744, Nicholas was the son of a well-known Quaker blacksmith, and the nephew of the mayor of Philadelphia. Nicholas's uncle had financed his education at Philadelphia Academy (University of Pennsylvania). When he completed his studies at the age of 15, he was readily accepted into Philadelphia's high society. At the age of 16, Nicholas was admitted to the Schuylkill Fishing Company, a prestigious city club. He was also one of the founders of the Gloucester Fox Hunting Club, and was a member of the Patriotic Association of Philadelphia, an organization whose membership included many of the city's prominent patriotic citizens. His marriage to the daughter of a well-established businessman further enhanced his social standing. When the Continental Congress began searching for a man to raise, train, equip, and command the newly authorized Continental Marines, Nicholas's name was at the top of their list.

While Esek Hopkins and Samuel Nicholas were organizing and outfitting their men and ships for service in the Continental Navy and Marines, the Naval Committee of the Continental Congress met in secret sessions to decide on a strategy, and assign missions to the Continental fleet. Politics complicated the process. Delegates were answerable to their powerful state assemblies and governors, who demanded a fair allocation of the scarce military resources to protect their states. Twelve of the 13 states bordered the Atlantic, and were subject to raids by the British navy. British ships prowled the coastline from New England to Georgia, interfering with commerce, and raiding seaport towns for supplies at will. Heated arguments ensued between the delegates as they attempted to formulate a naval strategy, and assign missions to the Continental fleet.

Beginning in 1775, 11 of the 13 states purchased ships, and organized small navies of their own to protect their coasts and waterways. Some state navies were established prior to the creation of the Continental Navy. Only two states, New Jersey and Delaware, never established their own navy. The state navies ranged in size from a single ship to small flotillas, but they were no match for the British fleets. Consequently, all 13 states wanted their shores protected by the new Continental Navy. The delegates to the Continental Congress from Maryland and Virginia presented strong arguments that they should be the first states to receive support from the

Continental Navy. Both states bordered the Chesapeake Bay, where commercial shipping was under threat. Lord Dunmore, the deposed royal governor of Virginia, had his own small navy of armed merchant ships that sailed back and forth across the Chesapeake, terrorizing the local inhabitants and capturing American merchant vessels.[6] The British navy had almost complete control of waters inside the Virginia Capes, which meant that Virginia and Maryland were insecure and vulnerable.

The Chesapeake Bay was of special concern to most delegates to Congress since it was a vital inland waterway for commerce between the states. The important trade centers of Annapolis, Baltimore, and even Philadelphia were dependent on free access to the Chesapeake. However, North and South Carolina and Georgia also expressed concerns for their own vulnerable coastlines. During the winter of 1775–76, the British had two frigates, two sloops-of-war off the Virginia coast, while other British ships took up stations off the Atlantic coast as far south as Georgia. Action to address the threat posed by the British navy was being demanded by all the southern state delegates to Congress, but there were competing demands from other delegations as well. The new Continental fleet of eight small warships was simply too small to meet the demands of all 13 states. Congress had to prioritize missions for the Continental Navy, and develop a naval strategy that would best support the war effort.

On November 29, 1775, Congress received information that there "was a large quantity of powder in the island of Providence," and the Naval Committee was instructed to take measures to secure the powder, and transport it to Philadelphia.[7] Since the supply of powder from Britain had been entirely cut off after the outbreak of hostilities, and domestic production of powder was incapable of meeting the army's demands in quantity or quality, gunpowder had to be procured from abroad. The British navy blockaded American ports to prevent the importation of gunpowder and other war materials so the army's supply of gunpowder continued to shrink. While preparations were underway to get the Continental fleet to sea, the commander-in-chief of the Continental Army, General George Washington wrote, "Our want of powder is inconceivable, a daily waste and no supply presents a gloomy prospect."[8]

Congress and its Naval Committee were well aware of the army's shortage of gunpowder, but failed to authorize a direct action mission to capture the gunpowder stored at New Providence in the Bahamas. Instead, the delegates bowed to political pressure from the southern delegates when they drafted the first orders for the American fleet. The Continental Navy's commander-in-chief received the orders from the Congress' Naval Committee on January 5, 1776. The orders directed Hopkins to first sail the fleet south to the Chesapeake Bay in Virginia where he was to "search out," attack and destroy all the "Naval forces of our Enemies . . ." then proceed immediately southward to the Carolinas to do the same, and then to sail directly northward to Rhode Island to "attack, take and destroy all the Enemies Naval force."[8] However, the final clause of the orders gave Commodore Hopkins some latitude once the fleet was at sea. It read:

> Notwithstanding these particular Orders, which 'tis hoped you will be able to execute, if bad Winds or Stormy Weather, or any other unforeseen accident or disaster you so to do, You are then to follow such Courses as your best Judgement shall Suggest to you as most useful to the American Cause and to distress the Enemy by all means in your power.[9]

On the chilling afternoon of January 4, 1776, four ships of the Continental Navy's fleet were ready to sail. Provisions were loaded, and the Continental Marines were on board. Sailors made last-minute preparations. Despite the frigid conditions and blustery winds, thousands of citizens, city officials, and members of the Continental Congress crowded the Philadelphia wharves to see the small Continental fleet set off. At 2:00 p.m., officers shouted orders, and Commodore Hopkins' flagship, *Alfred*, hoisted its ensign, signaling the fleet's departure. The American ships caught the current, and slowly slipped down the Delaware River, but the fleet did not get far. By the time the ships reached Reedy Island, the Delaware was almost frozen over. Ice closed in around the ships' hulls, and the Continental Navy's fleet was locked in the ice for almost six weeks. On February 11, 1776, the ice had melted, and the ships continued down the Delaware River. When the fleet reached Cape Henlopen, the southern cape of the Delaware Bay, the fleet dropped anchor to await the arrival of the two remaining vessels of the fleet, the sloop *Hornet* and the schooner *Wasp*. Both ships had been refitted at Baltimore, and joined the fleet on February 13.

While the fleet was anchored off Cape Henlopen, Commodore Hopkins issued new orders to his captains. The orders directed the six captains to sail south to Abaco Island in the Bahamas. Instead of sailing to the Chesapeake, Commodore Hopkins decided to conduct a seaborne raid on New Providence to seize the gunpowder stored on the island, without specific authorization from Congress. Hopkins later argued that as commander-in-chief of the Navy, he was exercising his discretion as outlined in the final paragraph of his orders. Nonetheless, it was a political blunder that alienated some members of Congress. Hopkins would eventually be held accountable for his actions.

The fleet set sail again on February 17, on a course that would take them straight to the Bahamas. With favorable winds, the ships made good progress for the first two days. However, during the night of February 19–20, the fleet sailed into a raging gale. As the storm at sea intensified, the American ships were separated. By dawn of February 20, two ships, the *Fly* and the *Hornet*, were nowhere in sight. Becoming separated from the fleet during the storm, and falling behind, the two ships followed the same course toward the Bahamas for two days before colliding with each other off Cape Hatteras. The *Hornet* lost her masthead, and attempted to reach the port of Charleston, but was driven off by a storm. The captain then decided to return to the Delaware. The *Fly* continued sailing toward the rendezvous point in the Bahamas.

Meanwhile, the remainder of the fleet continued on course, and arrived off the southwest coast of Great Abaco Island in the northern Bahamas on March 1, 1776. Approaching the island, the Americans spotted two coastal sloops belonging to New Providence. Hopkins quickly ordered his flagship, *Alfred*, to intercept and capture the enemy sloops, which they accomplished in short order. On the afternoon of March 1, the fleet and captured sloops dropped anchor in 12 fathoms of water off the "Hole in the Wall," on the remote southwest tip of Great Abaco Island.[10] New Providence was some 55 miles to the southwest, and approachable through the Northeast Providence Passage.

The "Hole in the Wall" was well known to most sailors and ship's captains of the period including Commodore Hopkins. It was named for a natural rock formation that jutted into the sea through which the waves had worn a hole. There were no inhabitants living near the "Hole in the Wall." Since there were no inhabitants living near the "Hole in the Wall," and they were still 55 miles from New Providence, Hopkins believed that he still had the element of surprise on his side, but that was not the case. British spies in Philadelphia had reported the American fleet's departure to British intelligence officers, but wrongly concluded that the fleet's destination was either New York or Boston. However, a British officer who had arrived in New Providence on February 25 had spotted the fleet off the Delaware Capes on his way south. His relayed this information to Montfort Browne, governor of the Bahamas, stating that American fleet was likely headed for New Providence. Then on March 1, Captain George Dorsett arrived in New Providence with more up-to-date information. Near Great Abaco on a whaling cruise, Dorsett had sighted the American fleet. Concluding that it was assembling for an attack on New Providence, he returned immediately to port to inform Governor Browne. The element of surprise was lost.

Despite the warnings, New Providence was ill-prepared to repel an attack. The poor state of readiness was the result of decisions made by British authorities. Several months prior to the arrival of the American fleet, General Gage, commander-in-chief of British forces in North America, had ordered the withdrawal of a detachment of the British 14th Regiment that was stationed at New Providence. After the Regulars departed, the New Providence militia assumed responsibility for the defense of the island. Major Robert Sterling commanded the island's three-hundred-strong provincial militia force. Since a majority of the militiamen were fishermen and seamen, the number present on the island at any one time fell well short of the number required to garrison the forts and defend the town.[11] Only one ship was on station at New Providence to protect the harbor and town. The armed schooner, *Saint John*, was anchored in New Providence harbor, but was barely seaworthy, and no match for the American warships.

Besides the lack of adequate defense forces, the colony's civil administration, namely Governor Browne, was incapable of decisive leadership and action. Browne had served as an officer in the British Army in the

West Indies during the Seven Years' War, and was twice wounded. He later served as lieutenant governor of West Florida before becoming governor of the Bahamas in 1774. Early in his tenure as governor, Browne left his post several times to travel to West Florida to pursue personal interests in land speculation. Despite the warnings that he received concerning the presence of the American fleet, Browne did not immediately call out the militia, or take any other action to prepare for an attack. Instead, he kept the information secret until the island's Colonial Council convened. While the governor was not solely responsible for the woeful state of New Providence's defenses, his inertia and apathy only made matters worse.

Commodore Hopkins and his captains were familiar with the waters surrounding the New Providence, its harbor, and the town itself. Many of them had served as captains, masters, navigators and mates on merchant vessels that sailed to the Bahamas prior to the outbreak of hostilities. Their knowledge, along with the information provided by the captains of the two captured sloops, gave the Americans a significant advantage as they finalized their plans for the raid.

In 1775, New Providence was a small sleepy colonial town consisting of a single street lined with wooden houses, surrounded by trees, shrubs, and gardens. The only public buildings in the town were a church, a jail, and an assembly-house. The town's residents included a few government officials, merchants, shipbuilders, fishermen, seamen, and laborers, numbering no more than a few hundred in total. The remainder of the island's population were planters and their slaves, who lived on plantations outside the town.

New Providence's harbor was protected from the sea and prevailing winds by Hog Island (present-day Paradise Island) This elongated island is located just off the shore of the town. The harbor had an eastern entrance, which was guarded by Fort Montagu; and a western entrance, which was guarded by Fort Nassau. Fort Nassau was a square palisaded stone fort dating back to the late 17th century. After its destruction by the French and Spanish in 1703, Fort Nassau was rebuilt in 1744, but by 1775 it had fallen into a state of disrepair. The fort had a total of forty-six 12- and 18- pounder cannon mounted on its walls and ramparts. However, the island's militia feared that the decaying walls would crumble and collapse if the cannons were fired.[12] Fort Nassau was vulnerable to attack by sea and land. It sat too close to the water's edge and was overlooked by high ground to the south. An enemy force landing on beaches outside the town could march into the hills behind the fort, and fire down on the fort's walls and ramparts, thus preventing the gun crews from firing their cannon at enemy ships forcing their way into the harbor.

The eastern passageway into the harbor was protected by Fort Montagu, a small square stone fort that mounted seventeen 12- and 18-pounders. It was located about two miles from town. Constructed during the 1740s, Fort Montagu was smaller than Fort Nassau, but was in a slightly better state of repair.

On March 2, Commodore Hopkins met with his ship captains, and marine officers to finalize the plan for the attack on New Providence. The landing force included 230 marines, and 50 sailors. Captain Nicholas commanded the marines, and the sailors were under the command of Lieutenant Thomas Weaver. Weaver was familiar with layout of the town and its defenses, having visited New Providence on several voyages. The plan called for the landing force to transfer to the two captured sloops and the sloop *Providence*.[13] The men would stay below deck until the vessels entered the harbor at dawn, where they would board whaleboats and row the final few yards to the beach. Once ashore, the landing party would immediately take possession of the town and its forts before any alarm could be raised. The rest of the fleet would stay just beyond the sight of land, until the landing force was ashore. The plan relied heavily on the element of surprise. The Americans were still unaware that the British knew of the American fleet's presence in the Bahamas.

During the afternoon and evening of March 2, the American sailors readied the ships' cannon, and checked the sails and rigging. The marines were issued muskets, bayonets, ammunition, and cutlasses before boarding the two captured sloops and the *Providence*. The marines were organized into two companies, which were commanded by First Lieutenant John Trevett and Lieutenant Henry Dayton. Both officers had served aboard merchant vessels before the war.

The American fleet departed its anchorage off Great Abaco Island on the evening of March 2, 1776. Early the next morning, the ships rendezvoused about three nautical miles north of the port of New Providence. Before the three sloops carrying the landing force could enter the harbor, Hopkins ordered the remaining ships to sail closer to the harbor entrance. That proved to be a serious mistake. At daybreak, an alert harbor pilot spotted the larger ships following the three sloops. He quickly ran to Governor House and notified Governor Browne. Sailors on the British armed schooner, *Saint John*, anchored in the harbor, also spotted the fast-approaching American ships. Browne went to the harbor to confirm the sighting, and after satisfying himself that the American fleet was indeed approaching the harbor entrance, he ordered the Provincial Council to assemble immediately at Fort Nassau. Governor Browne also sent a message to Captain Grant, the skipper of the *Saint John*, requesting that he move his armed schooner into the channel off Fort Nassau. However, the winds and tide delayed its repositioning.[14] The governor then proceeded to Fort Nassau to meet with the council, and direct the defense of New Providence. After a quick discussion with his council members, Browne ordered an alarm sounded by the firing of three rounds from Fort Nassau's cannons. Two of the three gun carriages collapsed when the cannons were fired. After the cannons fired, drummers began beating the long roll to call the island's militia force to arms.

Realizing that the element of surprise was lost, Commodore Hopkins signaled for a council of war with his captains to determine the next move. It was agreed that a forced entry into the harbor under the guns of the two forts offered little chance of success. Hopkins proposed moving the fleet to the opposite side of the island where the marines would be put ashore to attack the town from the rear. Those most familiar with the island and the surrounding waters pointed out that there was no anchorage on the western side of the island. Furthermore, there was no road connecting the western shore of the island with the town of New Providence. To reach the town, the marines would have to make a cross-country march of more than 20 miles, affording the island's militia time to prepare ambush positions along the route of march.

Lieutenant John Paul Jones recommended that the fleet sail to an anchorage in Hanover Sound, some six miles west of the town. From that location, the marines could board whaleboats, and conduct an amphibious landing under the cover of the *Hornet*'s guns. After landing, Captain Nicholas's marines and Lieutenant Weaver's sailors could first attack Fort Montagu before moving against Fort Nassau and New Providence. Commodore Hopkins agreed with the proposal. The *Providence* and the two captured sloops soon got underway, heading for the landing site, while the remainder of the fleet stood off Hanover Sound.

Under a bright noonday sun, the marines and sailors boarded the whaleboats, and began rowing toward a beach about two miles east of Fort Montagu. With their muskets at the ready, the marines leapt from the whaleboats into the knee-high surf and charged onto the beach. It was the first amphibious landing by the Continental Marines. The landing was unopposed. By 2:00 p.m. the entire landing force was ashore and ready to march.

When the marines landed, panic-stricken villagers fled the nearby village of New Guinea. The villagers, who were freed slaves, thought the Americans were Spaniards who intended to kidnap them and sell them as slaves. The British colonists and militia knew otherwise.

As the marines were coming ashore, Governor Browne and militia leaders were still making preparations to repel the invasion. Browne correctly assumed that the Americans intended to seize the 200 barrels of gunpowder stored at Fort Nassau. He wanted to ship the gunpowder off the island to prevent its capture, and proposed loading the powder onto the *Mississippi Packet*, which was anchored in the harbor. The captain of the *Mississippi Packet*, William Chambers, agreed, but reminded Browne that he would first have to unload a cargo of lumber consigned for Jamaica. Samuel Gambier, a highly respected member of the provincial council, argued against removing the powder, reminding the governor that it would be needed for the defense of the island. Instead he recommended that Chambers sail out of the harbor and shadow the American fleet to determine its intention. He further recommended that a strong detachment of militia be sent to reinforce Fort Montagu. The council agreed that the *Mississippi Packet* should shadow the American fleet, but when Chamber's ship attempted to leave the harbor, high winds and swells drove it back into the harbor. The council also agreed that Fort Montagu had to be reinforced, and at 9:00 a.m. Lieutenant John Pratt and 30 militiamen departed Fort Nassau to reinforce Fort Montagu. An hour later, another militia detachment, led by Lieutenant Burke, arrived at Fort Nassau. Burke was redirected to Fort Montagu to reinforce Pratt's detachment.

After the reinforcements arrived at Fort Montagu, Lieutenants Pratt and Burke began assigning gun crews, and moving shells and powder from the arsenal to the gun platforms. Lookouts spotted the American ships and the landings, which were only two miles from the fort. After learning that the Americans were coming ashore, the militia officers dispatched a 15-man patrol, led by Lieutenants Burke and Judkin, to reconnoiter the marine beachhead, and determine the size of the American force. When the patrol neared the beach, Lieutenant Burke went forward with a flag of truce to determine the marines' intentions. The marine commander told Burke that the "Congress of the United Colonies authorized his mission," and he intended to take possession of all powder and stores belonging to "His Majesty."[15] As soon as the truce ended, Lieutenant Burke ordered his men to withdraw to Fort Montagu by the shortest possible route.

When a courier from Fort Montagu arrived at Fort Nassau with news of the marine landings, the island's Provincial Council ordered Major Robert Sterling to march to Fort Montagu with additional reinforcements. Soon after, Governor Browne returned to Fort Nassau, and took personal command of the reinforcements.

When Governor Browne arrived at Fort Montagu, he weighed his options. He knew that the Americans could lay siege to Fort Montagu with only part of their force, while the rest of the force moved against Fort Nassau and the town—and Fort Nassau was now held by only a handful of militiamen. Browne therefore decided to evacuate Fort Montagu. Before spiking all of Fort Montagu's cannon, he ordered the firing of three parting cannon shots in the direction of the approaching marines.

When the cannon shots smashed harmlessly into the scrub pines on the flanks of the American column, Captain Nicholas halted his marines to confer with his lieutenants. He later wrote,

> As we approached the fort, (within about half a mile, having a deep cover to go around, with a prodigious thicket on one side and the water on the other, entirely open to their view,) they fired

three 12-pound shot, which made us halt, and consult what was best to be done; we then thought it more prudent to send a flag to let them know what our designs were in coming there.[16]

Captain Nicholas sent Lieutenant John Trevett to the fort under a flag of truce. About halfway to the fort, Trevett met Lieutenant Burke, who was coming from Fort Montagu under a flag of truce. Burke explained that he was under orders of the governor to "wait on the Commanding Officer of the Enemy to know his Errand and on what account he had landed his Troops."[17] Trevett escorted Burke back to Captain Nicholas. Burke revealed to Nicholas that the island's militia had withdrawn from Fort Montagu, and retired to Fort Nassau. He also told Nicholas that the fort's cannon had been spiked. Captain Nicholas told the lieutenant that he was only after the military stores on the island, and that he intended to meet with the governor the following morning.[18]

After learning that the militia had abandoned Fort Montagu, Captain Nicholas and his marines quickly took possession of the abandoned fort. After examining the spiked guns and searching the fort for hidden stores, Nicholas decided to spend the night at Fort Montagu rather than marching on to Fort Nassau and the town. Nicholas later explained his decision not to march immediately on the town—his men were exhausted having spent so much time crammed below decks on the sloops, and then marching overland in the tropical heat of the day to reach Fort Montagu; all without sleep or time to prepare rations.[19] Although Captain Nicholas was in the best position to evaluate the condition of his men, his decision not to move immediately on the town afforded the British time to prepare for an attack, and remove 200 barrels of gunpowder from the island.

As the Americans occupied the fort, Governor Browne was on horseback, racing ahead of his troops. Upon reaching the town he went straight to the governor's house, where he remained for the next few hours. Many of the dispirited militiamen left the retreating column to look after their families and property rather than return to Fort Nassau. When the governor returned to the fort after his hiatus, he took charge of the fort and began preparing it for battle. Still short of troops, Browne once again ordered his drummers to beat the long roll to reassemble the militia. Surprisingly, about half of the militia who had returned to their homes reassembled at the fort. With the garrison still short of men, Browne, in desperation, offered to arm any black man who joined the garrison. Only a few accepted his offer.

––––––––––––

After securing Fort Montagu for the night, Captain Nicholas dispatched a courier to Commodore Hopkins on-board his flagship, *Alfred*, to notify him that Fort Montagu was in American hands, and that he intended on marching on the town and Fort Nassau in the morning. Earlier that day, Hopkins had drafted a proclamation to the citizens of the town stating that his intent was to seize the powder and other military stores on the island, and that if the residents of the island did not attempt to interfere, he would do them no harm.[20] Apparently Hopkins did not consider that the British might attempt to remove the powder from the island for he kept his fleet anchored in Hanover Sound for the night, leaving the passageways to the New Providence harbor unguarded. It was a decision he would soon regret.

While the Americans settled in for the night, Governor Browne convened a council of war in New Providence with the island's leading citizens and militia officers in attendance. The majority agreed that Fort Nassau was not defensible given the condition of its walls, gun carriages and the lack of equipment and manpower. The next question on the agenda was what to do with the 200 barrels of gunpowder stored in the fort's magazine. Governor Browne insisted that the gunpowder would not be turned over to the Americans. Instead, he proposed to take it off the island. When the council members argued that the Americans might take retaliation by looting and burning the town, Browne agreed to leave a small portion of the barrels at the fort.

The evacuation of the powder began immediately. The powder was removed from Fort Nassau and moved to the harbor where it was loaded aboard the *Mississippi Packet*, and the British armed schooner, *Saint John*. One hundred and nineteen barrels were loaded on the *Mississippi Packet*, and another 43 barrels were rolled onto the *Saint John*. The two sloops slipped quietly out of the harbor at around 2:00 a.m. and set sail for British Saint Augustine, Florida.

With most of the gunpowder on its way to Saint Augustine, Governor

Browne and the Provincial Council discussed what other actions needed to be taken. Only a few militiamen remained at Fort Nassau. The others, realizing the poor condition of the fort and the unreliability of the gun carriages, deserted and returned to their homes after the gunpowder was moved to the ships. Governor Browne proposed moving a detachment of 40 militiamen from the governor's house to Fort Nassau, and the council agreed. When the detachment arrived at the fort and saw that only a few men were still at their posts, they quickly deserted. As morning approached, the council recommended that the governor order the evacuation of Fort Nassau. Although Governor Browne still favored making a stand, he soon realized that he had no supporters and was finally convinced to leave the fort, and return to his residence.

Captain Nicholas roused his men well before daybreak, and by dawn they had completed the one-mile march to the eastern edge of the town, where they halted. Fort Nassau was deserted, but the gate was locked and the British colors still flew over the ramparts. As the Americans prepared to enter the town, they were met by an emissary bearing another message from the governor which again asked their intentions. Nicholas replied with the same reply—we are here for the gunpowder. The emissary responded that the Fort Nassau garrison was waiting to receive him. After conferring with his officers, Captain Nicholas ordered the marines and sailors to march into the town. The Americans met no resistance from the residents or militia. Captain Nicholas then sent a guard detachment to take possession of the governor's house, and secure the keys of the fort.[21] The governor reluctantly complied, and the Americans took possession of Fort Nassau without a shot being fired.

After the British colors were replaced with the "Grand Flag of the United Colonies," Nicholas made quick count of the cannon and shot on hand before sending a message to Commodore Hopkins informing him that it was safe to bring ships into the harbor. The commodore's flagship and one escort vessel soon entered the harbor; the remainder of the fleet remained at anchor in Hanover Sound for two additional days before sailing to New Providence harbor.

While Captain Nicholas and his officers awaited the arrival of Commodore Hopkins, a group of marines spotted the governor and his council members preparing to depart the governor's house on horseback. It was clear that they intended to escape to the island's interior. When Captain Nicholas was informed of this development, he was faced with a quandary. He had no instructions from Commodore Hopkins on how to deal with the island's civil authorities, and was reluctant to take the governor prisoner. Lieutenants Trevett and Dayton had no such reservations, and argued that the governor and his party should be taken prisoner. The cautious Nicholas said they could do as they pleased.[22] The lieutenants proceeded to the governor's house, took Governor Browne prisoner, and took him to Fort Nassau where he was placed under guard.

After coming ashore, Commodore Hopkins was informed by Nicholas of the count of armaments, munitions, and other military stores found at forts Montagu and Nassau. Only 24 barrels of gunpowder had been found, and the Americans soon realised that the British had successfully removed a large amount of gunpowder from the island. Hopkins was less than pleased with this news, and went to meet with the governor. It was an acrimonious meeting. Governor Browne was indignant that he was under arrest, and Commodore Hopkins was irate that the British had outfoxed him. After the meeting, Hopkins ordered the governor's continued confinement at Fort Nassau. He was later permitted to return to the governor's house where he remained under guard. On March 10, Browne was informed that he was to be moved to the flagship *Alfred*. He protested, but to no avail. After boarding the *Alfred*, Governor Browne asked Commodore Hopkins the reasons for his confinement. Although the commodore responded that Browne's men had fired on the marines as they approached Fort Montagu, both men knew that the real reason was the governor's successful removal of the gunpowder from the island. Two other prisoners, Browne's secretary Lieutenant James Babbidge, and Thomas Irving, a British civil servant, soon joined the governor on board the *Alfred*.

After taking control of New Providence on March 4, 1776, the Americans spent the next two weeks inventorying the military stores at the forts, and moving the heavy cannon, shot, and shells overland to the harbor, where it was loaded on the American ships. It was not an easy task. A total of 88 cannon, ranging from 9- to 36-pounders, 15 mortars, 24 barrels of gunpowder, and thousands of shot and shells was listed on the inventories of the two forts, along with gun carriages, fuses, and other accessories.[23] Hopkins wanted to recover the entire inventory of weaponry and supplies to justify the raid. He also knew that, in addition to the critical shortage of gunpowder, the Continental Army was also critically short of artillery. When he learned that his own ships could not carry all the captured cannon and stores, he chartered a 150-ton Bermudan-built sloop, the *Endeavor*, from a private citizen of the island to transport a portion of the cannon and stores.

Relations between the American occupiers and the citizens of New Providence were generally peaceful, but there were some problems during the short occupation. Some of Hopkins' officers pressured him to permit the pillaging of private property, but the commodore insisted that civilian property rights be respected, and all violators received swift military justice.

Commodore Hopkins also had other concerns. He was most concerned about the health and welfare of his sailors and marines, as he knew that outbreaks of smallpox and tropical fevers were likely to occur with the onset of warmer spring temperatures. The Americans were also running short on food and other provisions, but a local merchant finally agreed to provide sustenance and other supplies under contract. Hopkins knew that once the *Mississippi Packet* and *Saint John* arrived in St Augustine, the British were likely to send a fleet to retake New Providence and destroy the American fleet. Therefore, it was critical that the fleet depart the Bahamas as soon as possible.

On Saturday March 16, the captured cannon, munitions and other military supplies were all loaded and secured. The marines were then withdrawn from the forts and embarked on the ships. Governor Browne asked to be permitted to go ashore to say farewell to his family, but the commodore denied his request. At 4:00 p.m. the commodore issued orders for the fleet to get under way and proceed to Block Island Channel off the New England coast.[24]

The Continental Navy's raid on the island of New Providence was a qualified success, but the planning and execution were far from flawless. There were serious political and tactical blunders made before and during the raid. Hopkins clearly did not have an authorization from Naval Committee to conduct the raid on New Providence. Sailing his fleet to the Bahamas instead of following his instructions to sail to the Chesapeake alienated most members of the Naval Committee. Although Commodore Hopkins initially received accolades for the capture of the badly needed cannon and other military stores, he later paid a heavy price for his actions during and after the raid.

At the tactical level, Hopkins's failure to blockade the New Providence harbor after the British detected his fleet's presence facilitated the removal of most of the gunpowder from the Bahamas to Florida without interference. Commodore Hopkins also failed to emphasize the need for speed with his subordinate commanders. Had the landing force proceeded directly to Fort Nassau after finding Fort Montagu abandoned, the British would not have had time to remove the gunpowder. However, the Naval Committee of the Continental Congress may have forgiven those blunders had Hopkins not erred badly after returning to American waters.

Except for an outbreak of smallpox, the return voyage was uneventful, until the fleet reached the waters off Long Island on April 4, 1776. That day, the American fleet captured the HMS *Hawk*. The following day the fleet captured the British ship *Bolton*, which was loaded with armaments and powder. Arriving off Block Island on April 6, the American fleet sighted the heavily armed HMS *Glasgow*. In a running sea battle, the outnumbered and outgunned *Glasgow* inflicted serious damage to the Continental Navy's ship *Cabot*, killing or wounding 12 officers and seamen including Commodore Hopkins's son. The American ships fought individually rather than acting together, and *Glasgow* defeated the American ships one by one. Although *Glasgow* was heavily damaged she escaped capture. The battered American fleet finally sailed into harbor at New London, Connecticut on April 8, 1776.

Commodore Hopkins received heavy criticism for his failure to capture the *Glasgow*, and there were a number of crew complaints against some of the captains of the fleet that resulted in investigations and courts-martial. Other complaints were lodged against Commodore Hopkins for his attempts to distribute the captured cannon and other military stores without the approval of the Naval Committee of Congress. Hopkins was finally called before the Naval Committee of the Continental Congress to explain his failure to follow the orders to patrol the Chesapeake, and his subsequent missteps during and after the New Providence raid.[25] Hopkins was subsequently censured for his actions by Congress, and after a further series of missteps and ill-advised actions he was forced out of the Navy in 1778.

The raid on New Providence was a seminal event in the history of special operations conducted during the American Revolutionary War. It was a joint operation conducted by the Continental Navy and Continental Marines, during which the Marines conducted their first amphibious assault on an enemy-held island. The operation also had strategic implications for the conduct of the war. The war was no longer confined to just the 13 colonies in North America. British colonies and bases in the Caribbean were at risk, and the supremacy of the British navy at sea was challenged. The New Providence raid also provided a valuable learning experience for officers of the Continental Navy and Marines, who would soon thereafter rise in rank and prominence. Once such officer was John Paul Jones, who was promoted to the rank of captain soon after the New Providence raid. Two years later Jones would carry the American War for Independence across the Atlantic to Europe, leading his own raid on the English coast, and then fighting one of the fiercest sea battles of the war in British waters.

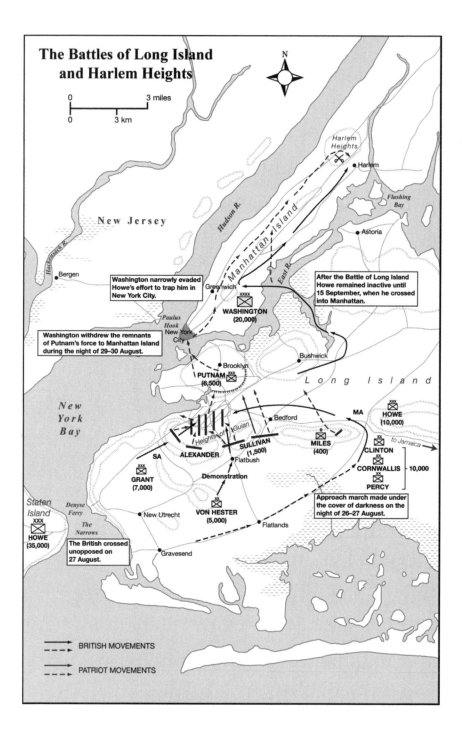

The Battles of Long Island and Harlem Heights

N

| 0 | | 3 miles |
| 0 | 3 km | |

Harlem Heights

• Harlem

Flushing Bay

New Jersey

Hudson R.

Manhattan Island

East R.

• Astoria

Hackensack R.

• Bergen

Washington narrowly evaded Howe's effort to trap him in New York City.

• Greenwich

After the Battle of Long Island Howe remained inactive until 15 September, when he crossed into Manhattan.

Paulus Hook

WASHINGTON (20,000)

New York City

Washington withdrew the remnants of Putnam's force to Manhattan Island during the night of 29–30 August.

• Bushwick

• Brooklyn

PUTNAM (6,500)

L o n g   I s l a n d

New York Bay

MA

HOWE (10,000)

• Bedford

Heights of Gutan

MILES (400)

to Jamaica

SA

SULLIVAN (1,500)

ALEXANDER

• Flatbush

CLINTON

CORNWALLIS — 10,000

GRANT (7,000)

Demonstration

PERCY

Staten Island

Denyse Ferry

• New Utrecht

VON HESTER (5,000)

Approach march made under the cover of darkness on the night of 26–27 August.

HOWE (35,000)

The Narrows

• Flatlands

The British crossed unopposed on 27 August.

• Gravesend

→ BRITISH MOVEMENTS

→ PATRIOT MOVEMENTS

3

KNOWLTON'S RANGERS

After spending an uneasy night, General Washington was up before dawn working on his correspondence. His headquarters was in a stately mansion owned by retired British officer and Loyalist, Colonel Roger Morris. The mansion sat atop the highest point on Harlem Heights. Washington's Continentals held a strong line of entrenchments on Harlem Heights on the northern plateau of Manhattan ten miles north of the city. From the balcony outside his study, Washington had a commanding view of the terrain to the south. Looking to the south with his glass, the general could see the spires of New York's churches far in the distance. To the west, he had an excellent view of the Hudson River, and to the east the Harlem River valley, and the small Dutch village of Harlem. The surprise British landing at Kips Bay on September 15, 1776, had forced Washington to order the withdrawal of his troops from lower Manhattan, and British troops quickly occupied the city. After failures in intelligence gathering during the Long Island campaign and the surprise British landing at Kips Bay, Washington decided to deploy a detachment of Lieutenant Colonel Knowlton's elite rangers well forward of his lines on Harlem Heights to gather intelligence, and provide early warning of a British attack. Washington was determined not to be surprised again. Suddenly the rattle of distant musketry interrupted the general's thoughts. His adjutant general, Joseph Reed, burst into his study with news that three British columns were sighted advancing toward the American positions. Washington ordered his adjutant to ride forward to an advanced post two and a half miles to the south to confirm the report before hastily completing his correspondence. The general then ordered the captain of his

Life Guards to mount an escort detachment, and saddle his horse. Washing-
ton was determined to see for himself if the reports of an attack were true.

GENERAL WASHINGTON WAS QUITE FAMILIAR WITH CAPABILITIES
of ranger units as a result of his service during the French and Indian
War. Ranger organizations such as Rogers' Rangers had gained fame supporting British operations against the French in Canada, and the regions
surrounding Lake Champlain and Lake George. The rangers conducted
reconnaissance patrols deep in enemy territory to gather valuable intelligence, and raided French outposts. In the days leading up to Lexington
and Concord, many ranger veterans of the French and Indian War volunteered to serve as minutemen in the Massachusetts militia. After war
broke out, many former rangers joined the ranks of the New England
militia regiments that fought at Bunker Hill. Several officers who had
served in Rogers' Rangers during the French and Indian War were appointed to high rank in the Continental Army under General Washington,
including Major General Israel Putnam and Brigadier Generals John Stark
and Moses Hazen. Other former rangers served as sergeants, lieutenants,
and captains in the Continental regiments and state militias. Washington
knew that he had a number of veteran rangers serving in the ranks of
the Continental Army, but did not think ranger units could adapt to the
European style of warfare waged by the British and his Continentals. The
campaigns of 1775 and 1776 changed his mindset.

From the beginning of the war, General Washington demonstrated a
keen appreciation of the value of intelligence, counterintelligence, and
special operations to assess British strengths and weaknesses and strike
vulnerable British targets. In 1777, his senior intelligence officer, Colonel
Benjamin Tallmadge, began organizing a network of spies operating behind British lines to gather intelligence on British troop strengths and dispositions. Tallmadge was also active in ferreting out British spies and
rogue intelligence officers in the employ of the British and overseeing
the interrogations of British prisoners of war. However, it was not until
the New York campaign of 1776 that General Washington recognized
the importance of timely battlefield intelligence and exploitation.

The 11-month siege of Boston ended on March 17, 1776. It was a re-markable success for the Americans and a humiliating experience for the British. The siege came to an end when the nascent American Army accomplished what some thought was impossible. On the night of Monday March 4, 1776, American troops occupied and fortified Dorchester Heights. The troops toiled throughout the night in unseasonably warm temperatures to complete their work, while American artillery pounded the British lines on the Charlestown Peninsula. Then before daylight on March 5, 20 of the heavy cannon captured at Fort Ticonderoga were pulled up the Dorchester Heights by teams of oxen, and manhandled into firing positions. At daybreak, the British were astonished to see the fortifications and menacing cannon overlooking the harbor and the city. Their own guns could not be elevated sufficiently to bombard the American positions on the heights. Bad weather over the next few days prevented the British from launching attacks on the American positions. On March 6, General Howe decided that he could no longer occupy Boston, and ordered an evacuation by sea. Over the next few days, almost nine thousand British troops and some eleven hundred Loyalists were crammed aboard British warships and transports. Then on March 17, after every man-of-war fired a 21-gun departing salute, the entire fleet of 120 ships weighed anchor and sailed out of the harbor, bound for Halifax, Nova Scotia. The siege of Boston was a stunning success. A rag-tag amateur American army had forced a powerful British army and fleet to withdraw from Boston and Cambridge. It took six weeks for the news to reach London. The news set off a firestorm in Parliament. On May 6, the duke of Manchester criticized his pro-government opponents in the House of Lords saying, "the fact remains that the army which was sent to reduce the province of Massachusetts Bay has been driven from the capital, and that the standard of the provincial army now waves in triumphant over the walls of Boston."[1]

No one knew for sure where the British would exact their revenge, but General Washington, after assessing the situation, correctly concluded that their next offensive would be directed against the thriving seaport city of New York. The victorious Continental Army was soon on the move, as regiment after regiment marched out of camp bound for New York, departing New England for the first time.

Over the next few weeks, the regiments of the Continental Army marched across Massachusetts, Rhode Island, and Connecticut. Upon reaching New London, Connecticut, a number of the regiments embarked on ships, and sailed down Long Island Sound to reach New York. By April 14, General Washington and most of the American army had arrived in New York.

Washington moved his headquarters into Number 1 Broadway, an elegant townhouse close to the battery at the southernmost tip of Manhattan. The commander-in-chief and his generals were soon poring over maps and charts of New York and its surrounding waterways, arguing how best to defend the city. It was no easy task.

The geography of New York and the surrounding areas is complicated, and defined by the rivers, waterways, and harbors surrounding it. Strategically, the geography favors an attacker, if he has overwhelming naval superiority. The British navy had that superiority. With hundreds of warships and transports, the British could land anywhere along the hundreds of miles of Atlantic coastline, or along the Long Island Sound shoreline. British warships and transports could also enter either the Hudson or East Rivers, and land troops on Manhattan Island. The British could also land troops on Staten Island or the northern shore of New Jersey and use those locations as staging areas to launch attacks against Long Island or Manhattan. In short, the British were capable of launching an invasion against New York from any direction, at a time and place of their choosing.

————————————

Soon after his arrival in New York, Washington began inspecting the existing fortifications and those that were under construction. He found the work on the defenses less than half complete, and time was growing short. After consulting with Major General Charles Lee, an expert on defense, Washington placed priority on fortifying Brooklyn Heights across the East River from New York City. Most of Washington's generals agreed that the British would land on the Atlantic beaches of Long Island, and then move south across the island to seize Brooklyn Heights before crossing the East River to take possession of New York City.

Governors Island also had to be fortified with gun emplacements and earthworks to prevent the British ships from entering the East River, and fortifications were needed along both banks of the Hudson River to prevent the British navy from sailing up the river and landing troops on Manhattan north of the city. Although the American troops worked day and night on the fortifications, everyone knew that it was a race against time.

Washington had other concerns as well. The stores of munitions and other military supplies in New York were inadequate to support the needs of the army during a long siege. Law and order in the city was a worry as malingering and the plundering of civilian homes and businesses by poorly disciplined troops was on the rise. Washington was also dissatisfied with the lack of intelligence on British troop movements and deployments. He recognized the need for an intelligence network that was capable of providing timely intelligence on British intentions, deployments, and early warnings of British attacks.

During late May, Washington was summoned to meet with the Continental Congress in Philadelphia, and did not return to New York until June 6. Shortly after his return, a Loyalist plot to assassinate the general and other key officers was uncovered. The assassinations were to take place at the moment the British fleet appeared off New York. The plot involved more than a dozen Loyalists including the mayor of New York, and two members of Washington's own Life Guard, causing the commander-in-chief to focus even more attention on intelligence gathering and counterintelligence.

On June 25, the lead ships of the British fleet arrived off Staten Island in the Lower Bay, just 10 miles below the Narrows. The British fleet had sailed from Halifax on June 9, and Washington had had no prior warning of its departure date from Halifax, or its anticipated arrival date in New York waters. That information did not reach Washington's headquarters until June 28, too late to be of any use. Within a few hours of the arrival of the first British ships, more than 40 additional ships had dropped anchor off Staten Island. The arrival of the British fleet spread fear among the patriotic citizens of New York, and jubilation among the Loyalists. Washington ordered the firing of alarm guns, and couriers were dispatched to alert the outlying forts and posts. By the evening of June 28, more than one hundred British ships were anchored in the Lower Bay.

General William Howe did not immediately land his troops. He decided to wait for the arrival of his brother, Admiral Richard Howe, who was sailing from England with a fleet carrying an additional twenty thousand troops. The long-anticipated landing on Staten Island did not occur until July 2, 1776. Most of the Patriot militia on the island promptly defected to the British, and joined the Loyalists. On the same day, the Continental Congress meeting in Philadelphia voted to "dissolve the connection" with Great Britain. When the news reached New York on July 6, spontaneous celebrations broke out in the American army camps and forts. The celebrations continued for the next few days as the Americans awaited General Howe's next move.

General Howe was in no great rush to begin offensive operations against New York. He still hoped that the dispute between Great Britain and its American colonies could be settled peacefully with offers of amnesty to the rebel political and military leadership. While Washington rejected Howe's peace terms, he continued to bolster New York's defenses, and improve the army's intelligence-gathering capabilities.

General Washington recognized the need for a force capable of operating behind the British lines, where it would gather intelligence on enemy dispositions, strike vulnerable enemy targets, and provide early warning of British attacks. Accordingly, Washington ordered the formation of a ranger unit made up of volunteers from five Connecticut, two Massachusetts and one Rhode Island regiment. A number of the men who volunteered were former rangers who had served during the French and Indian War. Washington selected Lieutenant Colonel Thomas Knowlton of Connecticut to command the rangers.

General Washington's decision to assign Lieutenant Colonel Knowlton as commander of the ranger unit was strongly influenced by Major General Putnam, a veteran ranger officer himself. Washington had also observed Knowlton's performance in the field during the siege of Boston, and considered him one of the best field officers in the Continental Army. Washington stipulated that Knowlton would take his orders directly from the army's commander-in-chief signifying the importance he placed on the rangers.

At 35 years of age, Thomas Knowlton was an officer who stood out among his peers in the Continental Army. At well over six feet in height, he was several inches taller than most of the officers and men of the Continental Army. With handsome facial features, and a muscular, trim frame, Knowlton possessed a natural military bearing. In addition, he had a proven record of heroic military service in two wars, and had served in all ranks from private to lieutenant colonel.

Lieutenant Colonel Knowlton was born in West Boxford, Massachusetts in November 1740, the sixth of eight children. When he was eight years old, Knowlton's father had moved the family to a four-hundred-acre farm near Ashton, Connecticut. Thomas and his siblings assisted their father on the family farm and carpentry business. Although he had a keen intellect, Knowlton had no more than the few years of basic studies that were taught in New England schools at that time.

In 1757, the 17-year-old Knowlton enlisted as a private in the 1st Connecticut Regiment for service during the French and Indian War. During his initial period of service, Private Knowlton experienced his first taste of combat in the same regiment as Captain John Durkee and Major Israel Putnam, both of whom trained and served with Roger's Rangers.[2] Knowlton rose rapidly through the ranks, achieving the rank of sergeant major by 1759, and by 1761, he was serving as a lieutenant in Captain Ledlie's 10th Company of the 1st Connecticut Regiment. Knowlton's promotions were the result of his courage and coolness under fire, and his demonstrated leadership qualities. When the British sent a fleet and invasion force to Cuba in the closing years of the Seven Years' War, Lieutenant Knowlton sailed to the island with the 1st Connecticut Regiment under its acting commander, Israel Putnam. The regiment participated in the campaign that led to the capture of the city of Havana. During the five-month siege of Havana and its aftermath, the British and Americans lost more than 2,700 men killed, and another 4,700 died of disease. Knowlton was one of a handful of survivors from his regiment who returned home the expedition unscathed.

After returning from Cuba in November 1762, Knowlton resumed his life as a farmer in Ashford, Connecticut. Following his marriage in 1759, Thomas Knowlton and his wife Anna raised a family of nine children. At the age of 33, he was appointed one of the selectmen of his town, an office usually held by much older men.

When news of Lexington and Concord reached Ashford in April

1775, Knowlton joined the Ashford Company of the Connecticut militia. Based on his experience and reputation from the French and Indian War, he was elected captain of the two-hundred-man company. His company soon joined the Patriot army that was assembling near Boston. Upon arrival, Knowlton's company was assigned to the 3d Regiment of Connecticut militia commanded by Colonel Israel Putnam, who would soon be promoted to major general in the Continental Army. Having observed Knowlton's performance during the French and Indian War and Cuban expedition, Putnam was fully aware of his courage, intellect, and leadership skills, and it was soon apparent that Knowlton was one of his favorite officers.

After weeks of inactivity and inaction, the militiamen soon became restless and bored with camp life. Many questioned why their leaders had not taken action to drive the British troops out of Boston. Pressure began to build on the Committee of Safety and the senior militia officers to begin offensive actions. Israel Putnam was a strong advocate of a plan to fortify a position on Charlestown peninsula. According to one eyewitness, Putnam went to Knowlton's quarters to solicit his opinion on this plan. Both men knew that fortifying Bunker Hill would provoke a strong British reaction and Knowlton told Putnam that he did not think the move was tactically sound, since the British could land at the neck of the Charlestown peninsula under the cover of their warships to attack Bunker Hill, and block the American force's only line of retreat. Putnam listened attentively to Knowlton, but was not inclined to follow his advice. Although he had reservations about the plan, Knowlton assured his commander that he and his men would support to the utmost any plan adopted by the senior leadership of the army.[3]

On the night of June 16–17, 1775, Thomas Knowlton's company joined Colonel William Prescott's regiment as it marched from Cambridge through the rolling countryside to the Charlestown peninsula. The regiment headed for Bunker Hill, which overlooked the Charles River and the city of Boston. Arriving on the peninsula, Colonel Prescott decided to fortify Breed's Hill, an elevation east of Bunker Hill, ignoring his explicit instructions from the Committee of Safety. Prescott later justified his decision by pointing out that although Bunker Hill was 50 feet higher in elevation, Breed's Hill was closer to the city of Boston.

After occupying Breed's Hill, Prescott's men worked feverishly through the night constructing a redoubt, and reinforcing a stone and rail fence that ran east from the redoubt to the Mystic River beach. At dawn, the British were astonished to see a strong redoubt on Breed's Hill flanked by a breastwork that extended down the hill terminating near a marshy stream. Beyond the stream was a hayfield that extended about 250 yards to the shoreline of the Mystic River. That parcel of land offered an avenue of approach to the rear of the redoubt on Breed's Hill, and it was undefended. At daybreak, Colonel Prescott spotted that weakness in his defenses, and quickly ordered Captain Knowlton to set up a defensive position across the hayfield. Knowlton positioned some of his men behind a post and rail fence that stretched across the field from the road to the banks of the Mystic River. Then he ordered his men to construct a parallel fence using rails from other fences, and fill the intervening space with freshly mown hay. About an hour after Knowlton established his positions, Colonel John Stark led his 1st New Hampshire Regiment into positions behind the fence closest to the hill. Knowlton and Stark's men were destined to play a critical role in the Battle of Bunker (Breed's) Hill.

At around 1:00 p.m., two thousand British Regulars under General Howe landed on the eastern side of the Charlestown peninsula. The British commander waited until his entire force had landed before moving against the American redoubt on Breed's Hill. As the Americans had anticipated, Howe split his force into two wings with one wing marching up Breed's Hill to make a frontal assault, while the other wing marched toward the American positions behind the rail fence to flank the American positions on the hill and cut off their line of retreat.

As the British advanced toward the rail fence, Captain Knowlton walked along the fence line in his shirtsleeves, musket in hand, to encourage his men all the while exposing himself to enemy fire. Knowlton's men beat back the first British attack, inflicting significant casualties on Howe's men and forcing them to fall back to reorganize for another attack. As a second attack took shape, Knowlton told his men to hold their fire until the British column was about 30 yards from the fence. Resting their muskets on the fence, the Americans then unleashed a deadly volley of musket fire into the British ranks. The slaughter was horrific. Bodies of the dead and wounded covered the field, and despite General Howe's personal exhortations, his shattered formations broke and fled. A British officer who accompanied Howe's assault described the action:

> As we approached, an incessant stream of fire poured from the rebel lines. It seemed a continued sheet of fire for near thirty minutes. Our Light Infantry were served up in companies against the grass fence without being able to penetrate. Indeed how could we penetrate? Most of our Grenadiers and Light Infantry [at] the moment of presenting themselves lost three-fourths, and many nine-tenths, of their men. Some had only eight or nine men a company left, some only three, four, and five.[4]

Despite their heavy casualties, the British were determined to take the American positions on Breed's Hill and its surrounding defenses. They therefore altered their plan for their third attack. While feinting another frontal attack, they directed their main attack against a gap between the breastwork of the redoubt and the fence held by Stark and Knowlton's men. Cannon were positioned to enfilade the breastwork on the left of the redoubt. Running low on ammunition, the Americans fired a final volley as Howe's troops stormed over the breastwork into the redoubt. Prescott's men attempted to club them with their muskets and pikes, but were soon forced to retreat. While the melee inside the redoubt continued, Knowlton's men maintained their positions along the fence line, preventing Howe's men from cutting off the American line of retreat from the hill. Knowlton held his position long enough to permit Prescott's main body and Stark's regiment to withdraw before ordering his own men to withdraw. Following the battle at Bunker (Breed's) Hill, the Continental Congress promoted Thomas Knowlton to major in the 20th Connecticut Regiment for his gallantry and leadership during that battle.

On January 8, 1776, General Washington directed Major Knowlton to conduct a night raid on Charlestown to burn houses occupied by British officers, and take the officers prisoner. It was a difficult mission, since the British still occupied both Bunker and Breeds Hill, and had sealed off the neck of the Charlestown peninsula. As darkness descended, Knowlton led two hundred hand-picked men in single file across a narrow milldam to reach the town. Knowlton had organized his men into three groups to search and fire the houses occupied by the British. Once across the milldam, Major Knowlton personally silenced a British sentry at a guardhouse, while his men took the remainder of the guard force prisoner. Knowlton's three groups then spread out to locate and fire the houses throughout the town. A total of 17 houses were set afire, and five officers were captured, causing chaos in the town and throughout the peninsula. Believing they were under attack, the British occupying Bunker Hill opened up with cannon fire, and British troops in Boston were called to full alert. In the confusion, Knowlton led his men safely back across the milldam with their prisoners without firing a shot or sustaining any casualties. General Washington personally thanked Major Knowlton and his men for their successful raid in the general orders dated January 9, 1776. Major Knowlton's leadership and courage earned him a promotion to lieutenant colonel, and put him at the head of Washington's short list of officers in whom he had special trust and confidence.

Soon after Knowlton's Rangers was formed, plans were made for them to carry out attacks on British ships stationed off Staten Island, and British installations on shore. Major General Putnam was the main advocate of the plan. Putnam wanted to attack the British ships using fire ships, while Knowlton's Rangers and Brigadier General Hugh Mercer's Virginia Brigade rowed across the Narrows to attack British shore installations on Staten Island. A series of mishaps involving the fire ships, and adverse weather, thwarted that part of the plan, but Knowlton and Mercer were determined to complete their part of the mission. Two attempts were made to cross the Lower Bay. On the first attempt, the boats ferrying the troops were unable to complete the crossing due to rough seas. The second attempt was cancelled a few hours before the scheduled crossing, due to a shortage of seaworthy boats.[5]

In 1776, the months of June and July were oppressively hot in New York and its environs. British ships loaded with troops continued to arrive at Staten Island, while the American troops worked around the clock in the summer heat to complete the defensive fortifications in New York and

Brooklyn. On August 1, a fleet of 45 British ships was spotted off Sandy Hook. On board were generals Clinton and Cornwallis and three thousand troops. The troops were returning from South Carolina after a failed attempt to capture the strategic seaport of Charleston. On August 4, an additional 45 ships arrived, further strengthening General Howe's command. By mid-August, thirty-two thousand British and Hessian troops were on Staten Island, more than enough to launch an offensive to capture New York. However, General Howe was in no hurry to attack.

Washington continued to receive reinforcements as well, however most were state militia regiments. For the most part, the state militia troops were inexperienced, and poorly armed and equipped. The American army also experienced a large number of desertions and illnesses. Outbreaks of dysentery and fever raged through the camps in New York and Long Island, leading to the death and incapacitation of large numbers of troops. General Heath estimated that some ten thousand soldiers in the fortifications and camps around New York were ill during the summer of 1776. Even Knowlton's elite Rangers had their share of men on the disabled list including one of Knowlton's company commanders, Captain Nathan Hale, who would soon undertake a dangerous mission.

While the American troops worked tirelessly on the fortifications, the generals pondered where and when the British would strike. General Nathaniel Greene of Rhode Island, who commanded the American troops on Long Island, predicted that the British would first attack somewhere on Long Island. Washington, on the other hand, expressed concern that an attack on Long Island could be a diversionary attack preceding an invasion of Manhattan. Believing that he could not afford to discount either scenario, Washington split the army into roughly two equal parts, stationed on both sides of the East River. In doing so, the American commander-in-chief violated one of the maxims of war: never divide your force when facing a superior enemy force.

At a critical moment in the New York campaign, Major General Nathaniel Greene was incapacitated due to illness. Washington was forced to evacuate Greene to Brooklyn, and temporarily replace him with General John Sullivan, who had just returned from Canada. Sullivan had little time to study the terrain and geography of Long Island.

Shortly after dawn on August 22, Clinton and Cornwallis launched an invasion of Long Island. After crossing the Narrows, four thousand troops were rowed ashore in flat-bottomed boats, landing on a wide, flat, and undefended beach at Gravesend Bay on the southwest tip of Long Island. By noon, the British had fifteen thousand troops and 40 field artillery pieces ashore arrayed against General Sullivan's modest force of six thousand men. The few American troops who were in the vicinity of the landing beach withdrew without firing a shot. As they withdrew, Sullivan's troops slaughtered cattle and burned fields of wheat and corn as well as farm buildings to prevent their use by the British. It mattered little. Once the British were ashore, Loyalist residents of Long Island welcomed the British troops with open arms, providing them with provisions and intelligence on American troop dispositions and fortifications.

The British moved quickly to secure and expand their beachhead before the Americans could react to the invasion. General Cornwallis advanced six miles to the north toward the American positions on Brooklyn Heights before he received orders to advance no further. Meanwhile, General Washington received news of the landings at his headquarters on Manhattan. The early reports grossly underestimated the number of troops that had landed on Long Island, meaning that Washington concluded that the invasion was no more than a feint. He was still convinced that the main attack would be directed against Manhattan. Washington sent a small force of 1,500 men to bolster the defenses on Brooklyn Heights. Later that same day Washington crossed the East River to Brooklyn to confer with General Sullivan, who reported only light skirmishing with British patrols. Washington then returned to his headquarters in New York. He was still convinced that the British landings on Long Island were a diversionary tactic.

On August 24, Washington decided to change the command arrangements on Long Island. He assigned overall command to General Putnam, who was replacing General Sullivan. Putnam crossed to Brooklyn the following day, August 25, bringing with him six battalions of reinforcements. That same day another five thousand Hessian troops crossed the Narrows from Staten Island raising the total number of troops under British command to twenty thousand, more than enough to launch attacks on the American positions. On August 26, Washington ordered more reinforcements to Long Island. In addition to battalions from Delaware, Maryland,

and Pennsylvania, Washington also ordered Lieutenant Colonel Thomas Knowlton and one hundred rangers to deploy to Long Island. Washington returned to Brooklyn that same day to confer with his senior commanders, inspect the defenses, and review the deployments of the American troops. Meanwhile British troops moved to positions within striking distance of the passes that led through a wooded ridgeline called Guana Heights forward of the main American defenses on Brooklyn Heights.

After conferring with his senior commanders, Washington announced his defensive plan. He wanted General Putnam to direct the overall defense from the fortifications on Brooklyn Heights, while generals Alexander and Sullivan deployed their troops along Guana Heights. Three major roads led through the narrow passes of Guana Heights toward Brooklyn Heights: the Gowanus Road was on the American far right nearest the Narrows; the Flatbush Road was in the center; and on the far left was the Bedford Road. Washington and his major subordinate commanders believed that the British would use one or more of those roads to pass through Guana Heights to reach the main American positions on Brooklyn Heights. General Alexander was assigned responsibility for defending the Gowanus Road approach with five hundred troops, while General Sullivan was to defend both the Flatbush Road approach, and the Bedford Road approach. Sullivan assigned a force of one thousand men, including Knowlton's Rangers, to defend the center, and another eight hundred men on the Bedford Road. It was a meager force to defend a ridgeline that extended for nearly four miles. Due to the hilly and heavily wooded terrain, it was extremely difficult for the various units to maintain contact with each other, but the rangers fought well on such terrain. Although, period battlefield maps do not depict precise ranger positions, it is likely that the Knowlton's Rangers were deployed well forward of the heights, where they could reconnoiter the British lines near the village of Flatbush.

As Washington and his generals finalized their plans, generals Howe, Clinton, and Cornwallis planned for their attack on Brooklyn Heights. It was General Clinton who proposed a plan for launching an attack using a fourth, and lesser-known, pass on the extreme left of the American lines. Jamaica Pass was almost three miles east of Bedford Pass, and was not much wider than a footpath. Clinton proposed sending a sizeable force through Jamaica Pass to flank the American positions on Guana

Heights, and then strike those positions from the rear. While this maneuver was underway, the British would also launch diversionary frontal attacks, applying pressure on the American troops defending the three major passes. If the attacks were executed as planned, General Sullivan's and General Alexander's troops on Guana Heights would be cut off from General Putnam's main defenses on Brooklyn Heights. With British troops to their front and rear, Sullivan's and Alexander's troops would have to either surrender, or face annihilation.

The existence of Jamaica Pass was not unknown to the Americans, but it was considered far too narrow and constricted to accommodate the passage of a large body of troops. Therefore, only a mounted patrol consisting of five inexperienced junior officers was sent to keep the pass under surveillance. That was a major mistake. Knowlton's one hundred rangers could have easily defended Jamaica Pass for several hours; long enough for General Putnam to reinforce his left flank.

Arriving late in the day on the eve of the attack, Knowlton's Rangers had little time to familiarize themselves with the terrain forward of the Flatbush Pass. The rangers moved forward of the American lines at dusk. By nightfall, the British were on the move. General Clinton took the lead with a British light infantry brigade. General Cornwallis followed with eight reserve battalions, and 14 artillery pieces. Marching silently, the long British column was led by three Loyalist guides who knew the area well. Generals Howe and Percy followed the main column with six additional infantry battalions, more artillery, and the baggage train. In all, General Howe boldly committed some ten thousand men to the attack through Jamaica Pass. All the tents were left erected in the British camps, and campfires were left burning to leave the impression that nothing was happening.

By dawn, the lead British units were through Jamaica Pass, and approaching Bedford road to the rear of the American positions on the Guana ridgeline. It took another two hours for the remainder of the British troops to file through the narrow Jamaica Pass, and move into attack positions behind the American defensive positions. The nine-mile night march was perfectly executed, and had been undetected by the Americans. The American patrol sent to keep watch on Jamaica Pass was captured before it could spread the alarm.

At 9:00 a.m., the British fired two cannon as a signal for the Hessians and British to begin their frontal attacks on the American positions on the center and right of the American positions on Guana Heights. By 11:00 a.m., General Sullivan's positions on the left and center of the ridge-line had collapsed. Those men who had not been killed or captured fled back toward the American lines on Brooklyn Heights. General Sullivan and hundreds of his men were captured. Only two regiments of General Alexander's command, one from Maryland and one from Delaware, held their ground on the American right. Alexander's troops were badly out-numbered and under heavy pressure.

When Knowlton's Rangers withdrew from their positions forward of Flatbush Pass during the Hessian bombardment, they were ordered to re-inforce Alexander's positions. However, as they fought their way toward Alexander's lines, the firing on the right suddenly ceased. Convinced that Alexander had surrendered, Knowlton ordered his men to withdraw to the American lines on Brooklyn Heights.[6] Threatened by the arrival of a large force of British light horse, Knowlton ordered his rangers to with-draw into the near impassible Gowanus marsh to evade their mounted pursuers. The rangers moved in small groups across the tidal marsh, and reached the safety of American lines on Brooklyn Heights without losing a man.[7] Knowlton's good judgment and quick decision-making had saved his command.

By early afternoon, after more than six hours of heavy fighting, the American units forward of Brooklyn Heights were completely defeated with the survivors fleeing in panic to reach the American lines on Brook-lyn Heights. American losses totaled more than three hundred men killed, with another thousand taken prisoner including three generals. British losses were between four hundred and seven hundred men.[8]

The British and Hessian troops were exuberant, and some of the British commanders, including General Clinton, wanted to continue the attack with an immediate assault on the American fortifications on Brook-lyn Heights. Exercising caution, General Howe overruled his subordinates and ordered a halt. After a nine-mile march overnight followed by six hours of heavy fighting, Howe concluded that his men had accomplished enough for one day. He also knew that the fortifications on Brooklyn Heights were much more formidable than those on Guana Heights.

As the day drew to a close, the Americans inside the fortifications on Brooklyn Heights remained on high alert in anticipation of an all-out attack. It never came. The last of the Americans to survive the day's fighting, many of them walking wounded, managed to reach the Brooklyn Heights under cover of darkness.

The following day, Washington ordered reinforcements to cross the river to reinforce Brooklyn Heights. With his forces holding only two square miles of Brooklyn with the East River at their backs, the Americans would be trapped if British warships sailed through the Narrows and entered the East River. The Americans sank old ships to block the mouth of the East River, but they did not totally block the entrance. As the day wore on, British and American sharpshooters traded shots and artillerymen fired registration rounds on enemy positions. Late in the day, a "nor'easter" began to sweep across Manhattan and Long Island, bringing with it with downpours, lightning and thunder. The temperatures continued to drop throughout the night further dampening the spirits of the troops.

The storm continued throughout the following day—April 29—drenching the troops and soaking the stores of gunpowder. After making his rounds on horseback with General Putnam, Washington called a council of war with his generals to discuss the possible evacuation of Brooklyn. The decision was unanimous; Brooklyn had to be evacuated before the British closed the trap. A call went out to assemble all available boats at the Brooklyn ferry landings, and secret movement orders were sent to the regiments holding the fortifications on Brooklyn Heights.

By nightfall everything was ready, and at 7:00 p.m., regimental commanders ordered their troops to assemble with their muskets and knapsacks. Officers told the men that they were going to make a surprise night attack on the British camps outside their lines. At 9:00 p.m., one by one the regiments stepped off into the dark rainy night on different routes that led to the ferry landings. Only a nominal rearguard remained on the heights. When the first troops arrived at the ferry landings, they found a small flotilla of boats manned by men from Colonel John Glover's 14th Continental Marblehead Regiment. Most of Glover's troops were Massachusetts sailors and fishermen who knew how to handle boats in rough seas.

By 11:00 p.m., the storm had passed, and the strong northeast winds had subsided. Troops were loaded on the whaleboats, and Glover's oarsmen began to row across the mile-wide stretch of water separating Brooklyn from Manhattan. The crossings continued throughout the night, as regiment after regiment was ferried across the East River. It was an extraordinary feat of seamanship, even for experienced sailors. Despite the swift currents and occasional gusts of wind, Glover's men rowed hour after hour to bring the overloaded boats across the river to Manhattan, and then return across the river for another load of troops, cannon, and supplies. The evacuation almost went awry when a regiment of the rearguard was ordered to begin marching toward the ferry landings prematurely. When Washington was informed of the situation, he galloped to intercept the column, and ordered it back to the trenches. With the rearguard back in place, the evacuation continued, but time was running out. At daybreak, a major portion of the army was still waiting to cross the river, and it was feared that the British would soon become aware that the Americans were withdrawing to Manhattan. Fortunately, a heavy fog descended on Brooklyn, concealing the troops and boats. The fog lifted only after the last American troops stepped ashore on Manhattan. More than nine thousand troops crossed the river that night. Not a single boat or man was lost during the evacuation, and none of the wounded or seriously ill were left behind in Brooklyn. When the British entered the abandoned American camps they found only three American deserters. The successful evacuation of the American army from Brooklyn was one of the most remarkable feats in American military history.

After the evacuation of the army from Brooklyn, Washington initially quartered his battered dispirited army in private homes and buildings in southern Manhattan. The army's tents were too wet to provide shelter, and the weather was still terrible. This arrangement did not sit well with New York's citizenry, and the troops made the situation worse by plundering houses and neighborhoods. Officers spent too much time in the city's taverns arguing about the reasons for their defeat on Long Island. Washington ordered a crackdown. Courts-martials, floggings, and frequent musters were ordered to restore discipline in the ranks. Meanwhile,

Washington considered his next move. Congress gave the commander-in-chief the authority to evacuate the city and Manhattan Island, but stipulated that the city could not be burned. Washington decided to keep his options open. He organized his regiments into brigades, then formed those brigades into "three Grand Divisions" to defend Manhattan. General Putnam's division, consisting of five brigades, was posted in the city on the southernmost tip of Manhattan facing the East River, while Nathaniel Greene's division, with six brigades, was posted ten miles to the north of the city on Harlem Heights. The third division, commanded by General Heath, was posted north of the Harlem River at Kingsbridge, where it could keep watch on the Westchester County shoreline of the Hudson River.[9] If the British landed a strong force along the shoreline, they would be able to cut Manhattan in half, trapping the American army in the lower half. Knowlton's Rangers were billeted near Washington's headquarters in lower Manhattan after their withdrawal from Brooklyn.

Washington was determined to make any British attack on Manhattan as costly as possible. To do this he needed information on where and when the British were likely to attack, and in what strength. Normal intelligence-gathering efforts were limited to posting men on high ground with telescopes to keep watch on the British camps across the East River, but they did not provide the detailed information Washington needed. So Washington summoned Knowlton to his headquarters, and asked him to find a volunteer with the proper qualifications who was willing to go behind British lines and gather information on British troop strengths and intentions.

Knowlton assembled his officers on the morning of September 10, and briefed them on the mission before asking for volunteers. No one stepped forward to volunteer for the mission. Finally, one of his most experienced officers, Lieutenant James Sprague, a veteran of the French and Indian War, broke the silence to express his reasons for not volunteering for the spy mission saying, "I'm willing to fight the British, and if need be, die a soldier's death in battle, but as for going among them in disguise and being taken and hung up like a dog, I'll not do it."[10] Knowlton made another appeal, but still no one volunteered, so he dismissed his officers. Sometime after the meeting, one of Knowlton's company commanders, who had been on the sick list with influenza, approached

Knowlton, and volunteered for the dangerous mission. That officer was Captain Nathan Hale, a 21-year-old Yale graduate from Connecticut.

Nathan Hale had enlisted in the Connecticut militia in 1775, soon after hostilities broke out at Lexington and Concord. He was soon elected first lieutenant of his company, which was part of Connecticut's 7th Regiment. He was promoted to captain on September 1, 1775, and was assigned as the second-in-command of the 7th Regiment's 3d company. Hale's company then marched to Cambridge, arriving on September 29, three months after the Battle of Bunker Hill. During the siege of Boston, Hale was appointed captain in the newly formed Continental Army, and was assigned to the 19th Continental Regiment.

After his regiment arrived in New York, Captain Hale was approached by his friend, Thomas Knowlton, who invited him to join the rangers as a company commander. Before joining the rangers, Hale led his own special operation. When he first arrived in New York from Boston, the young captain took note of a British sloop anchored in the Lower Bay, and guarded by the British warship, *Asia*. Hale's company was in dire need of provisions, and he knew that the sloop was laden with supplies. Selecting a few men from his company, Hale set out to capture the sloop and sail it back to the American lines on Long Island. After nightfall, Hale led his men along the shoreline of the East River behind the British lines. As they approached the sloop, Hale told his men to stay put, and then proceeded to wade through the water toward the bow of the sloop. He climbed up and over the bow, seized the tiller, and sailed toward back toward the American lines, while the crew slept below decks. Nathan Hale's daring night raid demonstrated his extraordinary courage, and made him a natural choice for a command billet in Knowlton's Rangers.

After volunteering for the spy mission, Hale's close friend and fellow Yale graduate, Captain William Hull, attempted to talk Nathan out of accepting the assignment. Hull, who knew Hale better than most, believed that the young captain was not the type to make a good spy, suggesting that he was too frank and open in his opinions, and "incapable of acting a part equally foreign to his feelings and habits."[11] Despite his friend's council, Hale refused to reconsider his decision, and began formulating his plans to carry out the mission.

On September 7, Washington convened another war council at his headquarters in the Mortier House north of the city. Washington informed his generals that he had received a letter from John Hancock, president of the Continental Congress. Hancock wrote that he wanted no damage done to New York, and that Washington had full authority to withdraw from New York, if he deemed it necessary. A minority of Washington's generals favored a full withdrawal from Manhattan, but the majority of the generals voted to resist any British attempt to capture New York. Washington believed that as long as the army held forts Washington and Lee on opposite shores of the Hudson, his forces had an escape corridor.

Meanwhile, General Howe, the British commander-in-chief, continued to make peace overtures to the Americans. He agreed to meet with three distinguished members of the Continental Congress, Benjamin Franklin, John Adams, and Edward Rutledge, at his headquarters on Staten Island. The meeting was held on September 9, but no peace agreement was reached.

With no hope of a peaceful resolution of the conflict, Washington's war council met again on September 12. Fearing that a British attack was imminent, the council agreed that the city had to be abandoned. On Saturday September 14, Washington ordered most of the army to move as quickly as possible north to King's Bridge, while four thousand troops under General Putnam were to remain in the city to cover the withdrawal. The wounded and sick were moved first, followed by the artillery, supplies and munitions. After the evacuation of the wounded and sick, the infantry regiments began marching north, strung out in long columns along the dusty roads leading out of the city. By late afternoon, most of the army was deployed on Harlem Heights, and farther north at King's Bridge. Washington moved his own headquarters that same night to the Morris mansion on Harlem Heights.

After reaching Harlem Heights, Washington ordered Lieutenant Colonel Knowlton to deploy his force of 150 rangers well forward of the main defensive line on Harlem Heights to watch for enemy movement, and provide early warning of an enemy attack. The rangers did not have long to wait. The British invasion date was set for the following day, Sunday, September 15.

Washington and his generals thought that the British landings would take place near King's Bridge, about 12 miles north of the lower tip of Manhattan near the confluence of the East and Harlem Rivers. General Clinton, who was to lead the assault, recommended just such a plan. A landing at King's Bridge would have trapped Washington's army on the lower half of Manhattan Island. However, General Howe rejected Clinton's plan. General Howe and his brother, Admiral Howe, were concerned that the dangerous currents at Hell's Point would make any landing in the King's Bridge area a high-risk operation. Instead, the British commander-in-chief selected Kips Bay for the amphibious landing. Kips Bay was a cove on the eastern shore of the island—extending roughly from present-day 32nd to 38th Streets—about four and one-half miles north of the battery on the southern tip of Manhattan (the cove has since been filled in). Kips Bay was an excellent place for an amphibious landing with deep water close to the shore, and a large meadow for assembling the troops after the landings. Once ashore, the British planned to march part of the landing force south to occupy the city, while the remainder of the army marched north to attack the American positions on Harlem Heights.

Kips Bay was defended by a Connecticut brigade under the command of Colonel William Douglas. Although the brigade had some 1,500 men assigned, only about one-third of the brigade was fit for duty and posted to the defenses at Kips Bay. Making matters worse, a number of the men were inexperienced replacements, who had never been under hostile fire. The men of Douglas's brigade, many of whom lacked muskets, took cover behind a crude breastwork, and in shallow trenches. At dawn, they were startled to see five British warships anchored just two hundred yards off shore. Benjamin Trumbull, a volunteer chaplain from Connecticut, described the scene in his journal: "A Little after Day Light on Sunday Morning Septr, 15 Two ships of the Line and three Frigates drew up near the Shore within Musket Shot of the Lines and entrenchments and came to anchor there in a proper Situation to fire most furiously upon our Lines."[12]

Around 10:00 a.m., more than 80 flat-bottomed boats, packed with four thousand redcoats and green-uniformed Hessians, pushed off from the far shore of the East River. When the boats were midway, the warships opened fire on the American lines with a furious cannonade. William Trumbull again described the scene writing, "All of a sudden, there came such a peal of thunder from the British shipping that I thought my head would go with the sound . . ."[13] The bombardment lasted for one hour as more than 80 cannon pulverized the crude American defenses at near point-blank range. The terrified American troops cowered in the shallow trenches and ditches. When the barrage lifted, the first wave of flatboats approached the shoreline, concealed by the powder smoke from the cannonade. When the smoke cleared, the shell-shocked survivors of the Connecticut brigade broke and ran. Once ashore, General Clinton's corps pushed inland for a quarter of a mile before halting.

General Washington could hear the bombardment from his headquarters on Harlem Heights. Hoping to rally the defenders, he rode toward Kips Bay, accompanied by a detachment of his life guards. About a mile inland from the beachhead at Kips Bay, Washington encountered a number of American troops, who were fleeing in all directions. He tried to rally the panic-stricken men with little success, and barely escaped capture when a group of Hessians arrived to finish off the fleeing Americans. Two brigades of Continentals rushed forward to reinforce the Connecticut brigade, but they too broke and ran when they saw their comrades fleeing for their lives. Once again Washington rode forward toward the enemy hoping his men would follow, but few did so. Washington's aides finally grabbed the bridle of his horse and led him off the field.

Meanwhile, the buildup of British troops at the beachhead continued, and by 4:00 p.m. some nine thousand British and Hessian troops were ashore. When British patrols reported that General Putnam's troops were abandoning the city and marching north, General Howe ordered a brigade to march south to occupy the city, while the landings continued.

General Putnam soon realized that his line of retreat was about to be cut, and began force-marching his 3,500 troops out of the city. Putnam's men marched north on the Post Road on the east side of the island. A mixed force of British and Hessians were marching south toward the city on the same road. Putnam's aide, Lieutenant Aaron Burr, convinced Putnam to follow another road that angled off toward the west side of the island before heading north along the Hudson River. At times, the American and British columns were moving in opposite directions little more than a quarter of mile apart.[14]

Meanwhile, the remainder of General Howe's forces began marching north on the Post Road toward Harlem Heights in the sweltering after-noon heat, paralleling Putnam's columns. When the British column reached McGowan's pass, they halted and encamped for the night. General Put-nam's men continued their march until they reached the safety of the American lines on Harlem Heights; it was well past sundown by the time Putnam's rearguard reached the heights.

Before dawn on September 16, Knowlton led his rangers forward of the American lines on a special reconnaissance mission. Washington want-ed to know if the British were preparing for an attack on Harlem Heights. The rangers headed south crossing the lowlands of the Hollow Way in the pre-dawn darkness before marching west toward the Bloomingdale Road and the Hudson River. Knowlton halted the column when it reached the Nicholas Jones farmhouse near the Hudson. After concealing his men around the farmhouse, Knowlton sent two of his men forward to locate the British positions. The men were instructed, ". . . to proceed stealthily without noise so as to avoid giving the slightest alarm."[15] When the scouts encountered a British force just after daylight, they fired at them before hastily withdrawing back to the farmhouse. Close on their heels were two battalions of light infantry from the British 42nd Regi-ment. As the British advance guard approached the rangers' position, Knowlton ordered his range men to open fire, and a hot 30-minute fire-fight ensued during which 10 rangers were lost.[16] Captain Stephen Brown wrote,

> They marched up within six rods of us, and then formed to give
> us battle which we were ready for; and Colonel Knowlton gave
> orders to fire, which we did, and stood theirs till we perceived
> they were getting their flank-guards around us. After giving them
> eight rounds apiece (1,000 shots), the colonel gave orders for re-
> treating, which we performed very well, without the loss of a man
> while retreating, though we lost about ten while in action.[17]

After retreating about one quarter-mile, Knowlton positioned his men behind a fence, but when he saw that he was far outnumbered by the British, he withdrew to a patch of woods to avoid being flanked, and cut off from the American lines. The rangers then poured fire into the British ranks as they approached the fence, inflicting a number of casualties. Joseph Plumb Martin, a 16-year-old private from Connecticut, observed the Rangers in action:

> Our people let the enemy advance until they arrived at the fence, when they arose and poured a volley upon them . . . There were, doubtless some killed, as I myself counted nineteen ball-holes through a single rail of the fence at which the enemy were standing when the action began.[18]

About this time, Joseph Reed, General Washington's adjutant general arrived on the scene. Reed later wrote in a letter to his wife,

> . . . an account came that the enemy were advancing upon us in three large columns . . . I accordingly went down to our most advanced guard (Knowlton's Rangers) and while I was talking with the officer, the enemy advanced guard fired upon us at a small distance. Our men behaved well, stood and returned fire, till overpowered by numbers were obliged to retreat. The enemy advanced upon us very fast.[19]

Moments later, General Washington arrived near the scene of the action, where he was informed that the on-going fighting was between Knowlton's Rangers and a three-hundred-man British force. About this time, the British force came into view and taunted the Americans by blowing their bugles in a series of calls usually reserved for fox hunting.[20] After observing the enemy formations, Washington decided on a plan to entrap the entire British force.

General Washington did not intend to bring on a major battle forward of his defenses on Harlem Heights, but he saw an opportunity to defeat the British advance guard. He decided to surprise the British by making a strong demonstration to their front with Colonel George Weedon's Virginia Regiment, while Lieutenant Colonel Knowlton's Rangers, and three companies of riflemen from Weedon's regiment, led by Major Andrew Leitch, encircled the entire British advance guard.

Washington's aide-de-camp, Tench Tilghman, described what happened next, "Unluckily Colonel Knowlton and Major Leitch began their attack too soon; it was rather in flank than rear. The action now grew warm. Major Leitch was wounded early in the engagement and Colonel Knowlton soon after, the latter mortally."[21] Sergeant David Thorp, a ranger orderly sergeant recalled that,

> There was orders to raise a company of "Rangers" of 150. I was one of them as an orderly Sergeant; About this (time) the enemy landed on York Island the next day after they landed, we had a very severe battle with the enemy, which was called the "Monday fight"—We, and brave commander Colonel who fell in the battle—He did not say "go boys," but, "come boys," and we always were ready and willing to follow him, and until he fell within six feet where I was—He begged to be moved so that the enemy should not get possession of his body—I was one who helped put him on the soldiers' shoulders who carried him off—He expired in about one hour . . .[22]

The heavily outnumbered rangers and Virginians continued the fight with "the greatest bravery," but they were in need of reinforcements. Observing that the fight was not going well on the flank, Washington ordered parts of Colonel Griffith's and Colonel Richardson's Maryland Regiments to support the rangers and Virginia riflemen. Tilghman wrote that, "These troops, though young, charged with as much bravery as I can conceive; they gave two fires and then rushed right forward, which drove the enemy from the wood into a buckwheat field, from whence they retreated."[23]

Having failed to encircle and capture the British force, Washington committed two Maryland regiments, and parts of other regiments that were near the action. At the same time, the British rushed reinforcements toward the fighting, committing nearly five thousand men to the battle. The fighting continued for hours with the Americans slowly gaining the advantage. In a letter to the president of the Continental Congress, Washington wrote,

> Those troops charged the Enemy with great Intrepidity and drove them from the Wood into the plain and were pushing them from

thence (having silenced their Fire in a great measure), when I judged it prudent to order a retreat, fearing the Enemy (as I have since found was really the case) were sending a large Body to support their party.[24]

Joseph Reed described what happened after Washington called off the pursuit, "The pursuit of a flying enemy was so new a scene, that it was with difficulty our men could be brought to retreat."[25]

British and Hessian losses were estimated at 90 killed and around three hundred wounded. American losses were considerably less, fewer than 30 killed and one hundred wounded. The Rangers lost at least 12 men and possibly more. A detailed report of Ranger losses has not been found.[26] The death of Lieutenant Colonel Knowlton was a devastating loss to the Rangers and the army. Washington appointed Captain Stephen Brown, one of Knowlton's company commanders, and a French and Indian War veteran, to take command of the rangers. In his general orders issued on September 17, 1776, Washington wrote, "The gallant and brave Col Knowlton, who would have been an Honor to any Country, having fallen yesterday, while gloriously fighting. Capt Brown is to take the Command of the party lately led by Col Knowlton—Officers and men are to obey him accordingly."[27] Knowlton's death was the beginning of the end of Knowlton's Rangers.

Details are sketchy concerning Nathan Hale's spy mission, but it is known that Captain Hale and his company first sergeant, Stephen Hempstead, departed the city on or before September 15, apparently unaware of the British landing at Kips Bay.[28] After departing the city, Hale and Hempstead traveled north and crossed the Harlem River to the Bronx, after which they traveled to Greenwich, Connecticut. Hale planned to cross to Long Island from Greenwich, but when he learned that British warships were prowling the sound off Greenwich, he decided to travel to Norwalk, Connecticut where a crossing was less likely to be intercepted. After his arrival in Norwalk, Hale convinced the captain of the schooner *Schuyler* to ferry him across Long Island Sound to the shores of Huntington, Long Island. Before setting sail, Nathan Hale exchanged his uniform for the garb of a Dutch schoolmaster, thereby changing his legal status from army combatant to spy. Nathan Hale probably stepped ashore near Huntington on the morning of September 16, parting company with his first sergeant for the last time. Ironically, Hale's spy mission on Long Island was no longer of any value. The British had landed at Kips Bay the day before, and were by now advancing toward Harlem Heights.

After departing Huntington, Hale made his way to Brooklyn, arriving on or about September 18. When and how Hale made his way from Brooklyn into the city of New York is unknown, however there were civilian ferries operating even after the British occupied the city. Even though the population of New York City was around twenty-five thousand, Hale was still at risk of discovery. He had been stationed in the city for five months prior to the British invasion, and had mingled freely with many of the city's residents. He could easily be spotted in a crowd being much taller than average, and possessing a distinct soldierly bearing. Nonetheless, he calmly went about his work, making drawings of several new British fortifications, and taking notes on British units stationed in the city. Three days after he entered the city posing as schoolmaster looking for work, a disturbing event occurred that would seal his fate.

Shortly after midnight on September 21, one or more unidentified arsonists set fires in the city. By 2:00 a.m., a large part of New York was ablaze, and civilians and British soldiers alike fled their living quarters, and ran through the streets to escape the flames. Fanned by a southwest wind, the flames soon engulfed at least one-third of the homes, churches, and buildings in the city. Entire blocks and neighborhoods were destroyed.

British soldiers apprehended several civilians who were carrying torches, matches, and combustibles that night, but Hale was not among them. Though the British later accused Hale of being involved in the arson, they had no actual proof of their allegations. It is doubtful that Washington would have risked the life of one of his best ranger officers to enter the city and organize a ring of arsonists to burn the city. Washington had been instructed by the Congress not to burn New York, and it is unlikely that he would have risked his career and integrity by ignoring his orders from Congress.

The fire burned itself out the following day, and the British apprehended Nathan Hale that same day. He was carrying maps, drawings, notes, and his Yale diploma on his person. Accounts differ on the circumstances of his capture, and possible betrayal. According to one account, Hale had a chance encounter in a tavern with Robert Rogers, who had commanded Roger's Rangers during the French and Indian War. By 1776, Rogers had volunteered to serve in the British Army with the rank of lieutenant colonel. He was given command of the Queen's Rangers, a Loyalist ranger unit. It is unknown whether the two recognized each other, but some accounts say that Hale revealed his true identity as he drank with Rogers.[29] Other accounts theorize that his own Tory cousin may have betrayed Hale. While either account may be true, it is also possible that Hale may have been stopped and searched by one of the numerous picket guards deployed around the city after the fire.

General Howe's daybook entry on September 22, 1776, merely states that, "A spy from the Enemy (by his own full confession) apprehended last night, was this day Executed at Eleven o'clock in front of the Artillery Park."[30] Apparently, General Howe thought that since Hale had revealed his true identity, and had on his person the incriminating drawings and notes, there was no need for a trial, which led to his speedy execution on the gallows. So ended the short life of Ranger Captain Nathan Hale, earning him entry into the pantheon of American heroes.

Knowlton's Rangers survived for two more months after the costly battle on September 16. On October 1, Major Andrew Colburn replaced Captain Brown and assumed command of the rangers, but he was wounded in action shortly thereafter, and forced to relinquish command. Captain Lemuel Holmes was the last officer to command Knowlton's Rangers.

On November 16, the entire ranger force was captured at Fort Washington. After defeating the Americans at the Battle of White Plains, the British surrounded the fort and were prepared to attack from all sides. The fort's commander, Colonel Robert Magaw, had requested that the rangers be attached to the garrison to bolster its security, and on the day of the surrender Captain Holmes and his rangers were the only security force deployed outside the fort. As the British tightened the cordon around the fort, Holmes and his men were forced to withdraw back to the fort, arriving just in time for the surrender. Five officers, including Captain Holmes, and 109 enlisted rangers were among those taken prisoner after the surrender of the fort.

After the capitulation, the rangers were marched to lower Manhattan and loaded onto prison ships anchored in the harbor. During their captivity, 10 rangers died as a result of the harsh conditions. A number of rangers were later paroled and subsequently returned to their parent regiments. Captain Holmes was also paroled after spending two years in captivity.

Although Knowlton's Rangers ceased to exist after the fall of Fort Washington, the ranger tradition survived within the American army. General Washington's employment of Knowlton's Rangers during the Long Island and New York campaigns did not take full advantage of their capabilities to undertake long-range reconnaissance missions, and raids against targets behind enemy lines. Instead, the rangers were deployed only a short distances from the American lines. On other occasions, they fought side by side with conventional infantry units as a light infantry force. While the rangers were capable of fighting as light infantry, it was not their primary mission, and did not take full advantage of their capabilities. Attaching the rangers to Colonel Magaw's doomed command at Fort Washington was a serious mistake and an irreplaceable loss to the Continental Army.

Washington's decision to send Ranger Captain Nathan Hale on spying mission into the city of New York, a mission for which he was ill-suited and unprepared, resulted in the loss of one of the army's most talented junior officers. However, the loss of Nathan Hale highlighted the need for a professional well-trained spy network, skilled in the use of codes and ciphers, dead drops, and secret writing materials such as invisible ink. It would take another two years to organize and train a spy network in British-occupied New York. The "Culper Ring" was fully operational by the summer of 1778.

4

WHITCOMB'S RANGERS

"July 23d. (1776)—Early in the morning I returned to my former place of abode; stayed there the whole day; saw 23 carts laden with barrels and tents going to St. John's. 24th stayed at the same place till about 12 o'clock then fired on an officer and moved immediately into Chamblee road. Being discovered retreated back into the woods and stayed all night, then taking the road and passing the guards till I came to Chamblee. Finding myself discovered, was obliged to conceal myself in the brush till dark, the 25th instant, on which I made my escape by the guards. I saw upwards of 40 carts preparing to go to St. John's and I judged there were laying at that place, and on the road about one full regiment of regulars."
— *Benjamin Whitcomb*, Journal of a Scout from Crown Point to St Johns Chamblee[1]

AS 1775 DREW TO A CLOSE, THE AMERICAN'S ILL-FATED CANADIAN campaign began to unravel. On the last day of the year, Major General Richard Montgomery and Brigadier General Benedict Arnold's forces launched an all-out assault on Quebec City in the midst of a blinding snowstorm. The battle was a disastrous defeat for the Americans; in three hours of fighting, one-third of the American forces in Canada were lost. Montgomery was killed and Arnold was seriously wounded. The British and Canadians suffered only light casualties. Following the unsuccessful attack, Arnold directed an unsuccessful siege of the city. The Americans suffered much more than the defenders during the harsh Canadian winter. Efforts to convince the French Canadians to join the American cause met with little success, while the British were able to boost loyalist sentiments among the citizens of the province, and the Native American tribes. On May 2, 1776, a fleet of 15 British ships entered the St. Lawrence River. On board were thousands of British and Hessian reinforcements led by General John Burgoyne. A few days later, Burgoyne's force arrived at Quebec to reinforce General Carleton's besieged garrison, forcing the American army to withdraw toward Montreal.

With the arrival of reinforcements, General Carleton soon made plans to mount a counteroffensive to drive the seriously weakened American army from Canada, and then continue the offensive to capture the strategically important forts at Crown Point and Ticonderoga on Lake Champlain. Seizure of the forts on Lake Champlain would hinder any future American offensives directed against Canada, and facilitate British efforts to gain control of the strategic Hudson River valley.

The American withdrawal from Canada proved more difficult than anyone anticipated, and very nearly ended in disaster. General John Thomas, sent to replace the fallen Montgomery, led the retreat from Quebec but he succumbed to smallpox as the army moved south along the Richelieu River. Benedict Arnold began preparations to evacuate the American garrison from Montreal. Meanwhile, a detachment of American troops was surrounded by a small British force and a large force of Indians and militia some 30 miles west of Montreal at a place called the Cedars. On May 19, Colonel Timothy Bedel, the American commander, surrendered his troops without a fight. It was a humiliating surrender for the troops, who believed that their commander had betrayed them. Bedel was subsequently court-martialed and cashiered from the Continental Army. Less than a month later, on June 8, the Americans suffered another defeat at Trois-Rivieres on the St. Lawrence River.

Following the American defeat at Trois-Rivieres, General Sullivan, the commander of American forces in Canada, ordered a complete withdrawal of American forces from Canada. The Americans were ordered to withdraw to Crown Point and Fort Ticonderoga on Lake Champlain. General Arnold's garrison at Montreal was the last American force to withdraw from Canada. Arnold's men marched to Saint Jean, where they joined the retreating American army, providing the rearguard as it withdrew toward Lake Champlain.

As the first bateaux carrying the remnants of the defeated American army arrived at Crown Point on July 1, they were met by Major General Philip Schuyler, commander of the army's Northern Department, and Major General Horatio Gates, the newly appointed commander of Fort Ticonderoga. Gates was responsible for the defense of the entire Lake Champlain area. Both men knew they faced monumental tasks. The American Northern Theater army had to be rebuilt and strengthened in the shortest possible time, and the defenses on Lake Champlain had to be significantly improved to block a British invasion.

After the capture of Ticonderoga and Crown Point by Ethan Allen's Green Mountain Boys in May 1775, the forts had supported American operations in Canada for a full year. However, little effort had been expended in repairing and improving the fortifications, and both forts were in terrible condition. Crown Point was not large enough to accommodate more than a token garrison, yet it served as the arrival point for the shattered American army after its withdrawal from Canada. The reorganization and rebuilding of the American Northern Department army began at Crown Point.

Although General Gates had never exercised independent command, and possessed little tactical or strategic experience, he proved to be just the right man for the job of rebuilding the American Northern army. His strengths lay in preparing regulations and standard operating procedures, and in logistics. Both areas were major weaknesses within the American army. When the defeated army arrived at Crown Point, it was completely disorganized and lacked standard regulations and procedures. Provisions, serviceable arms, ammunition, uniforms, medical supplies, and hospital facilities were all in short supply. Key leadership positions had not been filled, and morale and discipline were at an all-time low. Making matters worse, a large portion of the troops were infected with smallpox, dysentery, and other diseases, and were not fit for duty.

On July 7, General Schuyler convened a council of war at Crown Point, asking all five American general officers stationed in the American Northern Department to attend. Schuyler chaired the meeting. Other generals present were Major General Horatio Gates, and Brigadier Generals Benedict Arnold, John Sullivan, and Baron de Woedtke. The council made several important decisions. First, all five generals agreed that Crown Point should be evacuated, and that the American army's main defensive position should be at Fort Ticonderoga. It was further agreed that all the sick, including those infected with smallpox, would be evacuated to Fort George, where they would receive proper medical treatment. The generals further resolved that they should attempt to secure Lake Champlain by building and arming a small fleet of gondolas, row galleys, and bateaux. Other provisions were also made for the construction of roads, and additional fortifications to support Fort Ticonderoga. General Gates was a strict disciplinarian and master of details, and he soon set the plans into motion, knowing that he had little time to prepare for the British offensive.

By mid-July, General Schuyler was back in Albany organizing and supervising the logistical support of the Northern Department army, while General Gates moved the army from Crown Point to Ticonderoga. Repairs were soon underway at Ticonderoga. In addition to improving the fortifications at Ticonderoga, and establishing a workable logistic system to supply the Northern Department army, Gates was also wanted to gather intelligence on British preparations for an offensive down the Lake Champlain corridor. This required sending several deep-penetration patrols into Canada to gain information on British troop strengths, deployments and other preparations. To carry out the long-range patrols, Gates needed men who were intimately familiar with the terrain north of Lake Champlain in the Richelieu River Valley all the way to the St. Lawrence River. Depending on the route and destination, these patrols would have to traverse more than a hundred miles of rugged terrain, and the missions would take several weeks to complete. General Gates soon learned that he had in his command one of the best-qualified men to undertake such a mission—Lieutenant Benjamin Whitcomb.

———————

Benjamin Whitcomb was born in Lancaster, Massachusetts in 1737. When the French and Indian War broke out, he enlisted in the Massachusetts Provincials as an 18-year-old private. Soon thereafter, his company joined an expedition under General Sir William Johnson to seize Crown Point during the summer of 1755. Whitcomb participated in the battle of Lake George in September of that same year, when the Provincials defeated a force of 1,500 French and Indians commanded by the Baron de Dieskau. Whitcomb reenlisted in 1757, when Major General Louis-Joseph de Montcalm Marquis de Saint-Veran threatened to move on Albany after his victory at Fort William Henry. Two years later, Whitcomb joined General Jeffery Amherst's expedition against Montreal. After the capture of Montreal, Whitcomb's company marched across Vermont and New Hampshire to their homes in Massachusetts. During his service in the French and Indian War, Whitcomb became intimately familiar with the terrain in the Lake George–Champlain valley, and the Canadian lands along the Richelieu River north of Lake Champlain all the way to the river's confluence with the St. Lawrence River. After the French and Indian War, Whitcomb moved to Westmoreland, New Hampshire, and later to Maidenhead (present day Guildhall), in northern Vermont.

When the Revolutionary War broke out, Benjamin Whitcomb enlisted in Colonel Timothy Bedel's New Hampshire Regiment, and was appointed as a second lieutenant in Captain Samuel Young's Company. Whitcomb was later described as a man in his late thirties, tall and thin, with a rough pockmarked face and brown hair pulled back and tied in a queue. Like most hunters and woodsmen of the time, Whitcomb usually wore a sleeveless jacket, leather trousers, gray stockings, and shoes, with a gold cord tied around a broad, turned up felt hat.[2]

When Bedel's regiment was ordered to join the Continental Army in Canada, Whitcomb initially remained behind to recruit additional men for his company, but rejoined his company with the new recruits in May 1776. By that time, the Canadian campaign of 1775–76 was in disarray, and the army was withdrawing to Crown Point. Whitcomb's company was assigned to the rearguard during the withdrawal. On June 24, Whitcomb was promoted to first lieutenant, and the company reached Crown Point in early July. The 39-year-old veteran was afforded little time to rest.

Based on his experiences in the Lake George–Champlain Valley, and the Richelieu River Valley during the French and Indian War, Whitcomb was ordered to scout between Fort Ticonderoga and the British positions around Saint Jean sur Richelieu (Saint John) and Montreal in Canada.

The land north of Fort Ticonderoga was a vast wilderness covered in boundless forests, pathless woods, swamps, and lonely lakeshores. Steep foothills overshadowed by majestic mountains surrounded the lakes and river valleys. Cross-country movement was slow and difficult, and travel by canoe on the region's windswept lakes and swift-flowing rivers was hazardous. Subsistence in the wilderness was a challenge, even for experienced hunters like Benjamin Whitcomb and his rangers. Both he and his rangers preferred to travel either alone or in small groups to avoid detection and make good time on their long treks. They had to be constantly on alert for hostile Indian war parties bent on scalping and killing whoever crossed their path.

On the night of July 14, 1776, Lieutenant Whitcomb departed Crown Point with four men: two Americans and two French Canadians, headed for Saint Jean near Montreal, a straight-line distance of 120 miles. His mission was to scout along the Richelieu River between Saint Jean and Chambly south of Montreal counting boats and troops, and if possible, capturing a British officer for interrogation.

The patrol only covered seven miles the first night due to high winds. The following day, Whitcomb and his men reached the Onion River before being forced to halt due to strong winds and rain. The patrol hunkered down to wait out the storm. By the evening of July 17, the storm began to subside. That night, the patrol traveled 20 miles before it was forced to halt by another storm. On the evening of July 19, Whitcomb's patrol set off again. By daybreak of the 20th, the patrol had reached the head of the Missisquoi Bay, just north of the Vermont–Canadian border. Whitcomb's patrol continued moving north, following the Richelieu River towards Saint Jean. As the patrol neared Saint Jean, the two French-Canadian members of the patrol became uneasy, and were unwilling to go further; Whitcomb told them to return home. As he had had to send another patrol member back due to illness shortly after leaving Crown Point, it was now down to Whitcomb and one other man to complete the mission.

Whitcomb and his companion reached a point five miles from Saint Jean on the evening of July 20. They were close enough to hear drumbeats coming from the town. By noon of the following day, they were on the east bank of the Richelieu River opposite Saint Jean. The pair lay in wait on the riverbank for the rest of the day hoping to take a prisoner, but they saw no one. When they returned to the riverbank at daybreak the following morning, they were surprised to see 30 bateaux floating in the river, and a work party busy building more boats on the opposite shore.

Whitcomb kept the work party under observation hoping to take a prisoner, but the workers were closely guarded by a detachment of soldiers. After determining that his chances of capturing an officer in the area were remote, Whitcomb decided to head north along the Richelieu River to Chambly, a distance of some 15 miles. Along the way, they observed four bateaux loaded with barrels moving down the river. The two men soon happened on a French-Canadian cabin, where they found a canoe, enabling them to cross the river. At that time, Whitcomb and his companion were more than 120 miles deep in enemy territory.

Chambly was a French-Canadian settlement located less than 16 miles southeast of Montreal. The settlement had grown up around Fort Chambly at the foot of the Chambly Rapids on the Richelieu River. General Montgomery's forces had captured the fort in October 1775 during the ill-fated American invasion of Canada. During the American withdrawal the following spring, the fort had been evacuated and burned. Whitcomb knew that the British had between two and three thousand troops stationed in the St. Johns and Chambly area, and the risk of discovery—leading to capture or death—was extremely high.

After crossing the Richelieu undetected, Whitcomb proceeded cautiously along a road that led to Montreal. When enemy troops were sighted, Whitcomb twice led his companion into the woods where they concealed themselves, until the British troops passed by. Later in the day, Whitcomb observed 17 carts loaded with barrels moving south on the road followed by 27 armed Indians. That evening, when Whitcomb went searching for provisions, his only companion deserted, and most likely headed back to safer territory. The following morning, Whitcomb again concealed himself in the wood line, where he could observe the traffic moving along the road. About noon, he spotted a party of mounted British soldiers riding down the road. Seeing that the horsemen included a high-ranking officer, his aides, and a small escort, Whitcomb took aim and fired at the officer hoping to knock him off his horse. The officer was mortally wounded but managed to stay in the saddle. Pursued by the escort, Whitcomb retreated into the dense woods and managed to conceal himself in a hollow log. Realizing that it was far too dangerous to travel in daylight, Whitcomb hid in the woods until dark.

As soon as he determined that there were no patrols in the immediate area, Whitcomb began retracing his steps back toward Chambly. He was forced to slip back into the woods to bypass guards stationed along the road. Whitcomb remained in the Chambly-St. Johns area for four more days after shooting the British officer. He successfully evaded enemy patrols, and continued to count British troops and armed Indians traveling along the roads. On one occasion he barely escaped capture when a party of British Regulars spotted him. On July 27, Whitcomb set off on his long return trek to Fort Ticonderoga. Marching alone without the benefit of a compass, Whitcomb traveled down the west side of the Richelieu River and Lake Champlain in horrible weather conditions, finally reaching Fort Ticonderoga on August 6.

After reporting the considerable intelligence that he had gathered, Whitcomb finally learned the identity of the British officer he had shot. Brigadier General Patrick Gordon, commander of a brigade of British Regulars, had died of his wound several days after Whitcomb shot him. His death had set in motion a massive manhunt, and protests by the British military. Apparently, Gordon's aides got a good look at Whitcomb, and were able to identify most of his physical features. Major General William Phillips issued orders for British troops to hang Whitcomb and any members of his party immediately upon capture, and General Guy Carleton, governor of the Province of Quebec, offered a reward of 50 guineas for Benjamin Whitcomb, dead or alive. British authorities labeled Whitcomb as an assassin, claiming that it was against the rules of war to shoot officers from ambush, and demanding that he be turned over. American authorities responded by saying that, "as long as the British employed Indians to ambush and slaughter American soldiers and civilians," retaliatory actions, such as Whitcomb's, were justified.[3]

On August 19, General Gates ordered Whitcomb to undertake another scouting mission into the St. Johns–Chambly area with the stipulation that he was not to shoot anyone else. Ignoring the price on his head, Whitcomb set off for Canada the following day. Despite bad weather and being stricken with ague, he completed his mission gathering high-value intelligence on British troop dispositions and movements.

On September 5, Whitcomb departed on his third scouting mission to the Richelieu River Valley. By September 13, he was in the same area where he had shot General Gordon. Concealing himself near the road, he captured Colonel Skene, quartermaster of the 29th Regiment, and his enlisted aide. At first the colonel mistook Whitcomb for a Canadian civilian, and was convinced that this unkempt person was not a soldier. According to Whitcomb, the colonel offered him a bribe for his release, but Whitcomb refused to consider it. Having accomplished his mission, Whitcomb returned to Fort Ticonderoga with his prisoners, arriving on September 22. The two prisoners made no attempt to escape during the long trek, fearing that they would get lost in the wilderness, or be tracked down and killed by the notorious "assassin" Whitcomb.

The intelligence gathered by Lieutenant Whitcomb left little doubt that the British were preparing for a major offensive against the American forts on Lake Champlain before winter arrived. General Gates worked his troops day and night to improve the fortifications, while General Schuyler rushed supplies and reinforcements to Fort Ticonderoga. At the same time, General Arnold supervised a group of shipwrights and sailors who were building a fleet of ships and gunboats to engage the British fleet as it sailed down Lake Champlain toward Crown Point and Fort Ticonderoga.

The British offensive began when General Carleton's fleet, commanded by Captain Thomas Pringle, sailed onto Lake Champlain on October 9. Two days later the British fleet approached Valcour Island, where Arnold's much smaller fleet lay in wait. The American fleet fought valiantly, but it was outnumbered and outgunned by the British. After losing a number of ships, Arnold was forced to retire towards Crown Point under the cover of darkness. Bad weather slowed the badly damaged American ships as they sailed south. Arnold ordered the ships into Buttonmold Bay where they were purposely run aground, and set on fire. He then led the crews overland to Crown Point. Upon reaching Crown Point, Arnold concluded that the fort could not be held given the size of the British force. He burned the fort's barracks and storehouses and withdrew to Fort Ticonderoga. The following day the British landed troops and occupied Crown Point.

With a British army less than a dozen miles north of Fort Ticonderoga, General Gates recognized the need for a duly authorized specialized unit capable of conducting special reconnaissance and surveillance missions to provide early warning of enemy attacks. He recommended to the

Continental Congress that Whitcomb be promoted to the rank of captain in the Continental Army with full authorization to recruit two companies of rangers for the Continental Army.

After receiving General Gates' recommendation, the Continental Congress passed a resolution on October 15, 1776, authorizing Whitcomb to raise two independent companies of 50 men each to serve as rangers for the Continental Army. Whitcomb was appointed captain commandant of the ranger force with authorization to nominate officers for the two companies, subject to the approval of the commanding general of the Northern Department.[4] Whitcomb assumed command of one company and selected Captain George Aldrich to command the second company.

After spending more than two weeks at Crown Point, the British decided to probe the defenses of Fort Ticonderoga by sailing gunboats down Lake Champlain. On October 28, sentries at Fort Ticonderoga spotted the approaching gunboats and the fort's artillery opened fire. The gunboats quickly reversed course, and sailed back up the lake to Crown Point. As winter approached, Carleton knew that once Lake Champlain was frozen over, he would have no means of resupplying his army at Crown Point. He had no choice but to order his army to withdraw to Canada.

Recruitment of men to fill the ranks of the army's ranger companies began immediately, and continued throughout the winter of 1776–77. In January 1777, Captain Whitcomb dispatched Captain Aldrich to the Connecticut Valley to recruit additional men for the ranger companies. General Gates was convinced that the British would launch another invasion from Canada during the spring, and knew that he would need Captain Whitcomb and his rangers more than ever before.

In March 1777, the Continental Congress appointed General Gates as commander of the Continental Army's Northern Department, replacing General Schuyler. General Arthur St. Clair was placed in command of Fort Ticonderoga, but his arrival at Ticonderoga was delayed until early June.

As spring approached the Lake Champlain region, Whitcomb's ranger companies began patrolling the forests and woodlands in search of Indian and Loyalist raiding parties. On several occasions, Whitcomb and his rangers were sent out to track down and destroy enemy raiding parties. On one such mission, Whitcomb and his rangers tracked down and attacked an Indian raiding party led by an infamous Loyalist, Captain Samuel McKay. McKay was a British half-pay officer assigned to the Royal American Regiment, who had a price on his head because he had led attacks on unarmed civilians. On this particular raid, McKay's Indians spotted a group of American recruits camped near Lake George. The war party attacked at dawn, tomahawked four of the recruits, wounded their officer, and took 21 captives. Whitcomb's rangers caught up with McKay's raiders on their way north, and rescued several of the captives, although McKay escaped in the melee, and made his way back to Canada.[5]

In May, there were new reports indicating that a British force was amassing in Canada in preparation for a move south to attack Ticonderoga. Whitcomb's rangers moved north along the shore of Lake Champlain on the lookout for any signs of the British. General Gates was at Albany, when he received a report from Captain Whitcomb indicating that enemy troops had been spotted at Split Rock some 35 miles north of Ticonderoga. The British reconnoitering party then reversed course and sailed back toward Canada, leaving General Gates to conclude that the alarm over a British approach to Ticonderoga was premature.[6]

As May gave way to June, Whitcomb continued to send out small patrols to scout the woods surrounding Ticonderoga. The patrols reported that the woods were crawling with Indian scouting parties, but as yet there was no sign of a large British force. On June 28, one of Whitcomb's ranger patrols failed to return as scheduled. General Gates considered sending out Whitcomb with a larger ranger force to gather the intelligence he so desperately needed, but thought better of it—Whitcomb was too valuable to lose, and the garrison at Ticonderoga was too understrength to risk sending out a large party of rangers.

Little progress had been made on improving the defenses of Fort Ticonderoga during the winter and spring of 1777. General Schuyler recommended that certain improvements and repairs be made on the fort's southeast side, and that a large log boom be stretched across the waterway north of the fort to impede an enemy flotilla from landing troops near the fort. However, funds were in short supply, and the improvements at

Ticonderoga were never completed.[7] Moreover, there was still a manpower shortage at Ticonderoga, and illness continued to reduce the ranks of able-bodied men in the garrison. Requests for reinforcements throughout the spring had gone unanswered. By the end of June 1777, time had run out for General St. Clair and the garrison at Fort Ticonderoga.

On June 30, the main body of British and German troops under the command of General John Burgoyne arrived at Crown Point, 12 miles north of Ticonderoga. Burgoyne commanded a mixed force of British Regulars, Canadians, Loyalists, and Indians which numbered more than ten thousand men. General St. Clair's garrison at Fort Ticonderoga numbered around 3,800 men, but more than a quarter of the soldiers were unfit for duty.[8]

Burgoyne delayed his planned attack on Fort Ticonderoga for two days due to bad weather on Lake Champlain. On July 2, Burgoyne occupied Mount Hope, cutting off Lake George as a potential escape corridor for the Americans. The following day, the British launched a two-prong attack south against Ticonderoga and Mount Independence. The Americans delayed the British and Hessian advances from the outer works of Ticonderoga, but when the British placed their artillery on Mount Defiance that overlooked Fort Ticonderoga and Mount Independence, both forts became untenable. On the night of July 5–6, General St. Clair ordered the abandonment of both fortifications. Whitcomb's rangers withdrew with the rest of the Northern army towards Albany.

Before the evacuation of Fort Ticonderoga, Captain Whitcomb sent his deputy, Captain George Aldrich, to New Hampshire to recruit more men for the Rangers. On his return trip, Aldrich and his recruits joined Brigadier General John Stark near Bennington, and participated in the battle of Bennington on August 16, 1777, in which the Americans soundly defeated Lieutenant Colonel Friedrich Baum's mixed force of British, Hessians, Canadians, Loyalists, and Indians. Aldrich and his ranger recruits performed with distinction in that battle.

A month later, Whitcomb's rangers fought under General Gates during the epic battle of Saratoga. The rangers saw action at the battles of Freeman's Farm on September 19, and Bemis Heights on October 7. During the fighting, the rangers were attached to Dearborn's Light Infantry Battalion, part of the left wing of the army, which was commanded by

General Arnold. The portion of the battlefield where the rangers fought was heavily wooded with hills and ravines covered with clumps of brush, fallen trees, and rocks—the type of terrain in which the rangers fought best. At Freeman's Farm, Dearborn's Light Infantry Battalion with Whitcomb's rangers attached held the extreme left position of Arnold's left wing in the highest portion of the forest. Between the battles of Freeman's Farm and Bemis Heights, the rangers were employed in daily skirmishing and patrolling in the "no-man's-land" between the American and British lines. Captain Whitcomb was reportedly the first one to spot the British approach along Bemis Heights in the opening stage of that battle.

After the British surrender at Saratoga on October 17, 1777, Captain Whitcomb was promoted to the rank of major and assigned to a regiment that was being raised for an expedition to Canada. The regiment comprised five hundred volunteers, under the command of Colonel Timothy Bedel. General Lafayette was assigned to lead the expedition, but the expedition was cancelled when the Continental Congress failed to approve the army plan.

After the American victory at Saratoga, Whitcomb's rangers moved to Rutland, Vermont, near the border with Canada, where they established Fort Ranger. As senior Continental officer in the area, Major Whitcomb had command of the ranger companies along with several companies of militia, and a portion of Colonel Seth Warner's regiment. While stationed at Rutland, Whitcomb's men continued to scout and spy on the British in Canada. Whitcomb was credited with uncovering a plan for a British raid on American supplies and mills on both sides of Lake Champlain during October 1778. Whitcomb's rangers intercepted one of the raiding parties and forced it to withdraw to Canada.

Whitcomb's Rangers remained in Rutland throughout the fall of 1778. In early 1779, Whitcomb's Rangers moved to the upper Connecticut River Valley, known as the "Co'os," and established their headquarters at Haverhill, New Hampshire. The Rangers, augmented by additional companies from the region, assumed responsibility for the security of the area. In October 1780, a force of British and Indians set out to raid the Connecticut River Valley, but changed their plans when they learned that Whitcomb had assembled a force of five hundred men to defend the valley.

Whitcomb's Rangers remained as an "Independent Corps of Rangers" in the Continental Army, until the Continental Army's reorganization in early 1781. Under the reorganization plan, the rangers were assigned to the light infantry companies of the three New Hampshire Continental Line regiments.

Whitcomb's Rangers were distinct from other Continental Army and militia units. Their primary mission was scouting and intelligence gathering behind enemy lines, but they were also capable of fighting as a light infantry force when required. Only around 120 men served in Whitcomb's Independent Corps of Rangers. Most of the enlisted rangers were in their teens and early to mid-twenties, while most of their officers were in their thirties, with prior military experience from the French and Indian War. One of the youngest to serve was Private Abiel Chandler who enlisted in 1780, at the age of 15. Private Samuel Fifield was probably the oldest. He also enlisted in the rangers in 1780, at the age of 45. Regardless of their age, every one of Whitcomb's rangers was hand-picked by Benjamin Whitcomb and his officers, based on their stamina, woodsman skills and ability to operate alone or in small teams. They were capable of performing surveillance and reconnaissance missions in austere harsh environments, and conducting raids deep inside enemy-held territory with little or no outside support. Whitcomb's Rangers were the forbearers of today's US Army Rangers and Special Forces.

5

JOHN PAUL JONES' RAIDS
ON BRITAIN'S COAST

Whitehaven, April 28, 1778: Late last night or early this morning a number of armed men (to the amount of 30) landed at this place by two boats from an American privateer, as appears from one of the people now in custody. Whether he was left through accident or escaped by design is yet uncertain.

— *London Morning Post and Daily Advertiser*, April 28, 1778

SINCE ITS FORMATION IN 1775, THE CONTINENTAL NAVY, UNDER the direction of the Maritime Committee of the Continental Congress, focused on intercepting British shipments of supplies, materials, and troops to North America as well as disrupting British commercial shipping in the Atlantic and Caribbean. The Continental Navy's raid on New Providence in the Bahamas (January–March 1776), was only marginally successful, but it demonstrated the Navy's capability to conduct long-range out-of-theater strikes against British onshore installations.

The Continental fleet lost any credibility it had gained during the New Providence raid when it engaged the British warship *Glasgow* in a running sea battle on its return from the Bahamas. A shake-up of the Continental Navy followed soon after, based on complaints lodged against Commodore Esek Hopkins, the fleet's commander, and some of his captains for their performance during the raid, and the fight with the *Glasgow*. Other complaints arose based on the disposition of captured goods, and the

111

division of prize money. A number of investigations, and courts-martial followed. Though Hopkins was censured, he was not relieved as commander-in-chief of the Continental Navy at that time. The captain of the sloop *Providence*, Captain Hazard, was not as fortunate. Hazard was court-martialed based on a number of charges, including the embezzlement of his ship's stores. After being found guilty on several charges, he was relieved of his command, opening the way for an ambitious young officer, Lieutenant John Paul Jones. Commodore Hopkins selected Jones to command the *Providence*, with the temporary rank of captain, launching his historic career, and a new era for the fledgling Continental Navy.

John Paul Jones was born John Paul on July 6, 1747, in a traditional two-room cottage on the grounds of Arbigland estate on the west coast of Scotland. The estate sat on the northern side of the Solway Firth, part of the ancient Barony of Arbigland. Moors and 2,000-foot mountains overlook the rich farmlands bordering the firth. On a clear day, the English shore is clearly visible across the firth with the mountains of the Lake District looming in the background.[1] John Paul's father worked as a landscape gardener on the estate that was owned by Robert Craik, a Member of Parliament. Born the fourth of seven children, John spent his early years exploring the coastline, gazing at the merchant vessels and fishing boats sailing out of the firth toward the Irish Sea, and interacting with local fishermen and merchant sailors in the nearby sleepy port of Carsethorn. It came as no surprise to his family that he chose to pursue a career at sea. At the age of 13, John Paul was apprenticed to the owner of the merchant ship, *Friendship*. Although, the ship was a merchantman, she was armed with 18 cannon to ward off privateers, pirates, and commerce raiders.[2] The *Friendship* sailed from Whitehaven, a small town and port on the Cumbrian coastline west of England's Lake District. The ship made voyages to Barbados in the Lesser Antilles, and on the return voyages often visited ports in the American colonies before returning to England.

John Paul Jones' service on the *Friendship* afforded him the opportunity to learn the basic skills of seamanship including sail and line handling, navigation, helmsmanship, and gunnery. Jones also became familiar with the waters and ports along the English coast, as well as the Caribbean waters and ports, and those along the Atlantic seaboard of the American colonies. As a merchant sailor, Jones learned the importance of the cross-Atlantic trade to the British economy.

In 1764, the owners of the *Friendship* sold the ship, and Jones was released from his apprenticeship, having served only three years of the seven-year obligation. For the next several years, he served in billets as third mate, and then as a first mate on merchant and slave ships sailing between Whitehaven and Kingston, Jamaica. After becoming disgusted with the cruelty of the slave trade, he resigned his profitable first-mate billet on the slaver, *Two Friends*, while she was in port in Jamaica. He subsequently booked passage on the brig, *John*, which was returning to Scotland. The voyage led to a rapid advancement in his career as a merchant sailor. When both the captain and the ranking mate of the ship died of yellow fever during the Atlantic voyage, the 21-year-old Jones stepped forward to take command of the ship, and sailed it safely back to Kirkcudbright, Scotland. The ship's owners were impressed with Jones' leadership and seamanship skills, and offered him the command of the *John*. In 1769, Jones sailed from Scotland to Kingston, Jamaica, and repeated the same voyage a year later.

Although his crews respected the young captain, he was a stern disciplinarian and taskmaster. On a voyage to Tobago, Jones had his ship's carpenter flogged. The carpenter survived the flogging, but chose to leave Jones' ship in Tobago, and return to England on another ship. He died on the return trip, and his relatives accused Jones of causing the carpenter's death. After spending a short time in jail, Jones was exonerated, but the incident added to his reputation as a tough and harsh captain. In 1773, Jones was involved in another, more serious incident, involving a crewmember on the merchant ship, *Betsy*. After an Atlantic transit from England to Tobago, Jones became involved in a dispute with a crewmember over back wages. The crewman assaulted Jones, who in turn ran the man through with his sword. The dead crewman was a native of Tobago with many relatives and friends on the island. Fearing retribution by the slain crewman's family, and not trusting the impartiality and fairness of Tobago's courts, Captain Jones deserted his ship, and fled to Virginia, where his brother had taken up residence.[3]

Between 1773 and 1775, John Paul Jones kept a low profile in the American colonies. He wanted to become a landowner in Virginia, but he lacked the funds. The money that he had earned as captain of the *Betsy* was frozen in Tobago, due to the legal entanglements that resulted from his flight from the island's justice system. As the American colonies moved toward independence, Jones began to make important friends and contacts in Virginia, the Carolinas and Pennsylvania. As a member of the Freemasonry, he was introduced to several important persons in the Patriot movement, including Joseph Hewes, a successful North Carolina merchant and politician. Hewes served in the First Continental Congress, and was appointed to the Naval Committee. Hewes was instrumental in gaining an appointment for John Paul Jones in the newly organized Continental Navy. Jones' transformation from fugitive merchant captain to lieutenant in the Continental Navy was largely due to his political acumen, unbridled ambition, and determination.

John Paul Jones' appointment as first lieutenant of the Continental Navy's 30-gun frigate, *Alfred*, was confirmed on December 22, 1775. The 440-ton *Alfred* was one of eight converted merchant vessels assigned to the Continental Navy's first fleet under the command of Commodore Esek Hopkins. Hopkins selected *Alfred* as his flagship. Prior to the confirmation of his appointment, Jones had volunteered to supervise the conversion and outfitting of the *Alfred*, earning Hopkins's trust and confidence. The commodore rewarded Jones by giving him the honor of raising the first American flag on a Continental Navy ship. The ceremony was well attended by the prominent citizens of Philadelphia and members of the Continental Congress, giving Jones his first taste of fame.

Dudley Saltonstall of New London, Connecticut, assumed command of the *Alfred* on December 23, 1775, with John Paul Jones as his executive officer and second-in-command. Saltonstall received his appointment largely through his family's powerful political connections, but he had considerable experience as a merchant captain during the French and Indian War, and later as captain of a privateer sailing in the West Indies. However, his background and career were in sharp contrast to that his young Scottish executive officer, who had earned his position through hard work and proven abilities. Captain Saltonstall considered Jones his inferior, based on Jones' limited education and social standing, and gave him little credit or acknowledgement for his work in outfitting the *Alfred* and training her crew.[4] Jones disliked his captain at first sight, and complained of his "Rude Unhappy Temper," and snobbish manner.[5] As a result, the relationship between the two was cool, and fraught with tension and mistrust. On the other hand, Commodore Hopkins displayed a friendly attitude toward First Lieutenant Jones, and Jones remained loyal to his superior, until Hopkins denied him an opportunity for a command.[6]

Lieutenant Jones played a minor role during the New Providence expedition, but later claimed that he served as Commodore Hopkins' planning officer and strategist during the raid. That was a gross exaggeration, since Hopkins and Saltonstall both had first-hand knowledge of the waters and islands of the Bahamas. There is little doubt that the ambitious young lieutenant offered his advice to his superiors more than once on the raid. However, since the New Providence raid was John Paul Jones' first wartime experience as a naval officer, it is doubtful that his advice carried much weight with his superiors. After the raid, Jones' continued attempts to advance his career by exaggerating his own role in the raid, and by criticizing Saltonstall's performance as captain of the *Alfred*. Jones wrote to Congressman Hewes providing him with a mixed review of the raid, and criticizing Saltonstall's leadership. He did, however, praise Commodore Hopkins for completing the mission, and returning with the badly needed cannon, and a portion of powder that was stored at New Providence.[7] Hopkins, who had numerous critics in Congress, rewarded Jones for his loyalty and support by giving him command of the *Providence*.

During the late summer and fall of 1777, Jones sailed the Atlantic coast on voyages covering the sea-lanes from Nova Scotia to Bermuda. The voyages were in keeping with the Continental Navy's strategy of interdicting supplies meant for the British army units stationed in America, and disrupting British commerce and maritime activity off the American coast, thereby disrupting the British economy. After capturing several commercial prizes, and sinking a number of other vessels, the *Providence* returned to Newport, Rhode Island on October 17, 1776. Upon his arrival at Newport, Jones was informed that the Continental Congress had confirmed his rank as a permanent captain in the Continental Navy. Jones,

however, was not pleased with his standing on the seniority list of captains—he ranked 18th on the list of 24.[8] Jones was also disappointed that
he had not been given command of one of the Navy's larger ships, having
long aspired to command one of the new frigates. His protestations to
the president of the Continental Congress, Robert Morris, and his friend
Joseph Hewes on the Maritime Committee, went unanswered. Most of
the command appointments were based on regional representation in the
Congress, with a disproportionate share of appointments going to the
New England, and Middle Atlantic states where most of the ship-building
industry was located. Since he was not a native-born American, Jones was
at a distinct disadvantage. Despite his disappointment, John Paul Jones
was determined to continue his service to his adopted country.

Captain Jones' determination and devotion to his duties finally paid
off, and he was given command of the *Alfred*, the largest ship in the Continental Navy, in late October 1776. His sailing orders directed him to attack the British colliers that supplied coal to the British forces occupying
New York City, and to liberate American prisoners who were forced to
labor in the coal pits on Cape Breton Island, Nova Scotia. On November
1, 1776, the *Alfred*, accompanied by the *Hampton*, set sail from Providence,
Rhode Island. During the six-week voyage, the two ships ploughed
through high waves, and experienced harsh sailing conditions. As a result,
Jones was unable to liberate the Americans held captive on Cape Breton
Island. On a second voyage, Jones captured the British ship, *Mellish*, that
was carrying a cargo of winter clothing destined for General Burgoyne's
troops stationed in Canada. The captured clothing was sent to Washington's army. On the same voyage, Jones captured several other prizes, including two British colliers that were bound for New York City. Prior to
end of the *Alfred's* second voyage, Jones outran the 28-gun Royal Navy
frigate, *Milford*, and reached the safety of Boston with all four of his
prizes.

After arriving in Boston on December 16, 1776, Jones continued to
petition his superiors for a command more befitting his proven successes
at sea. He became even more irate when he learned that he was reassigned
to the *Providence*, a smaller ship than the *Alfred*. Jones viewed the reassign-
ment as a demotion, and blamed Commodore Hopkins for blocking his
advancement within the Navy. Jones was a strong advocate for projecting

American naval power to European waters, and on several occasions expressed his views directly to members of Congress. Jones was creating political waves within the Continental Navy, and the Congress. Some of his fellow officers and members of Congress believed that he was trying to advance his own career by disparaging his fellow officers within the Navy. His relationship with Commodore Hopkins continued to deteriorate during the winter of 1776–77, to the point where he only very nearly escaped court-martial. Still, there is no evidence that indicates that stubborn Scotsman seriously considered resigning from the Navy at that point in his career.

On June 14, 1777, Jones was offered command of a newly commissioned ship, the three-masted 20-gun sloop of war, *Ranger*. Jones was offered the command after Captain John Roche, the Navy's first choice, was suspended for unspecified misconduct. Although Jones aspired to command a larger ship than the *Ranger*, notably one of the new frigates, he was mollified by the fact that the *Ranger* was a new ship that was ideally suited for commerce raiding along enemy coasts.

By July 12, 1777, Jones was in Portsmouth overseeing the final fitting out of the *Ranger*, and recruiting a crew. Jones immediately identified several problems with the vessel. The 116-foot-long sloop had clean lines, and was clearly designed for speed, but she was over-rigged, and her masts and yardarms were too heavy for her size. This meant that *Ranger* was top-heavy, which would cause her to roll in moderate to heavy seas. That tendency had a detrimental effect on gunnery, since the cannon of that period required a fairly stable platform to insure accuracy. Jones also thought that the *Ranger* was too light a ship to mount 20 cannon, so he reduced the number of guns to 18. Moreover, the ship's sails were of poor quality, and likely to tear in strong winds. Jones had little time to correct those problems at Portsmouth before setting sail for France. The procurement and installation of lighter masts and yards would have to wait until he arrived in France. Otherwise, the *Ranger* would have missed her sailing date.

Recruiting a crew of 140 able-bodied sailors and a complement of qualified officers from the Portsmouth area also presented a major challenge. Due to time constraints, it was not possible to recruit sailors and marines from ports far from Portsmouth. Some recruiting efforts were launched in Providence, Rhode Island, and Boston, but the vast majority of the crew signed on from Portsmouth and the surrounding areas of New Hampshire. To entice men to sail on the *Ranger*, Jones made promises of liberal prize monies, regular pay, and bonuses for signing, all payable over the first year. Jones had only limited power to make good on those promises. Disputes over pay would continue to plague Jones throughout his time as captain of the *Ranger*. Nevertheless, Jones was able to recruit a full crew of officers and sailors. All five of the officers, and two-thirds of the men were from Portsmouth. This helped build a cohesive crew, but placed Jones at a disadvantage when he attempted to enforce discipline among the crewmembers. As an outsider and a foreign-born captain, Jones realized that he lacked the total support of his officers or crewmembers, but he was unconcerned, since he anticipated a new assignment once he reached France. Jones believed he was being sent to France to command the frigate, *L'Indien*, which was under construction in Holland under the authorization of the Paris-based American Commissioners.

On the morning of November 1, 1777, the *Ranger* weighed anchor and sailed out of Portsmouth harbor bound for France. On board were a full crew and five officers. Jones's first lieutenant was a former merchant seaman, Thomas Simpson, of Portsmouth. Simpson was nine years older than Jones. The *Ranger*'s second lieutenant was Elijah Hall, who was also a former merchant seaman and shipbuilder from the Portsmouth area. Thirty-one-year-old Captain Matthew Parke and 22-year-old Lieutenant Samuel Wallingford were the two Continental Marine officers aboard the *Ranger*. Parke was a veteran of the New Providence raid with three years' experience as marine officer under his belt. Wallingford was a new and inexperienced marine officer. Prior to his appointment as a marine officer, Wallingford served an officer in the New Hampshire militia. *Ranger*'s midshipman was David Wendell of Portsmouth, and the ship's surgeon was Harvard-educated Doctor Ezra Green of Portsmouth. Doctor Green kept a diary that provides a day-by-day description of the voyage of the *Ranger*.

The *Ranger* carried important dispatches for the Paris-based American

Commissioners, including news of the stunning American victory at Saratoga. Jones planned to personally deliver the dispatches to Benjamin Franklin, the senior American commissioner, hoping to receive confirmation of his appointment as captain of *L'Indien*.

Despite her flaws, the *Ranger* completed the Atlantic transit in 31 days, and arrived at the mouth of the Loire on December 2, 1777, along with two enemy brigs taken as prizes in the Bay of Biscay. After taking a French pilot on board, the *Ranger* proceeded to Paimbouef, the closest deep-water port to the city of Nantes.[9] After arriving in Nantes, Jones did not immediately set off for Paris to deliver the dispatches as planned, but instead sent them on. Having observed *Ranger*'s seaworthiness during the voyage, Jones knew that the ship needed repairs and modifications before she could undertake another voyage. There were also problems with the crewmembers. The Continental Congress had not, as yet, granted authorization for the crew's pay and allowances. Realizing the seriousness of their complaints, Jones paid his crewmembers using his own funds. After insuring that the immediate problems of his crew and ship were satisfied, Jones set out for Paris in late December.

Upon his arrival in Paris, Jones reported to Benjamin Franklin, the senior American commissioner to the French government. Jones realized that he needed Franklin's support to advance his naval career. Franklin immediately recognized that Jones was an aggressive and stalwart navy captain, who was capable of winning victories at sea. However, he also noted that Jones lacked political and diplomatic skills, and was completely naive about the intrigues of the French court. Franklin therefore decided to establish a positive nurturing relationship with the young captain, who was 40 years his junior. As senior American commissioner, Franklin had formulated his own plans for a trans-Atlantic naval strategy, and he needed aggressive American navy captains like Jones to implement the strategy. However, not all the American commissioners shared Franklin's enthusiasm for Captain John Paul Jones. Charles Lee, the second-ranking commissioner, disliked Jones from the start, probably because Jones was foreign-born. Lee had little faith and confidence in Franklin's abilities as high commissioner. John Adams was another commissioner who didn't share Franklin's opinion of Jones. Adams spent time with Jones in Paris, and at Nantes. He also corresponded with Jones on naval matters. Adams recorded his impressions of Jones in his diary writing that, "Eccentricities and irregularities are to be expected of him. They are in his character; they are visible in his eyes. His voice is soft and small; his eyes have keenness, and wildness and softness in it."[10] Despite the opinions of Lee and Adams, Franklin was determined to help Jones secure a larger ship, and advance his career, but not immediately.

While in Paris, Franklin broke the news to Jones that he would not command the *L'Indien*. The American commissioners had run out of funds to pay the private shipbuilders in Holland, and the contract was broken. The ship was later sold to the French government. Jones was disappointed, but took Franklin's advice to use his time in Paris to develop his own contacts with influential French citizens. He soon made the acquaintance of the wife of a wealthy merchant fleet owner, who was also a member of King Louis XVI's privy council. The woman's husband also had important connections with the French government and navy, and was involved in matters related to the American Revolution. Jones hoped that by befriending the woman, he could advance his efforts to secure command of a larger warship.[11]

In late January 1778, Jones returned to the *Ranger* in Nantes. He was disappointed by what he found, as the crew was even more disgruntled than when he had left for Paris. Although Jones advanced the crew a partial pay from his own funds, and disbursed prize money for the two captured brigs, the sums were not nearly what the crewmembers had been promised at the time of their enlistment. First Lieutenant Thomas Simpson informed Jones that the crew had refused to work on the ship during the harsh winter weather, and that the most of the crew thought that the *Ranger* should return to Portsmouth. While re-establishing his authority as captain of the *Ranger*, Jones finally received some good news. The commissioners had issued sailing orders for the *Ranger*.

The orders were written and signed by Benjamin Franklin and Silas Deane on January 16, 1778. Charles Lee's and John Adams's signatures were conspicuously absent from the document. The blanket orders gave Jones wide latitude in planning his next cruise stating that, "we advise you after equipping the *Ranger* in the best manner, for the Cruise you propose, that you proceed with her in the manner you shall judge best, for distressing the Enemies of the United States, by Sea, or otherwise, consistent with the Laws of War, and the Terms of your Commission . . ."[12] The only specific instructions in the orders was a list of French ports to which Jones should send any British ships taken as prizes. The orders also cautioned Jones not to undertake any actions that would bring complaints from France, Spain, or other neutral powers, and that if he made any "attempt on the Coasts of Great Britain," he should not return immediately to a French port, unless forced to by the weather, or pursuit by the enemy.[13] The latter stipulation was added to the orders because the alliance between France and the United States was in final negotiations, and would not be signed for another month. Jones' only disappointment with the orders was that he was instructed to inform his crewmembers that they would have to "Rely on the Justice of the Congress" for their pay and promised bonuses. He had hoped that the commissioners would have at least authorized a partial pay from their own funds.

Jones had started planning the *Ranger*'s voyage before he received his official orders from the commissioners. He planned to depart France and sail into the Irish Sea where he would disrupt British commerce off the coasts of England, Ireland, and Scotland by capturing or sinking merchant ships, and attacking onshore facilities at British ports. Jones wanted to create a climate of fear and consternation among the British population to erode public support for the war. Jones's plans for the *Ranger*'s cruise reflected the views of Robert Morris, president of the Continental Congress, who stated nearly a year earlier that the most effective use of American ships against the British was "to surprise their defenceless Places and thereby divide their Attention and draw it off from our Coasts,"[14] Jones was keenly aware that he had enemies in Congress, the Navy, and even among the commissioners in France, and was careful to follow the broad strategic guidance of the nation's civilian leadership.

———

After receiving his instructions from the commissioners, Jones spent the next few weeks making repairs on the *Ranger*, and procuring supplies for the mission. New sails were hung, swivel guns were mounted in the fighting tops, and the bow ports were modified so that the guns could be trained forward in a chase. Quantities of winter clothing, and provisions were also purchased, and barrels of gunpowder were brought aboard, along with dozens of pistols, cutlasses, and blunderbusses.[15]

On February 13, 1778, one week after the United States and France signed an alliance, the *Ranger* sailed down the Loire to Quiberon Bay, where a French fleet lay anchored. When the *Ranger* entered the bay with the Stars and Stripes flying in the breeze, Jones fired a salute to the senior French admiral's flagship. The French returned the honor. For the next few weeks, the *Ranger* sailed along the French coast in the Bay of Biscay. Jones wanted to test the modifications made to the *Ranger,* and hone the skills of his crew. He was well aware that he had only limited support from his officers and crew. Most were anxious to begin taking prizes, but wanted no part of Jones's plans to raid British ports. Undeterred by this lack of support, Jones continued firming up his plans for the raids.

On March 3, 1778, the *Ranger* departed Quiberon Bay, and sailed northwest toward Brest. The *Ranger* arrived at the little port of Cameret, about eight miles south of Brest on March 8. Both the inner and outer ports at Brest were crowded with French navy ships, and there was no safe anchorage for the *Ranger* at that port. Jones traveled to Brest every few days to meet with Admiral le Comte d'Orvilliers. He had requested that the French Navy provide a frigate and tender to accompany the *Ranger* on her voyage to the Irish Sea. The admiral was impressed with the American navy captain and his bold plans, and offered Jones suggestions and support. Meanwhile, Jones kept his crew busy making even more modifications to his ship to increase her speed, maneuverability, and seaworthiness. Eight of the *Ranger*'s crew deserted at Cameret, but local French authorities apprehended seven of the American sailors, and returned them to the *Ranger.*

On March 23, the *Ranger* sailed the short distance to Brest, affording the crew the opportunity for shore liberty in the military port. Once ashore, several crewmembers attempted to desert. A few of the deserters were apprehended, and returned to the *Ranger* where Jones had them confined in irons. After 10 days in Brest, the *Ranger* returned to Cameret for a final scraping and caulking of the sloop's hull, and other modifications. Carpenters moved the masts further aft, sail makers shortened the sails on the lower spars, and the ballast was repositioned.

Before going to sea, Jones took the time to settle one of his major personnel problems. Marine Captain Parke had been unhappy and disruptive ever since the *Ranger's* arrival in France. He had anticipated an assignment to a frigate under Jones's command. When he found out that both he and Jones would continue to serve on the *Ranger*, he began to treat the crewmembers harshly, and the other officers petitioned Jones to dismiss him. The crew also resented the fact that Captain Parke received a large share of the prize money. Since Parke had previously requested a discharge, and was a disruptive influence, Jones finally decided to dismiss him and temporarily replace him with Lieutenant Jean Meijer of the Swedish army.[16]

The *Ranger* was refloated on April 4, and then sailed down the bay accompanied by the French frigate *Fortunee*, and a tender. However, poor weather prevented both ships from reaching the open sea, and they were forced to return to port. While the ships waited for better weather, Lieutenant Wallingford conducted small-arms practice for the marines, and navy Lieutenant Simpson exercised the ship's gun crews. On April 8, the weather cleared, and the American and French ships put to sea.[17]

By that time, Jones had established three objectives for his attack on the British Isles. First, he planned to disrupt British maritime commerce by raiding a British port to destroy ships at anchorage, and the onshore fortifications. He was convinced that the attack would cause panic in the surrounding countryside. Jones believed that the attack was justified, since the British had raided and attacked American costal cities and ports. Secondly, Jones hoped to capture a high-ranking British official, who could then be exchanged for American sailors held captive by the British. Although the British and Americans regularly exchanged prisoners, American sailors taken prisoner by the British were often treated as rebels and pirates, and left to rot in British prisons under the harshest of conditions. Finally, Jones planned to attack British merchant ships along the coasts of the British Isles, and either sink them, or take them as prizes. Jones did not intend to engage British warships in sea battles unless he had a clear advantage in firepower, or was forced to do so.

The French ships returned to Brest as the *Ranger* approached the Irish Sea. Soon after entering the Irish Sea, the *Ranger* sank one small British cargo carrier, and captured another. Jones ordered a prize crew to sail the captured ship to Brest.

On the morning of April 18, the *Ranger* was off the Point of Ayre

The Voyage of the "Ranger"
March 3 – May 8, 1778

on the northern tip of the Isle of Man, when a lookout spotted the British Revenue cutter, *Hussar*. Jones tried to pose his ship as a Scottish merchantman, but the deception failed as the cutter drew near. Jones then ordered his crew to fire a broadside into the cutter. The captain of the more agile *Hussar* managed to outmaneuver the *Ranger*, and escape with minor damage. *Hussar* then fled toward shallow waters off Scotland's coast. Jones gave up the chase after the *Hussar*'s captain skillfully maneuvered his vessel between the shoals at the entrance of Luce Bay. Jones chose not to risk entering the shallow waters of Luce Bay. The *Ranger*'s surgeon, Doctor Ezra Green, wrote in his diary that the cutter, "slipped through our fingers," and could have been taken with "great ease, if Jones had permitted his marines to fire on the cutter's crew when the *Hussar* first approached the *Ranger*'s "lee Quarter."[18] Jones knew that the *Hussar*'s captain would soon alert the British Admiralty that there was an American warship operating in British waters off the coast of Scotland. Therefore, he had to move quickly to accomplish his objectives.

During the next few days, *Ranger* sank a schooner and a sloop near the entrance of the Firth of Clyde. Jones' crewmembers wanted to take both ships as prizes, but he ignored their pleas. On April 20, Jones learned from the crew of a small fishing boat that the HMS *Drake*, a 20-gun sloop-of-war, was anchored near the mouth of the Belfast Lough. Jones immediately ordered his ship to enter the lough, but the crew refused. Jones was furious, but finally convinced the crew that the *Ranger* could easily enter the lough under the cover of darkness and surprise the *Drake*. Jones planned to bring *Ranger* alongside the *Drake* and then sweep her decks with gunfire before grappling and boarding her. *Ranger* entered the lough around midnight, but overshot the *Drake* as she attempted to come alongside. There was no opportunity for a second chance. Heavy winds began to blow, and in the words of Surgeon Green, the *Ranger* was, "oblig'd to cut and run out, which we were very lucky in effecting."[19] The crew was exhausted by the failed attempt on the *Drake*, and more disgruntled than ever before. Jones ordered his ship to continue standing off the Belfast Lough, hoping to try again the following night, but the weather worsened, and the attack on the *Drake* was abandoned.

Jones then set sailed southeast across the Irish Sea to conduct a raid on Whitehaven, the very port that he had left 18 years earlier, when he first went to sea on the *Friendship*. Jones knew the sea approaches to Whitehaven, the layout of the port, and its fortifications like the back of his hand. It had been more than a century since the last enemy attack on British soil, and Jones was confident that Whitehaven was not prepared for an American raid.

When Jones briefed his officers on his plan, they stubbornly argued against their captain's orders, stopping just short of mutiny. Navy Lieutenants Thomas Simpson and Elijah Hall encouraged dissent among the crewmembers pointing out that the raid posed an unnecessary risk, and was unlikely to result in any prize money for the crew. When Jones called for volunteers, both Simpson and Hall refused to go ashore with their captain feigning illness. Jones continued to enlist volunteers as *Ranger* crossed Solway Firth, and bore down on Whitehaven. It was April 22, and snow covered the land on both sides of Solway Firth.

Late in the day the winds grew faint, and by midnight the *Ranger* was still miles away from Whitehaven. Jones knew that the sloop was unlikely to reach Whitehaven harbor before daylight. Thirty marines and 10 sailors had volunteered for the mission. Two small boats were lowered, and Jones ordered his raiders over the side. Jones took command of one boat with Lieutenant Meijer as his second, and Marine Lieutenant Wallingford commanded the other, with Midshipman Ben Hill as his mate.[20] Rowing against the tide, it took three hours for the assault force to reach Whitehaven's inner harbor. According to Jones's account of the raid, it was near dawn by the time the boats reached the outer pier.[21] Jones then ordered Wallingsford's boat with "necessary combustibles," to the northern end of the harbor instructing the marine lieutenant to burn as many of the merchantmen anchored there as possible.[22] Leaving Lieutenant Meijer with the boat and crew, Captain Jones then led his own detachment toward the walls of the fort. After scaling the walls of the fort, Captain Jones and his raiders spiked all the cannon, while the sentinels slept in the guardhouse. After locking the sleeping British sentinels in their own guardhouse, Jones posted his own sentinels on the ramparts. He and Midshipman Green then ran a quarter-mile to the southern fort and spiked all the cannon.

Meanwhile, a traitor emerged in the ranks of the assault force. David Freeman, who had signed on the *Ranger* for the sole purpose of making his way home to Ireland, had volunteered to go ashore with the assault force. After landing at Whitehaven, Freeman deserted, and alerted the townsmen that a raid was in progress. By the time Jones and Green made their way back to the other fort, townspeople were emerging from their houses, and gathering in the streets. Surveying the harbor Jones saw that not one of the numerous merchant ships was afire. The raiders led by Lieutenant Wallingford and Midshipman Hill had failed to carry out their part of the mission. According to one contemporary account, Wallingford's boat landed at the Old Quay slip, after which the men proceeded to a public house where they "made free with liquor."[23] Wallingford told Jones that he was unable to set the ships afire because he was unable to light the combustible material. As a large crowd of citizens moved toward the harbor, Jones secured a lighted candle from a house, and set the collier, *Thompson*, on fire using a barrel of tar to spread the blaze. The flames soon reached the rigging and set the mainmast ablaze. As Jones and his men retreated toward their boats, hundreds of the town's residents tried to smother the flames on the *Thompson*. Others followed Jones and his raiders in a menacing manner, but keeping at a safe distance. Jones was the last to board his boat. He stood on the pier with sword in hand, daring the Englishmen to approach. None did. As the raiders rowed toward the *Ranger*, they were fired on by one of the fort's cannon that had been overlooked by the raiders. However, the fire was inaccurate, and boats were soon out of range. By six in the morning, the raiders were back on board the *Ranger* leaving only one deserter ashore. There was no bloodshed on either side during the raid.

The American raid on Whitehaven was only a limited military success in terms of material damage. The town's citizens extinguished the fire on the *Thompson*, and the spiked cannon were quickly repaired. British estimates of the damage done to the *Thompson* and port defenses ranged from £250 to £1,250 sterling.[24] Even though the damage was negligible, the raid was a psychological victory for the Americans. Newspaper headlines spread the news of the raid across the British Isles. Whitehaven's *Morning Post and Daily Advertiser* edition of April 28, 1778, provided a detailed account of the raid, including the identities of the *Ranger*'s officers. Many of the details were based on the interrogation of the *Ranger*'s deserter. The article, however, misidentified the *Ranger* as an American privateer rather than a Continental Navy warship. As news of the raid spread across Britain, ports were put on alert and militias were mobilized. When the extra edition of the Whitehaven paper was reprinted in the London *Morning Post*, the British government began to feel the heat. On April 29, the *Morning Chronicle and London Advertiser* published a letter from Edinburgh that criticized the provost and magistrates of Dumfries for, "The ruinous state of the fortifications of many of our sea-port towns" and "the want of necessary range of fortifications seems almost inexcusable."[25] The Royal Navy also came under heavy criticism for failing to protect the coasts with its "wooden walls"[26] British newspapers also gave Jones wide notoriety among the public, describing him as a renegade Scot, who had fled criminal charges for killing a crew member in Tobago, while he was captain of the *Betsy*. As the voyage of the *Ranger* continued, John Paul Jones quickly became a name recognized in nearly every household in Britain.

After the Whitehaven raid, Jones wasted no time in pursuing his second objective for the voyage. He was determined more than ever to take a high-ranking British official prisoner, who could then be exchanged for American prisoners held in the British Isles. Jones selected as his target Dunbar Douglas, fourth earl of Selkirk, a Scottish representative peer in the British House of Lords. The earl of Selkirk was a well-known and respected dignitary in Scotland, and was probably targeted by Jones for practical reasons. The earl's manor was just a short sail from Whitehaven, on St. Mary's Isle on the Scottish side of Solway Firth, not far from the Arbigland estate where Jones was born. There is little doubt that Jones selected the earl because he was familiar with the manor, and probably could recognize the earl on sight as he had been an occasional guest at Arbigland when Jones was growing up. Whether the British government would have considered the exchange of a large number of American prisoners for the Scottish peer remains a matter for speculation.

Shortly after Jones's party boarded the *Ranger* off Whitehaven, Jones ordered the ship to head for Solway Firth. By 10:00 a.m. the *Ranger* arrived at the entrance of Kirkcudbright Bay in Solway Firth. The *Ranger* lingered in deep water under reduced sail while the Jones and his team prepared to go ashore in small boats. St. Mary's Isle is actually a peninsula, and could only be reached by small boats passing through an intricate tidal channel. Jones was familiar with the bay, and all the landmarks that aided navigation, as well as the terrain features and buildings on the peninsula.

Captain Jones, Lieutenant Wallingford, Master David Cullam, and a dozen marines and sailors boarded the *Ranger's* cutter and rowed ashore, making landfall at the point of isle between 10:30 and 11:00 a.m. After posting an armed guard with the cutter, Jones, accompanied by his two officers and a well-armed squad of marines and sailors, proceeded up a path that led to the mansion. Along the way, they encountered the estate's head gardener. Jones identified his party as a press gang seeking recruits for the Royal Navy. In his conversation with the gardener, Jones learned to his dismay that the Earl was absent from the estate, and therefore out of reach. At that point, Jones was prepared to abort the mission and return to the *Ranger*, but Lieutenants Wallingford and Cullam objected arguing that the crew was entitled to at least loot the Earl's mansion, since there were no prizes earned at Whitehaven. They also reminded Jones that the British often looted and burned private homes along the American coast. Both officers claimed that some of their own acquaintances and friends had had their homes looted and burned by British raiding parties. Jones reluctantly gave his approval, but imposed some restrictions on his men. He stipulated that Lieutenants Wallingford and Cullam and some of the men could go to the mansion, demand the family silver and carry it off, but under no circumstances were they to search the house for additional loot, or demand anything else of the occupants. Jones's decision to allow his men to loot the mansion placed him in an embarrassing situation that he would later regret. It tarnished his reputation as a gentleman.

Inside the Selkirk mansion, the earl's wife, her daughters and eight-year-old son, and four house guests had just finished breakfast when a member of the household staff spotted a group of armed men surrounding the house. After sending her children, guests, and maidservants upstairs, the countess and her butler met Wallingford and Cullam at the door. The pair identified themselves as officers of the American sloop, *Ranger*, under the command of Captain John Paul Jones, and stated that they had orders to carry off the household silver. Lady Selkirk judiciously complied with the demands. When the servants had filled the sacks, she coolly asked for a receipt, and offered the two Americans a glass of wine before they departed with the silver. The entire episode lasted about 15 minutes.

After leaving the mansion, the two officers assembled their men, and returned to the boat where Captain Jones was waiting. After boarding the cutter, the raiders rowed back to the *Ranger* and sailed down the firth headed for the Irish Sea. They were fortunate to escape. for within a half an hour armed volunteers from Kirkcudbright arrived to search the isle for the raiders.

The St. Mary's Isle raid was a dismal embarrassing failure for Jones and his crew. Although Jones was familiar with the target area, he had no current intelligence on the earl's whereabouts, or security arrangements on the St Mary's Isle. Failures in operations such as this one highlighted the need for detailed planning and target intelligence. The only positive outcome of the raid was the psychological effect it had on the populace. Jones's reputation as a fearsome adversary was spreading rapidly along the coastlines of Great Britain. Jones himself was concerned that the looting of the earl's mansion had put a stain on his reputation, and wrote a series of letters attempting to justify his actions. In an attempt to clear his name and status as a gentleman, Jones later attempted to return the Selkirk silver, after compensating his crew for its value in prize money.

Rather than sailing south toward St. George's Channel to exit the Irish Sea, Jones set sail for the Belfast Lough on Ireland's northeast coast, where he had last seen the British warship *Drake*. By daybreak of April 24, the *Ranger* was off Carrickfergus at the entrance of Belfast Lough. Jones planned to enter the lough, and attack the *Drake* in broad daylight, but once again he lacked the support of his crew. As he approached the lough, Jones closed the ship's gun ports and ordered his crew to stay out of sight below decks. The crew took the opportunity to hold a meeting to decide whether or not to fight. Jones's second-in-command, Lieutenant Simpson, urged the men not to fight. Lieutenant Meijer learned that the crew were plotting to take over the ship, and warned Jones. Captain Jones in turn addressed his crew reminding them of the large amount of prize money that could be earned by capturing a British warship. The crew then agreed to fight.

Meanwhile, Captain Burden, commander of the *Drake*, became increasingly suspicious of the unidentified ship lying off the entrance of the lough. He therefore sent one of his lieutenants out in his gig to investigate. When the lieutenant boarded the *Ranger*, Jones identified himself and his ship, and took the lieutenant and his crew prisoner. When the lieutenant and his party failed to respond to recall signals from the *Drake*, Captain Burden prepared his ship for battle. Jones decided to lure the *Drake* out of the lough in order to fight in the open sea, where he had more room to maneuver. *Ranger* slowly worked her way out of the bay, struggling against the tide and unfavorable winds. The *Drake* took the bait and followed the *Ranger*. Once both ships were in open waters, Jones allowed *Drake* to approach within hailing distance. As she approached, the British ship raised her colors, and the *Ranger* responded by hoisting the American Stars and Stripes flag. When the two ships were within hailing distance, the Englishman challenged the Americans to identify their ship. "The American Continental Ship *Ranger*" replied the *Ranger*'s master. With little more than an hour to sunset, Jones decided it was time to begin the sea battle.[27]

The two ships were well matched. Both were sloops of war with the *Drake* having a slight advantage in firepower mounting twenty 6-pounders, while the *Ranger* mounted eighteen 9-pounders. The *Drake* also had a larger crew, so it behooved Jones not to maneuver close enough to the British ship to allow the enemy crew to grapple and board his ship.

Captain Jones later published his own vivid account of the battle, writing:

> The Drake being astern of the Ranger, I ordered the helm up, and gave her the first broadside. The action was warm, close and obstinate. It lasted an hour and four minutes, when the enemy called for quarters; her fore and main-topsail yards being both cut away, and down on the cap; the top-gallant yard and mizzen-gaff both hanging up and down along the mast; the second ensign which they had hoisted shot away, and hanging on the quarter gallery in the water; the jib shot away, and hanging in the water; her sails and rigging entirely cut to pieces; her masts and yards all wounded, and her hull also very much galled.[28]

After the *Drake* "called for quarters," Jones ordered a boarding party to the ship to disarm and take the crew prisoner, and survey the damage. The boarders found the decks running with blood. Torn pieces of sail, rigging, broken spars and splinters from the damaged masts and spars were strewn across the deck. The dead and wounded lay among the debris, while the sullen survivors lined up to surrender their arms.

During the action, both ships raked each other's decks with grapeshot and musket fire, inflicting casualties on the crews. The *Drake* suffered more losses than the *Ranger* losing her captain and four sailors killed, and 19 others wounded, including her first lieutenant. The remainder of the *Drake's* 160-man crew was taken prisoner. The *Ranger's* casualties included Marine Lieutenant Wallingford, and seaman, John Dougall, who were killed in the action, and six wounded, including a gunner and Midshipman Powers, who lost an arm. Lieutenant Wallingford took a musket ball to the head while directing the fires of his marines.

The *Ranger* suffered considerable damage, but was still seaworthy. Nonetheless, it was a remarkable victory for a Continental Navy ship and her crew operating in enemy-controlled waters. Captain Jones had no formal training as a naval officer, while his adversary, Royal Navy Captain Burden, was a veteran of several sea battles during his long career as naval officer. Despite their distain for Jones, the New England crewmembers of the *Ranger* fought valiantly during the engagement with the *Drake*.

British newspapers covered the sea battle, and tried to identify the reasons for the British defeat and the American victory. One correspondent reported that the *Drake's* powder was "too weak," while another advanced the theory that the ship's gunners undercharged their guns, because they had been "secreting large quantities of powder," and selling it for their own profit. Therefore, the correspondents claimed that the "*Drake's* shots could not penetrate *Ranger's* hull."[29] Others reported that the American ship had heavier guns than *Drake's* 6-pounders.[30]

Playing down the loss of the *Drake*, the British Admiralty acted quickly to try to intercept and capture the *Ranger* and her crew. The HMS *Stag* and HMS *Doctor* were already searching the Irish Sea for the *Ranger* even before the *Drake* was captured. After the battle, the 36-gun frigate *Thesis* sailed from Glasgow to patrol the North Sea, and the sloop-of-war *Heart of Oak* sailed from Liverpool to search the Irish Sea. On May 1, the 36-gun *Boston* sailed from Waterford to join the hunt.[31]

On April 25, the day after the battle, Jones ordered the crews of both ships to begin repairing and refitting the two ships. A brigantine out of Whitehaven approached the two ships for a closer look, and was captured by the Americans. After putting a prize crew on board, the brigantine was sailed for Brest, where it was sold, adding to the prize money. That evening a solemn ceremony was held at sea. Captain Burden of the *Drake,* and Lieutenants Wallingford and Dobbs (who had died of his wounds), were all buried at sea with full military honors. The repairs were completed by the following morning, and the *Ranger* got underway. Jones appointed Lieutenant Simpson as prize master of the *Drake,* and ordered him to take station close off the *Ranger*'s starboard quarter, and continue the same course as the *Ranger.* If the two ships were separated by bad weather or enemy action, Simpson was instructed to sail to France on his own.[32]

Captain Jones decided that his best chance of escaping any pursuers was to sail around the northern coast of Ireland, and then follow a course south along Ireland's west coast before setting a direct course for France. It was a wise decision, since most of his pursuers were searching the Irish Sea for his ship and the captured prize. By May 4, the *Ranger* and her prize had successfully made their way down Ireland's western coast, and were near the French island of Ushant, off the Brittany coast. At that time the *Ranger* had the *Drake* under tow, but when Jones spotted another potential prize, he ordered the tow line cut to give chase. According to Jones, he shouted orders to Lieutenant Simpson, prize master of the *Drake,* to follow him. Instead, Simpson continued to sail for Ushant and the French port of Brest, later claiming that he had misunderstood Jones orders. After determining that the ship he was pursuing was a neutral Swedish ship, Jones turned south and caught up with the *Drake.* By that time, Jones was furious with Lieutenant Simpson. He relieved Simpson of his duties as prize master, and placed him under arrest. It is not clear whether Simpson deliberately disobeyed his captain's orders, or simply didn't hear the shouted order. It didn't matter. Jones had had enough of Simpson, who had undermined and challenged his authority as captain of the *Ranger* throughout the cruise.

On May 8, 1778, the *Ranger,* with her prize in tow, sailed into Brest harbor completing the cruise. Other than French Admiral d'Orvilliers, no high-ranking French or American official was on hand to congratulate

Jones and his crew for their successful cruise and victory over the *Drake*. There were no parades or congratulatory speeches honoring *Ranger*'s captain and crew. Instead, Jones was beset with problems that required resolution. First, he had to arrange for repairs to the *Ranger*, making her fit for sea. He also had to negotiate for fair prize money for his crew. Additionally, he needed to find a replacement for Lieutenant Wallingford. Fortunately, he was able to find one rather quickly. On 26 May, the American agent at Nantes recommended William Morris, who, according to the agent, was more motivated by patriotism, and a desire to serve than "a desire to enrich himself."[33] Jones agreed with the agent's assessment of Morris and appointed him as lieutenant of marines on the *Ranger*. Last but not least, Jones had to decide what to do with Lieutenant Simpson, who was still under arrest.

Jones knew that Simpson was responsible for much of the unrest and discontent among the crew of the *Ranger*, and was convinced that he had attempted to incite a mutiny before the battle with the *Drake*. He also believed that Simpson was, at least in part, responsible for the failure of the Whitehaven raid. The lieutenant was adamantly against Jones's plan, and withheld his support and endorsement, making his views known to the crewmembers prior to the raid. On the other hand, Jones knew that the crew of the *Ranger* held Simpson in high regard, and that they viewed his arrest as unjust.

The American commissioners in Paris showed little support for Jones in the Simpson affair. They suggested that Jones be more flexible in the matter, and informed him that they desired to see Simpson released on parole and returned to America, where he would face a court-martial that would decide his guilt or innocence. Jones acceded to the commissioners' wishes, and Simpson was released on parole. Five weeks later Simpson was released from parole, and to Jones's dismay, was given command of the *Ranger*, as it was preparing to sail for America. The crew warmly received Lieutenant Simpson, and the *Ranger* soon set sail for America, accompanied by two other American ships. Captain John Paul Jones remained behind, traveling to Paris to begin his efforts to secure command of another ship.

John Paul Jones's 1778 raids on Britain's coast, and victory over the Royal Navy's HMS *Drake* were bold undertakings by the American Navy's "first sea warrior." In September 1779, Jones gained fame, glory and praise, when, as captain of the *Bonhomme Richard*, he defeated HMS *Serapis*. While Jones's victory over the *Serapis* overshadowed his raid on Britain's coast, it does not diminish the importance of the *Ranger*'s cruise, which was a great psychological victory over the British. One could make a comparison with Doolittle's raid on Tokyo in April 1942. The British populace believed they were invulnerable to American attacks on their homeland just as the Japanese were similarly convinced in 1942. While neither of the raids inflicted significant material damage, they did create doubts in the minds of their citizens about their leaders' competence, and their war policies. Moreover, both raids boosted American morale on the home front when it was most needed.

6

PARTISAN WARFARE
IN THE NORTHERN THEATER

I take the liberty of giving to you as my opinion also, that the way to annoy, distress and really injure the Enemy on their march (after obstructing the Roads as much as possible) with militia, is to suffer them to act in very light Bodies as the Enemy's Guards in front flanks and Rear must be exposed and may be greatly injured by the concealed and well directed fire of men from Ambush. This kind of annoyance ought to be incessant day and night and would I think be very effectual.

— George Washington to militia Brigadier General
Philemon Dickinson, June 5, 1778

THE REVOLUTIONARY WAR WAS AS MUCH A PARTISAN WAR AS IT WAS a conventional war in which British regular forces maneuvered and engaged American Continental troops in European-style campaigns and battles. In contrast, partisan warfare was not conducted along fixed lines using European-style tactics, but rather consisted primarily of skirmishes, ambushes, and attacks directed against enemy supply lines, lines of communications, and outposts in enemy controlled areas and contested areas. Current US military doctrine and terminology does not use the term partisan warfare, but uses two terms that are roughly equivalent to partisan warfare during the American Revolutionary War. The first is "irregular warfare." The US Military's Joint Publication (JP) 1-02 defines irregular warfare as, "A violent struggle among state and non-state actors for legitimacy and influence over the relevant population."[1] The same publication defines "irregular forces" as "Armed individuals or groups who are not members of the regular armed forces, police, or other internal security forces."[2] Another term, "guerilla warfare," more closely parallels the American partisan warfare waged during the Revolutionary War. Guerilla warfare is defined today as "Military and paramilitary operations conducted in enemy-held or hostile territory by irregular, predominantly indigenous forces." A guerilla force is described as, "A group of irregular, predominantly indigenous personnel organized along military lines to conduct military and paramilitary operations in enemy-held, hostile, or denied territory."[3] The major difference between present-day irregular and guerilla warfare, and partisan warfare waged during the Revolutionary War, is the type of forces employed.

During the American Revolutionary War, Patriot forces engaged in partisan warfare were predominantly organized militia forces raised by state or county authorities. The origins of American militia organizations can be traced back to the Indian wars and the French and Indian War, when colonial militia units defended frontier outposts and settlements. Compulsory militia service became an established practice in all American colonies long before the Revolutionary War. During the French and Indian War, American colonial militia units also augmented regular British forces in operations directed against the French and their Indian allies. The preparedness and quality of American militia units and their leadership varied widely from state to state, and county to county. Militia units in contested areas were generally more effective than those based in more secure areas. The most effective militia units were those with minimum organization and maximum individual responsibility. These units were highly maneuverable, and capable of swift decisive action. Ambushes, raids, and attacks on enemy outposts were among their favorite tactics. On the other hand, even the most effective militia units suffered from high personnel turnover, lax discipline, and the tendency to question orders thought to be unreasonable.

Although the contributions of militia organizations to the war effort in the South, and in upstate New York are widely known, state militias in New England and the Middle Atlantic states also participated in partisan warfare, in addition to supporting Continental Army forces during major campaigns and battles.

Militia forces were engaged in all levels of the war. When mobilized for active service, they supported regular forces by defending endangered areas, harassing the movement of British forces, disrupting their supply lines, gathering information, and reconnoitering and foraging for regular forces. When militia forces were not in direct support of Continental forces, they were engaged in almost constant partisan warfare with Americans who remained loyal to the British crown. Loyalists or Tories formed their own militia organizations, which operated to uphold British rule in contested areas by suppressing their rebellious neighbors. Partisan warfare during the American Revolutionary War was vicious and brutal, splitting families, and pitting neighbor against neighbor. Noncombatants as well as combatants were at risk, and casualties were high on both sides. Nonetheless, most historians now agree that militia forces, whether fighting in direct support of regular army forces, or fighting on their own for control of the countryside contributed immeasurably to the war effort, and had a major impact on the final outcome of the war—independence from Great Britain.

For the most part, the last five months of 1776 were a disaster for Washington's army. The American army was defeated in the Battle of Long Island in August, barely escaping destruction. The following month the British occupied New York City, and the American army was pushed northward, first to Harlem Heights, and then to White Plains. As Washington withdrew, he left behind some six thousand men to defend two forts, Fort Washington and Fort Lee, on opposite sides of the Hudson.

After defeating the Americans at the White Plains on October 28, General Howe marched his army south to capture Fort Washington, the last remaining American bastion on Manhattan. Meanwhile, Washington's army withdrew north toward the Hudson highlands, eventually crossing the Hudson River at Peekskill. Washington then split his army, leaving generals Charles Lee and William Heath to guard the passes though the New York Highlands with eight thousand men, and then marched the remainder of his army south into New Jersey.

After Fort Washington surrendered on November 16, 1776, Washington ordered General Nathaniel Greene to evacuate Fort Lee on the western side of the Hudson. Washington then marched his demoralized army across New Jersey in the direction of Trenton. Meanwhile, General Howe dispatched a portion of the British army under General Cornwallis to pursue and destroy Washington's army. Cornwallis's mixed force of British, Hessian, and Loyalist troops pursued the Americans as they retreated southward hoping to bring on a major battle. Washington's exhausted and demoralized army finally crossed the Delaware River into Pennsylvania in early December.

By the time Washington's army crossed the Delaware, its strength had dwindled to fewer than two thousand men. During the long retreat from New York, New Jersey militia units simply melted away, company by company, as their enlistments expired. Upon reaching their homes, the militiamen, for the most part, remained inactive as the British extended their control over New Jersey. As British forces spread out across the state, Loyalists came out of hiding, reaffirming their support for the British. Many took up arms to prove their loyalty, and took revenge on their Patriot neighbors. General Howe and his field commander, General Cornwallis, welcomed their support, and extended a British and Hessian chain of garrisons throughout New Jersey to support and protect their Loyalist supporters. Soon the Patriots and those who chose to remain neutral began to suffer under the British occupation.

Despite written guarantees of safety from General Howe, looting, the burning of homes and barns, murder, and rape became common occurrences in New Jersey, particularly in areas near Hessian outposts, and in those counties with large Loyalist populations.[4] According to Moore's *Diary of the American Revolution,* "The whole track of the British army is marked with desolation and a wanton destruction of property . . . The fences destroyed, houses deserted, pulled in pieces or consumed by fire, over a rich and once well-cultivated and well-inhabited country . . . "[5] The British admitted that there was a great deal of plundering, but attempted to shift much of the blame to the Hessians.[6] A Hessian officer later wrote that "there was much plundering," and that "It has made the country people all the more embittered rebels."[7]

During the early days of the British occupation of New Jersey, the state's militia was disorganized and inactive, leaving the civilian population unprotected. During the campaigns on Long Island and Manhattan, and during the long retreat across New Jersey, Continental Army officers often characterized militia units as unreliable and unpredictable. Nevertheless, those campaigns enabled Washington to recognize the limitations of the militia, and how to capitalize on their strengths. He later became convinced that local militia organizations could be of great value in preventing the British from establishing uncontested control over large areas of occupied territory.[8]

Monmouth County, New Jersey was one county where the rising violence against those who supported the Revolution was nearly intolerable. Washington referred to it as "an insurrection of the Tories in Monmouth County."[9] The county stretched for ninety miles along the Atlantic seaboard from Sandy Hook and Raritan Bay in the north to Little Egg Harbor in the south. A heavily forested area known as the Pine Barrens covered much of the county's interior. Most of population of Monmouth County lived in the northernmost townships and in Stafford Township in the southernmost area of the county.

When twenty-five thousand British troops landed at Staten Island and Sandy Hook on June 29, 1776, hundreds of Loyalists rose to support the British. By July 1776, the county's population was about evenly split between those who supported the Revolution, and those who remained loyal to the king. When the Continental Congress voted favorably on the Declaration of Independence on July 2, 1776, Monmouth County erupted into a confused state of insurrection.[10] Patriot militia units from surrounding counties were sent to Monmouth County to help suppress Loyalist uprisings. On November 24, Washington sent a regiment under Colonel David Forman, a native of Monmouth, to suppress the Loyalists. Forman was under strict orders from Washington not to engage in plundering of Loyalist property unless it was about to fall into British hands. Forman did not follow his orders to the letter. After his arrival in the county, he encouraged a Patriot vigilante group to begin confiscating Loyalist property and estates, igniting a bloody and bitter civil war in Monmouth County.[11] General Howe ordered troops, who were in winter quarters near the county, to support Monmouth's Loyalists. By the end of December 1776, the Loyalists had the upper hand in the county.[12]

After the American victories at Trenton on December 26, 1776, and Princeton on January 3, 1777, Washington's army went into winter quarters in the hills around Morristown in northern New Jersey. General Howe then decided to withdraw from his outposts in southern and central New Jersey, and occupy only a strip of land in northeast New Jersey running from New Brunswick to Perth Amboy. Howe did not plan for a winter campaign in New Jersey, but remained concerned that Washington's army was encamped just 30 miles from New York City.

After the battle of Princeton, General Washington formulated a strategy for the winter of 1777. Washington's plans did not include an attack on British-occupied New York City during the winter months, but he was determined not to give the British army any rest. He therefore planned a campaign of harassment and interdiction using small detachments of Continentals and militia. Those forces would attack British outposts, supply depots, and intercept British foraging parties as they searched the countryside for forage for their horses and other plunder. Washington knew that General Howe could not feed his troops and their horses solely from foodstuffs and forage shipped from Britain, and was reliant on his men foraging in the countryside. Washington knew that if British foraging parties were attacked, the British would have to send escort forces with them, of up to two thousand men in strength.[13] Washington also ordered the Continentals and militia to clear horses, wagons, and other livestock from all areas near the British lines to prevent their confiscation and use by the British in a spring campaign. Thus, Washington's winter campaign was essentially a "forage war."

Inspired by Washington's successes at Trenton and Princeton, Patriot militiamen, who felt powerless after Washington's army withdrew to Pennsylvania, were eager to take the offensive against the British and their Loyalist allies. Washington knew that his Continentals were not capable of impeding all British efforts to gather supplies from the countryside, and the success of his winter war depended in large measure on the militias.

New Jersey militia units and local partisans played a major role in the winter war of 1777, at times operating on their own, and when necessary supported by detachments of Continentals. In late January 1777, Colonel Philemon Dickinson led four hundred New Jersey militia in a an attack on a British foraging party near Somerset Court House in north central New Jersey. The militia captured 40 wagons filled with forage and other foodstuffs, along with one hundred horses, and several prisoners. Dickinson would later become the overall commander of the New Jersey militia. On February 1, some five hundred Continental light infantry and four hundred New Jersey militia, under the overall command of Colonel Charles Scott, attacked a two-thousand-man British foraging party near New Brunswick in Middlesex County. After the heavy fighting, the British withdrew, leaving behind a number of wagonloads of hay. It was a costly defeat for the British, who sustained around one hundred casualties, while the American losses totaled 24 killed and wounded.

As the winter wore on, the militiamen and Continentals continued to enjoy success, improving their tactics on each mission. Intelligence became an important factor in their success. Spies reported where the British intended to search for supplies, and the Americans arrived in those areas during the hours of darkness, and established multiple ambushes along the roads leading to those areas. The Americans also lured British raiding and foraging parties by having local farmers drive herds of beef cattle close to their lines. When the British took the bait and attempted to capture the herds, Patriot infantry and cavalry would ambush the British raiders.[14]

As Washington predicted, the British continued to increase the size of their foraging parties. On February 8, General Cornwallis, Howe's senior commander in New Jersey, led his own foraging party into Middlesex County. The foraging party included 1,750 British and Hessian troops and a section of artillery. As the British approached Quibbletown, American riflemen opened fire on their column. Initially, the American marksmen stood their ground, but were finally forced to retire when the British artillery drove them from positions.

The New Jersey counties closest to New York City and Staten Island were the most vulnerable for British foraging. Foremost was Bergen County on the west side of the Hudson River opposite Manhattan. Prior to the war, Bergen County had a vibrant economy, based on the sale of its agricultural products in the markets of New York City. Bergen County's population included a large number of "Jersey Dutchmen," whose ancestors had founded the Dutch colony of New Amsterdam. Most were prosperous farmers with strong ties to the Dutch Reformed Church. The most important town in Bergen County was Hackensack. Located on the Hackensack River, the town had excellent shipping facilities, and access to major roads running through the county, making it a center of trade, travel and communication.

When the British army marched triumphantly into New York City in September 1776, life in Bergen County was nearly intolerable. The county was in a state of almost constant state of warfare, roamed by British foraging parties in search of food, forage, and plunder. The foragers were based at Paulus Hook and Bergen Point, and from those locations they had easy access to the farms and towns in Bergen County. Foraging parties of up to four hundred men frequently raided the Hackensack valley.[15] Repeated raids by the British disrupted the county's economy, threatening the economic survival of the farmers. Some of the Dutch farmers signed loyalty oaths to the king, and joined the ranks of the Loyalists, but others were determined to resist the British incursions. The American victories at Trenton and Princeton, breathed new life into the resistance movement in the county. Most of the farmers and merchants realized that the county's militia had to be strengthened and reorganized under new leadership.

One of the emerging militia leaders in Bergen County was Major John Mauritius Goetschius, who had been appointed as an officer in the county militia in 1775. Goetschius was a natural-born guerilla leader. He scrapped the old militia formations and drills prescribed by drill manuals of that day, and suspended the use of the fife and drum. [16] In lieu of traditional drills and musters, Goetschius and his second-in-command, Sam Demarest, trained their men in ambush techniques, hit and run raids and defensive patrolling. Goetschius knew that the militiamen's first priority was the protection of their own homes and farms. He therefore developed an organizational strategy that would allow his men to undertake both offensive and defensive missions. Each company was divided into groups. At night, one group conducted patrols and sentry duty, while another armed group remained on standby.

Another notable militia leader in Bergen County was 30-year-old John Outwater, also of Dutch ancestry. Outwater's militia company became active in early 1777. Most of the members of Outwater's company were farmers from the area surrounding Hackensack. The company was assigned the missions of patrolling the Hackensack River to guard against enemy raids from the Loyalist posts at Paulus Hook, and halting illicit trade with New York. Outwater's company had limited success in harassing Loyalist trade and foraging operations, but kept the farms around Hackensack under Patriot control.

Middlesex County, opposite Staten Island, was another New Jersey county heavily targeted by British raiding parties. On a clear frosty Sunday morning (February 23, 1777), a British force under the command of Lieutenant Colonel Charles Mawhood landed on the beaches of Middlesex County. Mawhood's force included a light infantry regiment, a detachment of grenadiers, and an infantry brigade, supported by a few light artillery pieces. A train of wagons for collecting forage in the county accompanied Mawhood's troops. John Peebles, an officer of the Royal Highland Regiment, wrote a vivid description of his experiences during the raid. Peebles led the advance guard of Colonel Campbell's 52nd Regiment as it swept through Middlesex County. After passing through the town of Woodbridge, Peebles's men saw their first action of the day. Peebles described the action in his diary:

> . . . when we marched about a mile and a half westward, I discover'd a body of Rebels on a hill which I acquainted Colonel Campbell of, Very Well says he I'll manouvre them, he accordingly gave orders for the Detachment to form & desir'd me to move on the edge of a wood in our front, as we came forward the Rebels disappeared, & I kept moving on thinking the whole detachment were coming after, but it seems they made a turn to the left while I went on the track of the enemy, & soon saw a body of them go into a wood where they halted, I sent a Corp'l to Col. Campbell to acquaint him with the situation, but the detachment being a good way off at this time he was long in coming back,—The Rebels seeing my small party drawn up & nobody near them sent out a party of 30 or 40 to bring us on to engage, I went up and met them and receiv'd their fire from behind a fence. I moved on to a fence in front & order'd my men to fire, which we continued to do each other for a few minutes when they gave way . . . I don't think we hit above 3 or 4 of them. I had two wounded . . .[17]

Catamount Tavern Monument, Bennington, Vermont. Tavern was a meeting place for Ethan Allen and his officers. The expedition to capture Fort Ticonderoga began here. Monument is situated near the site of the pole that had a stuffed catamount atop it. Notice the catamount is snarling to the west toward New York. *Author's photo.*

Fort Ticonderoga, New York, as seen from Mt. Defiance (Sugar Loaf Hill) with Vermont in the background and Lake Champlain looping around the peninsula. In July 1777, the British placed artillery on Mt. Defiance from which vantage point their cannon could rake Ft. Ticonderoga (foreground) making the fort untenable for American forces. *Author's photo.*

Fort Ticonderoga cannon. Cannon were capable of firing accurately to destroy British warships and troop ships sailing south on Lake Champlain. After Ethan Allen's capture of Fort Ticonderoga, a number of British cannon were moved overland to the Boston area and placed on Dorchester Heights forcing the British to evacuate the city. *Author's photo.*

Fort Ticonderoga mortar battery. Mortars are capable of high-angle fire to destroy enemy targets at short ranges. *Author's photo.*

The interior of Fort Ticonderoga, New York. Officers' quarters on right; enlisted barracks on left. *Author's photo.*

Fort Ticonderoga, New York. Entrance way in inner wall of fort leading to parade ground and barracks. A lone British sentry guarded the entrance when Ethan Allen leading 83 men stormed the fort. *Author's photo.*

Fort Ticonderoga, New York, reconstructed officers' quarters. The fort's commandant, British Captain Delaplace was asleep in his quarters on the second floor when Ethan Allen's men stormed the fort. *Author's photo.*

Ruins of barracks at Fort Crown Point, New York. After capturing Fort Ticonderoga, Ethan Allen dispatched Seth Warner to seize Crown Point, capturing additional cannon and other armaments. *Author's photo.*

Memorial to Colonel Seth Warner, Bennington, Vermont. Seth Warner was one of Ethan Allen's subordinate commanders on the expedition to seize Fort Ticonderoga. Warner later led a detachment of Green Mountain Boys during the Battle of Bennington in August 1777. *Author's photo.*

Saratoga, New York. Whitcomb's Rangers saw action at Freeman's Farm during the battle as part of the left wing of the American army commanded by General Arnold. *Author's photo.*

Saratoga National Historical Park, New York. General Benedict Arnold's "Boot Monument" located near Breyman's Redoubt commemorates Arnold's leg wound received when Americans stormed the redoubt. This is the only American monument to Arnold on American soil. Arnold's name is conspicuously absent from the monument. *Author's photo.*

Patrick Ferguson's Grave, Kings Mountain Battlefield, South Carolina. Ferguson led American loyalist troops during the October 1780 battle. Ferguson was the only British regular in the battle. Ferguson was killed in the closing minutes of the battle as he attempted to break out of his encircled force. *Author's photo.*

Marker of spot where Lieutenant Colonel Patrick Ferguson fell during the Battle of Kings Mountain. Ferguson was shot from the saddle as he attempted to break out of his encircled position. *Author's photo.*

American Monument, Kings Mountain National Battlefield Park, South Carolina. Monument is located on the site of the Loyalist wagon camp, the last point of resistance. *Author's photo.*

Monuments marking spot where 25-year-old Major William Chronicle of South Carolina fell mortally wounded while leading his men during an assault up the steep slope at Kings Mountain. Veterans of the battle placed original marker on left in 1815. *Author's photo.*

Moving artillery captured at Fort Ticonderoga overland to Boston.
Courtesy National Archives and Records Administration.

Flag raising on the Continental Navy ship *Alfred*, flagship of Commodore Esek Hopkins.
The *Alfred* was one of six American ships that sailed to the Bahamas during the raid on
New Providence Island. *Courtesy of U.S. Naval History and Heritage Command.*

Continental Marines and Sailors landing on New Providence Island, Bahamas, on March 2, 1776. The Americans hoped to capture the store of gunpowder on the island. The operation was commanded by Commodore Esek Hopkins.
Courtesy of U.S. Navy Art Collection, Washington D.C.

Captain John Paul Jones, Continental Navy. During April 1778, Jones, while captain of the Continental Navy ship *Ranger* conducted raids on the English coast and captured the HMS *Drake* after a sea battle off the coast of Ireland.
Courtesy of the Naval History and Heritage Command.

Americans led by George Rogers Clark attack Fort Sackville. British
Lieutenant Governor Hamilton surrendered Fort Sackville to the
Americans led by George Rogers Clark on February 25, 1779.
Courtesy of the National Archives and Records Administration.

George Rogers Clark's march to Vincennes. During February of 1779, Clark led a small force of Americans on a daring 180-mile-long winter march to recapture Vincennes and Fort Sackville.
Courtesy of the National Archives and Records Administration.

Continental Navy ship *Ranger*, commanded by Captain John
Paul Jones, receiving the salute of the French fleet at
Quiberon Bay, France, February 14, 1778.
Courtesy of U.S. Naval History and Heritage Command.

American troops led by General Washington retreat from Long Island. On the night
of 29–30 August 1776, Washington evacuated his troops from defenses on Brooklyn
Heights, and crossed the East River to Manhattan without the loss of a single life.
Knowlton's Rangers were among the last troops to evacuate.
Courtesy of the National Archives and Records Administration

After the skirmish, Peebles was ordered to retire back to Colonel Campbell's location. Campbell's force then continued their march and soon saw another body of rebels emerging from a swamp. Colonel Campbell ordered Peebles's detachment to advance to a fence at the edge of woods where the rebels had taken cover. After Peebles's men opened fire on the rebel force a sharp fight then ensued. By that time, Peebles's small detachment numbered no more than 14 or 15 men. Two Grenadier companies then rushed forward to support Peebles, but they came under galling fire from their right flank. The grenadiers suffered several casualties and were soon ordered to retire. Peebles remained in position until he had only one wounded man with him at the fence line. Having used up all his ammunition at the advancing rebels, Peebles "took to his heels" and ran back to Colonel Campbell's column, barely escaping with his life. Colonel Campbell then ordered up his reserves, but they were slow in arriving. When they finally arrived, Campbell's men fired a heavy volley into the woods, temporarily driving the rebels off. Campbell then had his wounded loaded onto wagons before another party of rebels appeared in his rear. The rebels, however, were quickly driven off when the British took them under fire. The British column then moved on, but it was continually harassed by sniper fire from rebel parties on the British flanks and rear. The British responded with artillery fire to drive them off. As Campbell's troops withdrew toward Woodbridge, they encountered another large group of rebels that were attempting to cut them off. The British charged the rebels, and again drove them off. Finally reaching the shoreline at Perth Amboy between 7:00 p.m. and 8:00 p.m., Campbell's force were totally exhausted and had collected almost no forage during the expedition.

Total British losses during the foraging raid were 69 killed and wounded, and six men missing. Peebles's advance guard alone lost 26 men killed, wounded, and missing. Peebles wrote, ". . . what pity it is to throw away such men as these on such shabbily ill managed occasions."[18] Colonel Campbell blamed the expedition's commander, Colonel Mawhood, for his heavy losses during the raid, claiming that his regiment was not well supported. While British foraging expeditions did not always end in failure, many met with heavy resistance from militia troops and small detachments of Continentals.

While the partisan war continued unabated in New Jersey during the winter months of 1777, a similar war was being fought in the neighboring state of New York. The Hudson River provided the British an excellent avenue of approach into the Highlands region of New York. With their naval superiority, the British were in complete control of the lower Hudson. Loading their troops on transports, the British were able to sail unopposed upriver, land their troops, collect supplies, and then sail back downriver to New York City. In 1777, two major American forts guarded the Hudson River. Fort Montgomery was located at the confluence of Popolopen Creek with the Hudson River in Orange County, and Fort Constitution was located further upriver on Constitution Island opposite West Point. Both forts were too far upriver to protect the lower reaches of the Hudson. Major General Alexander McDougal of the Continental Army had overall responsibility for the defense of the Hudson Highlands. When he assumed command in February 1777, McDougal had only six hundred Massachusetts militia, a New Hampshire regiment, and four small Continental regiments to defend the entire region. With those troops, McDougal had to defend the mountain passes that led into the area, provide garrisons for the forts, and protect the settlements downriver from the forts. Since he had only a limited number of Continental troops, McDougal relied on local militia to defend the towns south of Fort Montgomery.

In mid-March, General Howe, who was aware of the rebel weaknesses along the lower Hudson, ordered a raid on Peekskill located some 40 miles upriver from New York City. An American supply depot with large quantities of military supplies, barracks, and mills was located at Peekskill, and Howe wanted it destroyed. Around noon on March 23, a British raiding party consisting of five hundred men and four artillery pieces landed near Peekskill.

After taking up positions on Drum Hill, the British opened fire on the town, and the American positions on Fort Hill. General McDougal received advance warning of the British raid, and arrived before the landings. He ordered the removal of some of the supplies, and burned the rest along with the barracks, and storehouses. He then withdrew his outnumbered force of some 250 militia to a hill about two miles from the town. The British raiders then moved into the village and finished destroying the remaining supplies, workshops, storehouses and wagons. Meanwhile, McDougal sent a message to Fort Constitution, ordering the fort's commander to send reinforcements.

The British raiders remained in the area during the night of March 23–24, and on the following day marched toward McDougal's position. McDougal decided not to stand and fight, and instead ordered a withdrawal. He could not risk losing the only force defending the lower Hudson Valley. The area was far too important to the Americans, since the large Fishkill supply depot, a major logistical center for the army, was also located in the region.

When McDougal withdrew, he left behind a small detachment of reinforcements from Fort Constitution to cover the withdrawal. As darkness approached, the 80-man detachment led by Lieutenant Colonel Marinus Willet fixed bayonets and attacked the flank of the British column's advance guard, overwhelming it. Willet's troops then moved forward, and began sniping at the main force using trees and stone walls as cover. The British quickly fell back to their position on Fort Hill, and began preparations to leave the area. At around midnight, the British troops retreated to their ships, and sailed back to New York City. Willet's counterattack killed nine British soldiers and wounded four. Overall British losses during the raid were 13 killed and four wounded, while Colonel Willet reported two men killed and five wounded. The British did not return to the Highlands in force for another six months.

Another battleground in the forage war was Westchester County, New York. Located on the east side of the Hudson just north of British-occupied New York, the county came to be known as "Neutral Ground" between the two armies.[19] The residents of the county were evenly divided in their support for the Patriot and Loyalist causes, and due to its proximity to New York City, the county was a favored area for British foraging parties. The county was also the home base of the notorious Loyalist cavalry leader James DeLancey. In 1777, DeLancey was appointed captain of an elite troop of light horse, called the Westchester Chasseurs. The troop roamed the county collecting supplies and forage, and frequently clashed with Patriot militia.

William Duer, a New York State senator, attempted to organize the Westchester militia into ranger companies composed of men who knew the ground in the county, but by April 1777, fewer than two hundred militiamen were actively defending the county, even though some 1,400 men were on the militia rolls. This gave the British and Loyalists a significant advantage in numbers, and they sent out foraging parties on a daily basis collecting horses, hay, and cattle. Washington recommended to the New York authorities that they remove or destroy all forage and livestock from areas of the county in close proximity to the British lines.[20]

Without question, Washington's winter campaign strategy for 1776–77 was successful. The main British army in New York remained undefeated, but so did the American army. By the spring of 1777, the British held only a strip of territory between Perth Amboy and New Brunswick. Moreover, in New Jersey alone, there were at least six hundred battles, skirmishes, and other acts of violence between January and April 1777.[21] Additionally, British troops were afforded little time to rest and recuperate during the winter months. Since British troops were unaccustomed to winter campaigning, their combat effectiveness and morale were seriously degraded during the winter of 1777. Total British losses in the New Jersey campaign, including the major battles at Trenton, and Princeton were 2,887 men. Of those losses, 954 occurred during the forage war, and another two hundred were sustained in other small-unit actions.[22] General Howe was not able to launch his Philadelphia campaign until late July 1777 due to the losses, and the overall poor condition of his troops. He had hoped to receive fifteen thousand reinforcements from Britain by spring, and march his army overland from New York to capture Philadelphia in the late spring or early summer of 1777. When he received only a handful of reinforcements, he decided to sail south to the Chesapeake, and land his army at the northern end of the Bay to approach Philadelphia from the south.

The winter campaign also sealed the fate of the New Jersey Loyalists. The resurgence of the Patriot militia, and restoration of civil authority crushed the Loyalists as a viable military and political force in the state. The British withdrawal from most areas of the state left the Loyalists few choices. They could either move to British-occupied New York City, or remain at home and look after themselves. Many of those who fled to New York joined regular Loyalist units in the British Army, such as the Queen's Rangers and the King's American Regiment. Those who remained behind faced Patriot revenge. Some of the more notorious Loyalist leaders were hanged, or received prison sentences. Others had their property seized. Some simply switched sides, and enlisted in the state's militia, or joined the Continental Army. A few fought on, waging a persistent guerilla war, but they were never able to overpower the Patriot militia and the civil government.[23]

From 1777 onward, partisan warfare became an integral part of theater campaigns for the duration of the war. On the American side, highly mobile state and local mounted militia units were increasingly used to conduct joint special operations with Continental cavalry and dragoon units such as Lee's Legion, and William Washington's cavalry. Additionally, state and local infantry militia were fought side by side with Continental line units in major battles. On the British side, Loyalist forces, such as Tarleton's Dragoons and the King's American Dragoons continued to play an important role for the duration of the war.

7

THE RISE OF PARTISAN WARFARE
IN THE SOUTHERN THEATER

The night was black as tar, and a steady drizzle of rain soaked the long column of horsemen as they rode along the muddy backcountry road. The flintlocks of the men's long rifles were wrapped in blankets and hunting shirts to keep them dry. Dawn broke gray and gloomy, and the drizzle turned to a soaking rain. Just after sunrise, the horsemen forded the rain-swollen Broad River, and proceeded at a slow gait along a winding path that led toward a looming mountain ridgeline less than ten miles distant. Early morning mists covered the mountain like a white shroud. The men and horses were weary and hungry after their night-long ride, but their commander refused his subordinates' requests for a breakfast halt. The mounted men grumbled and cursed their leaders. During short halts, they munched on hard, dry kernels of Indian corn, sharing some with their near-starving horses. Others chewed on pieces of dried beef that they carried in their wallets and saddlebags. By noontime the Patriots were within three miles of the mountain. Tensions continued to rise after scouts reported capturing a Tory girl, who revealed that she had been in the enemy camp earlier that morning. Their prey was camped in the saddle of a ridgeline that ran off the southern end of the mountain. Some of the scouts and guides were familiar with the area having used the same campsite while hunting deer and wolves. By 3:00 a.m., the Patriots were moving silently through the woods at the base of Kings Mountain.

VIRGINIA AND THE CAROLINAS WERE SPARED FROM INVASION AND occupation by British troops for more than two years after General Henry

150

Clinton's failed attempt to capture Charleston in 1776. However, the region was not free of conflict. On the contrary, there was almost constant inter-necine warfare between bands of Patriots and those who chose to remain loyal to the Crown. Most of these bands were loosely organized, and their actions were designed primarily to instill fear and terror, and intimidate their neighbors who had opposing views on independence from Great Britain. The raids resulted in senseless killings, pillaging, and looting, often for personal gain or revenge, rather than principle. After five years of this irregular warfare, neither side had gained the upper hand, however, the year 1780 would bring a dramatic change to the war in the southern states.

After a series of strategic failures and setbacks in the northern theater, culminating with the American victory at Saratoga in the fall of 1777, fol-lowed by France's entry into the war in 1778, Lord North's government began focusing on a new strategy that would enable Britain to at least retain her southern colonies. The strategy, however, was flawed. It over-estimated Tory strength and latent Loyalist sympathies in the population. This was especially true in the hinterlands of the southern states. None-theless, the British adopted the new southern strategy, which called a series of campaigns focused on the south. General Sir Henry Clinton, commander-in-chief of British forces in North America was responsible for implementing the strategy. His plan first called for British forces to capture Savannah, Georgia, while British agents incited their Indian allies to attack American settlements along the southern frontiers from Virginia to Georgia. The next target of British forces was the port of Charleston, South Carolina. Following the capture of Charleston, British forces supported by the Loyalists were to advance into South Carolina, where they would pacify the interior and separate it from the American "over the mountain" settlements (settlements west of the Appalachians). After securing South Carolina, the British would open communications with North Carolina Loyalists and invade that state, bringing it under British control. Finally, once Georgia and the Carolinas were secure, the British would focus their attention on Virginia.

Complying with the new strategy, General Clinton sent 3,500 troops from New York and New Jersey, under Lieutenant Colonel Archibald Campbell, by sea to capture Savannah, while another British force ad-vanced from Florida to attack the port city from the rear. Recognizing the threat, Congress appointed Major General Benjamin Lincoln as commander of the Southern Department in October 1778. Lincoln arrived in Charleston on December 4, 1778. He marched south in an attempt to save Savannah from capture, but the British halted his advance at the Savannah River, and Savannah fell to the British on December 29. In 1779, a combined Franco-American expedition led by Admiral d'Estaing and General Lincoln was launched to oust the British from Georgia, but after a month-long unsuccessful siege of Savannah, the Americans and French withdrew in October.

British successes in Georgia convinced General Clinton that the time was ripe for his campaign against South Carolina. The departure of Admiral d'Estaing's fleet from the southern coast opened the way for Clinton to sail south from New York toward Charleston. The invasion force of some 7,600 troops sailed from New York on December 26, 1779. The fleet was battered by a series of winter storms off the North Carolina capes, but still managed to reach Edisto Inlet 30 miles below Charleston on February 11, 1780. Rather than attempting to sail directly into Charleston harbor, as he had done in 1776, Clinton ordered his army to land on Simmons Island and approach the city by an overland route. Through the rest of February and the first half of March, the British advanced slowly to reduce the American fortifications guarding the southern approaches to Charleston harbor. Then on March 10, Clinton's second-in-command, Major General Lord Charles Cornwallis, crossed to the mainland. After receiving reinforcements, Clinton crossed the Ashley River on March 29, and began constructing siege lines three days later. On April 8, the British fleet forced its way past the guns of Fort Moultrie, and entered Charleston harbor. General Lincoln's Charleston garrison was reinforced in early April, with the arrival of 1,500 Virginia Continentals bringing its total strength to 5,500 men. However, the Americans were still outnumbered two to one. On April 14, Lieutenant Colonel Banastre Tarleton attacked and routed a detachment of American troops led by Brigadier General Isaac Huger at Monck's Corner north of Charleston, completely sealing off the American army's only route of escape. Realizing the seriousness of the situation, General Lincoln offered to evacuate the city, provided that his troops were allowed to depart unmolested. Clinton refused the request.

The siege continued throughout the remainder of April and into early

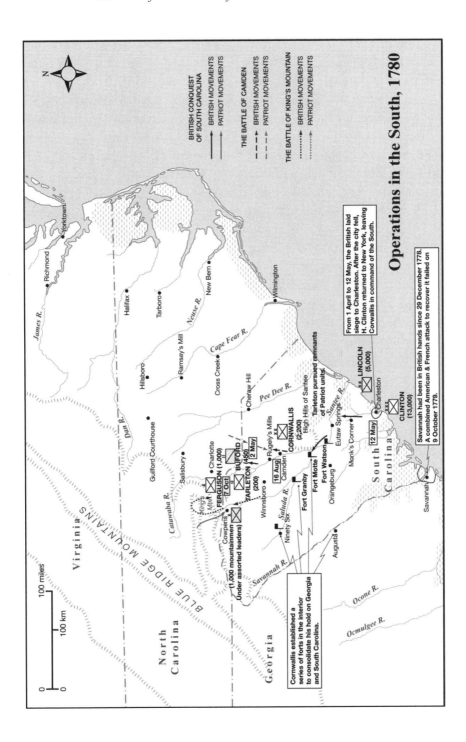

Operations in the South, 1780

May. During this period the American lines were under constant bombardment. Ground attacks were also launched against the city's outer defenses. As the siege lines drew closer to the city, British bombardments set fire to several buildings inside the city, and Charleston officials petitioned General Lincoln to surrender. Finally realizing that his army's situation was hopeless, Lincoln decided to surrender on May 11. The following day, a lone Continental drummer boy beat a parley, and guns on both sides grew silent. Charleston, America's fourth largest city, and its 5,500-man garrison surrendered on May 12.

The American Continentals marched sullenly out of their trenches, and stacked their weapons in an area between the two lines of trenches, while the militia troops were marched into the city where they laid down their arms. General Clinton's surrender terms were harsh. The Continental troops, including all of their officers, were held as prisoners of war. Clinton hoped to exchange the Continental troops for British soldiers taken prisoner at Saratoga, however, the exchanges never took place, and the Continental-enlisted soldiers were left to languish under deplorable conditions aboard prison ships in Charleston harbor, and on barren barrier islands. Large numbers of Continental prisoners died of disease and starvation before they were finally liberated. The militia received better treatment. Ignoring the advice of many of his own officers and influential South Carolina Loyalists, Clinton paroled almost all of the South Carolina militiamen. Only a few of the most obstinate rebels were held as prisoners. Some eight hundred militiamen were permitted to return to their homes with the promise that they would never again take up arms against their king. It was a decision that General Clinton, and his successor Lord Cornwallis, would soon regret.

Soon after the surrender of Charleston, General Clinton began preparations for his return to New York, fearing that the Americans and their new French allies would attempt an attack on that city. Before his departure, Clinton provided Lord Cornwallis with specific guidance on how the war to secure the southern colonies was to be carried out. The relationship between the two generals had frayed during the siege, and they would never again see eye to eye on strategy and tactics. As commander-in-chief in North America, Clinton was not prepared to give his subordinate complete autonomy.

Broadly stated, Clinton's instructions to Cornwallis were to first pacify South Carolina and then, with Loyalist support, invade and reclaim North Carolina. Having secured the Carolinas, Cornwallis's army could then move north into Virginia where, with reinforcements drawn from New York, he would bring that state under full British control. Leaving Cornwallis with a mixed force of 6,400 British Regulars, two Hessian regiments, and Loyalist troops from New York and New Jersey, General Clinton departed for New York in early June. He took with him nearly eight thousand troops which, had they remained in the Carolinas, may have guaranteed a successful southern campaign.

While long columns of British and Hessian troops began filing up the gangplanks of Royal Navy transports in Charleston harbor, Cornwallis began launching operations into the interior of South Carolina. He planned to subjugate and pacify the "back country," by first mopping up the last remaining remnants of the southern Continental Army in South Carolina and Georgia, and then extending Loyalist control from the coastal areas to the Piedmont region and beyond.

Before his departure, Clinton had already ordered three columns of British and troops into the interior. One column marched northwest toward the Loyalist outpost at Ninety Six, about 180 miles from Charleston, while another marched toward Augusta. Lord Cornwallis led the largest column with 2,500 troops and five fieldpieces. Cornwallis marched toward Camden, 130 miles north of Charleston. His immediate concern was a force of 350 Virginia Continentals led by Colonel Abraham Buford. The Virginians had been on their way to reinforce the American garrison at Charleston when they learned the city had fallen to the British. Buford then reversed course, and began marching north to link up with reinforcements that were marching south from Virginia. Realizing that the Americans had a ten-day lead on his slow-moving column, Cornwallis ordered Lieutenant Colonel Tarleton to give chase with the British Legion.

Born in Liverpool, England in 1754, Banastre Tarleton was the son of a wealthy merchant and one-time mayor of Liverpool. He studied at Oxford University and intended to pursue a career as a lawyer. However, after his father's death he quickly squandered most of his inheritance on women and gambling. In 1775, the 21-year-old Tarleton was able to purchase a commission as a cornet in the 1st Dragoon Guards. That December, he embarked as an unattached cavalry officer with troops under the command of Lord Cornwallis bound for service in America. After participating in Cornwallis's unsuccessful attempt to capture Charleston in 1776, Tarleton applied for service with the 16th Light Dragoons.

After the British capture of New York, Tarleton participated in a dragoon raid that led to the capture of General Charles Lee in New Jersey. Tarleton's actions during the raid earned him a promotion to major. After further service in New Jersey and Pennsylvania, Tarleton was promoted to lieutenant colonel in 1777, and given command of the British Legion, which was composed primarily of American Loyalists. Two years later, Tarleton's Legion sailed south with generals Clinton and Cornwallis to capture Charleston. During the siege of Charleston, he was ordered by Clinton to cut off the rebel communication and supply lines between the backcountry and Charleston and accomplished that mission by defeating an American force at Monck's Corner. He remained determined to teach the rebels a lesson they would never forget, and earn a reputation that would stay with him for the duration of the war and beyond.

Tarleton set off with a mixed force of his own legionnaires, a detachment of British dragoons, and a 3-pound cannon, to intercept Buford's column. Tarleton pushed his men and horses to the limit, and, after nearly two and a half days of hard riding, he was within striking distance of Buford's column. Buford was warned of Tarleton's approach, and fled north into an area known as the Waxhaws. As Tarleton closed on Buford's column, the Americans formed a line of battle. By that time, Tarleton realized that his troops and their mounts were exhausted from the chase, and were in no condition to fight. Therefore he decided on a bold gamble. He halted his advance guard, and sent an officer forward to demand that the Americans surrender, overstating his own numbers. Tarleton's surrender terms were harsh ending with a warning, "If you are rash enough to reject the terms," Tarleton wrote, "the blood be upon your head."[1] Buford's reply was just as terse; "I reject your proposals, and shall defend myself to the extremity."[2] By that time it was nearly 3:00 p.m. Once he received Buford's reply, Tarleton had little choice but to attack.

Buford deployed his rearguard in an open wood, and continued his withdrawal. Tarleton's bugler signaled for a charge, and a "furious attack was made on the rearguard, commanded by Lieutenant Pearson."[3] Not a single member of the rearguard escaped, and Pearson "was inhumanely mangled on the face as he lay on his back."[4] Tarleton's force then closed with Buford's main body as it was moving across open ground. Tarleton attacked with his infantry in the center and cavalry on both flanks, and the 3-pounder in the rear. According to one account they "advanced to the charge with the horrid yells of infuriated demons."[5] Buford's Virginians held their fire until Tarleton's dragoons were almost among them, leaving themselves little or no time to reload. Buford, realizing that further resistance was hopeless, ordered his men to ground their arms, and hoisted a surrender flag. According to an account written by Tarleton seven years after the battle, his own horse went down in the charge, and "slaughter commenced before Lieutenant-Colonel Tarleton could remount another horse."[6] The slaughter began when the American ensign, who was attempting to raise the white flag, was cut down by one of Tarleton's horsemen with a saber blow. The Virginians scrambled to recover their arms to defend themselves, but they were too disorganized to put up a firm resistance. Tarleton's dragoons and infantry were among them, slashing and stabbing. Wounded survivors tried to conceal themselves beneath the bodies of their comrades, but according to the few American survivors, the enraged British went over the ground "plunging their bayonets into everyone that exhibited any signs of life, and in some instances, where several had fallen one over the other, these monsters were seen to throw off on the point of the bayonet the uppermost, to come at those beneath."[7] Tarleton was finally able to remount, and regain some control over his men, but it was too late to achieve anythink meaningful.

One hundred and thirteen of Buford's men lay dead on the field, and another 150 were so badly maimed that Tarleton was forced to parole them. Only 53 Americans, many with non-life threatening wounds, were taken prisoner. Colonel Buford managed to escape with his few remaining men on horseback. The British lost only five killed and 12 wounded in the fighting. At sunset, the severely and fatally wounded were loaded onto wagons, and transported to the Church of the Waxhaws where Scotch-Irish women from the local community dressed their wounds, and comforted the dying.[8]

Buford's defeat at the Waxhaws led the British and their Loyalist allies to believe that they had control over most of South Carolina, but that was far from true. Although patriot sentiments and morale were at a low ebb, news of the British massacre at the Waxhaws spread rapidly throughout the southern states, motivating many with Whig sentiments and those who otherwise might have remained neutral, to form volunteer militia companies to protect their homes and settlements from the ruthless Tarleton. "Tarleton's Quarter!" soon became their rallying cry. With Cornwallis's army on the march, and the American Southern Continental Army seemingly helpless to defend the Carolinas and Georgia, the war in the summer of 1780 became a partisan war.

Before his departure for New York, General Clinton issued a proclamation demanding that all citizens support their king's cause in suppressing the rebellion, effectively cancelling previously issued paroles and truces, and eliminating the possibility that anyone could remain neutral. Clinton's proclamation also demanded that every eligible male serve in the Loyalist militia when requested, and all citizens were encouraged to take an oath of allegiance. While many complied, others resisted and joined a growing number of Patriot bands led by paroled and prewar militia leaders such as Francis Marion, Thomas Sumter, and Andrew Pickens. The ranks of the Patriot forces swelled as Tory units and British troops spread out across the backcountry, foraging, and raiding the farms and plantations of those suspected of supporting the rebel cause. The raiders carried off slaves and livestock, and torched the homes, barns, and crops of suspected rebels.

At first, the loosely organized Patriot bands concentrated their efforts on protecting their homesteads and taking revenge on local Tories by attacking their homes and properties, but as British troops moved into their territories, the Patriot bands became increasingly bold, attacking British and Tory outposts and campsites, and ambushing supply trains, couriers, and small detachments of British and Loyalist troops. Before long, Cornwallis and his subordinate commanders were forced to assign a significant number of escort troops to move supplies and garrison his outposts and forts in the interior. By late June 1780, a full-scale partisan war raged across the Carolinas and Georgia.

Even though partisan bands of Patriots were threatening British supply lines and lines of communication, Cornwallis was already making preparations for an invasion of North Carolina. Realizing that a campaign in that state would require substantial Loyalist support, Cornwallis encouraged his Loyalist contacts in North Carolina to begin stockpiling supplies. He also admonished them to remain inactive pending his arrival in the state. Lieutenant Colonel John Moore, a Tory officer in the Royal North Carolina Volunteers, was sent by Cornwallis to gauge the amount of Loyalist support in the area around his home, near Ramsour's Mill, about 35 miles northwest of Charlotte. Cornwallis also cautioned Moore not to commence any actions that might alert the rebels of his plans to invade the state. Moore reached his home on June 18 and—despite Cornwallis's instructions—he immediately assembled some 40 Loyalists from the area to spread the word of the pending British invasion. Moore was soon joined by Nicholas Welch, another Tory officer. Welch offered gold coins to anyone who would swear allegiance to the British Crown. Word spread quickly, and cash-strapped farmers from throughout the region joined the Loyalist ranks. Within days, some 1,300 armed and unarmed Loyalists established a camp on a low ridgeline near Ramsour's Mill to hear the exhortations and impassioned tales of British victories in South Carolina. Such a large gathering in the backcountry did not go unnoticed by local Patriots, and the stage was set for the first major battle between Loyalist and Patriot forces in North Carolina.

When word reached Charlotte of the large Loyalist assemblage at Ramsour's Mill, General Griffith Rutherford dispatched Colonel Francis Locke with a small force of militia to the area to disrupt the Loyalist meeting. Gathering small units of Patriots along the way, Locke arrived in the vicinity of the Loyalist camp with approximately four hundred men. Despite their numerical disadvantage, Locke and his captains decided to approach the enemy camp in a night march, and then launch a surprise attack at dawn.

Locke's column arrived in the vicinity of the enemy camp in the pre-dawn hours of June 20, 1780. A group of mounted militia under captains Fall, Brandon, and McDowell led the column.[9] The horsemen encountered a small Loyalist picket force less than half a mile from the enemy camp. The pickets opened fire on the Patriots, then quickly withdrew toward the camp on the ridge. The mounted Patriots pursued the pickets down the moonlit road, and then turned right and pursued them up the ridgeline. When the horsemen were within 30 yards of the camp, they opened fire on Loyalists as they attempted to form a defensive line. When the Loyalists realized that the attackers were few in number, they quickly regained their composure, "and poured a destructive fire" into the rebel horsemen killing Captain Fall and several of his men.[10] The survivors of the charge quickly retreated back down the slope in great disorder, passing through the Patriot infantry, who were advancing toward the camp. The emboldened Loyalists charged down the slope in pursuit of the horsemen, and the two opposing forces collided firing into each other at near-point-blank range. With no time to reload in such close proximity and lacking bayonets, the fight soon turned into a frontier-style brawl. The opponents went at each other with rifle butts, hunting knives, rocks, and fists. Since neither side wore uniforms, the only way to distinguish friend from foe was by an improvised form of identification: Loyalists wore pine tops in their hats, and Patriots wore paper squares in the lapels of their jackets. As the combatants tried to re-form their lines, more and more Patriot infantry began to move forward and the Patriots were able to extend their lines, overlapping the Loyalist flanks. Captain Hardin, who was experienced in Indian styles of warfare, led a group of his men forward and established a firing position, unleashing a galling fire on the Loyalist left flank.[11] With their flank turned, the Loyalists had no choice but to retreat back up the ridge.

After reaching the crest of the ridge, the Loyalists fled down the reverse slope to where another group of Loyalists had gathered. The Patriots pursued the Loyalists to the top of the ridge, then halted when they saw a new Loyalist line forming behind the ridge. After sizing up his losses, Colonel Locke decided to hold his newly won ground. Initially, Locke had only 86 effectives to defend his hard-won ground on the ridge, but after repeated efforts to gather those scattered in the action, he managed to assemble a total of 110 men. Still, with 170 men killed or wounded, and more missing, he was still outnumbered. Realizing his perilous situation, Locke sent messengers to General Rutherford, who was approaching with reinforcements, urging him to hasten.

However, Lieutenant Colonel Moore and his Loyalists had had enough, and retreated before the arrival of rebel reinforcements. The carnage on the field was horrible. When Patriot reinforcements arrived two hours after the battle, the dead and most of the wounded were still lying where they had fallen.[12] No reports of casualties were submitted after the battle, but one participant recalled that 56 dead lay on the side of the ridge that had seen the heaviest fighting, and many others lay scattered on the flanks and over the ridge toward the mill. The same source wrote that around 70 men were killed on each side, and another hundred were wounded on each side, and "fifty Tories were taken prisoners."[13] One historian and author estimated a casualty rate of 28 percent among participants, a higher casualty rate than most Revolutionary War battles between trained regular troops.[14]

The Loyalist defeat in western North Carolina curtailed recruiting, and support for Cornwallis's move into North Carolina, delaying it until late September 1780.

Lieutenant Colonel Moore, the Tory commander, escaped back to Camden, South Carolina, where Cornwallis had established his headquarters. When he learned of the defeat of the North Carolina Loyalists, Cornwallis was livid and wanted to court-martial Moore for disregarding his orders and inciting a premature uprising among the Loyalists. However, he relented realizing that he still needed Loyalist support to suppress the rebel partisans, who were growing bolder and more active by the day.

The month of July 1780 brought an upsurge in rebel partisan attacks throughout South Carolina. On July 12, Captain John McClure, one of Thomas Sumter's key lieutenants, virtually wiped out a British dragoon scouting party from Tarleton's Legion. Loyalist Captain Christian Huck of Philadelphia led the scouting party. The fight occurred at Williamson's plantation, near the headwaters of Fishing Creek in York County, South Carolina. Thirty-five members of the scouting party were killed including Captain Huck, another 30 were wounded, and a large number were taken prisoner. Only 24 Loyalist survivors managed to make their way back to Tarleton's camp. The rebels suffered only one casualty. The lopsided Patriot victory helped raise morale among the Patriots, and led to an upsurge in enlistments.

Colonel Thomas Sumter was emboldened by his subordinate's success at Williamson's plantation, and decided to attack a Tory outpost at Rocky Mount. Dubbed the "Carolina Gamecock" by his men, Sumter served throughout the war. He was promoted to the rank of brigadier general, and lived long enough to earn the distinction of being the last surviving American general of the American Revolution.

A Virginian by birth, Thomas Sumter later moved to South Carolina and settled in Stateburg in the High Hills of Santee (present day Sumter County), where he married and became a successful plantation owner. He participated in the successful defense of Charleston in 1776, and then crossed the state to pacify the Cherokees on the western frontier. He then returned to his plantation, and was not present during the siege and surrender of Charleston in 1780. Nonetheless, he remained near the top of the British Army's most wanted list. In late May 1780, a squadron of Tarleton's dragoons was dispatched to capture Sumter. When he learned that the British were searching for his plantation, Sumter fled to safety. When Captain Charles Campbell and his dragoons rode up to Sumter's plantation house, they were informed that he had fled. Frustrated, the dragoons burned the plantation house and outbuildings, while Sumter's invalid wife and 11-year-old son looked on in horror. When Sumter learned of the event, he donned his uniform and buckled on his sword swearing to drive the British and their Loyalist allies from the state once and for all. Since he was well known throughout the backcountry for his courage and determination, the "Carolina Gamecock" had little difficulty recruiting men who were willing to fight for the Patriot cause.

By late July, Sumter had assembled several hundred mounted partisans for the purpose of attacking British outposts north of Camden, South Carolina. He also recruited the services of Major William Davie, a prominent North Carolina Patriot.[15] Sumter planned to attack a 150-man detachment of New York Tory Volunteers led by Lieutenant Colonel George Trumbull at Rocky Mount with a force of five hundred men, while Major Davie moved to threaten a Tory force at Hanging Rock, to dissuade them from reinforcing Trumbull at Rocky Mount.

When Sumter arrived at Rocky Mount on July 30, he found that the Loyalists had positioned themselves in two log-houses and a loop-holed building. The houses and building were surrounded by an abatis of sharpened tree branches.[16] Undeterred by the enemy's defenses, Sumter launched an unsuccessful and costly assault on the sheltered enemy troops. He then tried to burn the buildings, but a thunderstorm extinguished the flames. After a short eight-hour siege, the frustrated Sumter abandoned the effort and withdrew. In the meantime, Davie arrived in the vicinity of Hanging Rock only to learn that he was outnumbered. While conducting a reconnaissance of the area, Davie spotted three companies of mounted infantry halted at a farmhouse, and attacked them in full view of the Loyalist garrison. After cutting the ranks of Loyalists to pieces, and capturing 60 horses and one hundred rifles and muskets, he rode off to link up with Colonel Sumter.[17]

After regrouping and receiving Davie's reinforcements, Sumter and Davie planned another attack on the Loyalist stronghold at Rocky Mount. The plan called for three separate columns to march independently toward the encampment, followed by a attack at dawn. The plan almost went awry when the three attacking units became intermingled just as they reached Rocky Mount. Despite the confusion, Sumter's men managed to overrun the encampment, and began plundering the stores, which included a significant amount of rum. At that point, good order and discipline broke down as the men helped themselves to the liquor. As British reinforcements began to arrive in the area, Major Davie, commanding a more disciplined force, had to rescue Sumter's unruly partisans. Despite the breakdown in discipline in the Patriot ranks, the Loyalists suffered some two hundred casualties in the fighting.

Colonel Sumter and his men were not the only Patriot forces active in the escalating partisan war. Forty-eight-year-old South Carolinian Francis Marion was a veteran of the French and Indian War, during which he served as militia lieutenant in a campaign against the Cherokee along the Georgia and South Carolina frontier. In 1775, he was commissioned as a captain in the 2d South Carolina Regiment, and participated in the defense of Fort Sullivan in Charleston harbor during General Clinton's failed 1776 attempt to capture Charleston. Later the same year, Marion was commissioned as a lieutenant colonel in the Continental Army by Congress, and in the spring of 1780, he served under General Lincoln during the 1780 siege of Charleston. By happenstance, Marion was not captured by the

British after the surrender of the city. At the time of the surrender, Marion was outside the city, recuperating from a broken ankle.

Soon after the fall of Charleston, Marion organized a small band of partisans, probably no more than 70 men, and began launching small-scale attacks on British and Loyalist units. Marion's partisans began their operations in late July 1780, in an area of South Carolina bounded by the towns of Cheraw, Kingstree, and Georgetown. Since he was born and raised in the area, Marion knew the terrain like the back of his hand. The region was ideally suited for guerilla warfare with thick woods, tangled thickets, winding silt-filled rivers, fetid marshes, and inhospitable swamps. Marion's partisans established a number of secure camps and supply bases in the seemingly impenetrable swamps and marshes, from which they launched attacks against Loyalist militia and British supply lines. After the attacks, Marion's men would withdraw to one of their secret camps hidden deep in the swamps. Local residents, sympathetic to the Patriot cause, acted as auxiliaries for Marion's guerillas, providing food, medicine and other supplies and gathering intelligence on British and Loyalist units and their activities. While living in the camps, Marion's men slept in lean-to shelters, and crude shacks protected their gunpowder and supplies from the rain. Nearby bridges were stripped of their wooden planking, fords were obstructed with debris and deadfall, and boats were hidden or sunk to deny the enemy access to the base areas. Marion's guerillas stayed on the move and never spent more than a few nights in any one camp.

Unlike Colonel Thomas Sumter, Marion was a master tactician who never risked the lives of his men unnecessarily. His attacks were well planned, and he never attacked a numerically superior force head-on. Due to the small size of his band, Marion usually attacked small supply columns, or ambushed small detachments of Tories and British soldiers. When he had a sufficient number of men on hand, he conducted raids on enemy supply depots and encampments.

When General Horatio Gates assumed command of the Continental Army's southern army at the end of July 1780, Colonel Marion rode to his headquarters located at Rugeley's Mill, North Carolina, and reported for duty. Gates was unimpressed with the soft-spoken Marion, and his small band of ragged partisans. He ordered Marion to return to South Carolina to burn bridges and boats along the Santee River. Gates was preparing to attack the British garrison at Camden, and wanted to prevent British reinforcements from reaching Camden prior to the attack.

―――――――

While Marion and his followers were burning bridges and boats along the Santee in the eastern portion of South Carolina, partisan warfare continued to rage in the northwestern portion of the state. Local Loyalists supported by the Queen's Rangers were attempting to gain control of the area. During the summer of 1780, the Loyalists established two strong outposts in the region, Fort Prince and Fort Thicketty. The Loyalists launched raids from the forts attacking Patriot settlements, and collecting forage and food supplies from local farmers. Fort Thicketty was located about 10 miles southeast of the Cowpens near Goucher Creek. The fort was first constructed to protect settlers from marauding bands of Cherokees. After occupying the old fort, the Loyalists repaired and improved the fortifications, turning it into a formidable bastion. Captain Patrick Moore, a local Loyalist, commanded the Fort Thicketty garrison and boldly stated that the fort was too strong "for the rebels to take it."[18] Captain Moore had a personal score to settle with the rebels: he had fought alongside his brother, Lieutenant Colonel John Moore, at Ramsour's Mill, and while both had escaped capture, their British allies had scorned them afterward. Moore was determined to restore his good name as a loyal subject of the Crown.

Alarmed by the Tory raids and pillaging along the frontier, colonels Charles McDowell, Isaac Shelby, and Elijah Clarke, organized a force of six hundred men to launch a surprise attack to capture Fort Thicketty. The Patriot force began marching toward the fort at sunset on the evening of July 25. By daylight the following morning the Patriots had the fort surrounded. Colonel Shelby sent an emissary to the fort to demand the surrender of the garrison, but Captain Moore replied "that he would defend the place to the last extremity."[19] Colonel Shelby then moved his men forward, halting them within musket range of the fort's walls, before giving Moore a second chance to surrender. Obviously intimidated by the size of the Patriot force arranged before the fort, Moore accepted the terms, and surrendered the fort without firing a shot.

The Patriots captured the entire garrison of ninety-three Loyalists and a British sergeant major, who had been sent to the fort to drill and discipline the Loyalists. Also captured were two hundred muskets, and a large supply of powder and shot. The capture of Fort Thicketty was a major setback for British and Loyalist efforts. Captain Moore was heavily censured by the British for his cowardly surrender.

The months of August and October 1780 brought changes to the partisan war in the southern theater. After his arrival in late July, General Gates met with Continental Army officers and partisan leaders from the region. Gates was determined to march from Charlotte into South Carolina to attack the British post at Camden, and he needed militia and partisan support. Gates' small army of Continentals departed Charlotte on July 27, and crossed the Pee Dee River on August 3. After crossing the river, he was reinforced with two thousand militia, bringing the total strength of his army to some 4,500 men. Meanwhile, after learning of Gates' march into South Carolina, Lord Cornwallis marched north from Charleston to reinforce the British post at Camden, arriving on August 9. With the reinforcements, the British garrison at Camden numbered around 2,200 men. Rather than wait at Camden for the Americans to attack, Cornwallis began pushing north of the town to intercept the Americans. Late in the evening of August 15, the American and British forces made contact about five miles north of the town. Both forces pulled back for the night, and prepared for a major battle the following day.

General Gates unwisely placed his militia on his left flank opposite Cornwallis's best troops. Cornwallis opened the battle by attacking the American militia, easily breaking their lines, and sending them into flight. The Continentals counterattacked the British left and came close to breaking the British line, but were halted when the British assaulted their exposed left flank. After putting up a stiff resistance, Gates' Continentals were forced to withdraw. Cornwallis then ordered his cavalry commander, Lieutenant Colonel Tarleton, to attack the American rear. The retreat soon turned into a rout as the relentless Tarleton pursued the Americans for more than 20 miles. Gates fled the field, outdistancing his retreating troops.

Camden was a crushing defeat and major setback for the American Southern army. It would take months to rebuild to army under its new commander, Major General Nathaniel Greene. Meanwhile, Lord Cornwallis planned a campaign to invade North Carolina to exploit his victory at Camden, and crush rebel resistance in the Carolinas once and for all. As he lacked sufficient regular British troops to achieve his goal, he would still have to depend heavily on Loyalist partisan militia to crush the remaining rebel resistance. Cornwallis realized that as he moved north, his supply lines and lines of communication from the port of Charleston would still be vulnerable to the rebel partisan forces led by Thomas Sumter, Andrew Pickens, and the elusive Francis Marion, so he ordered Tarleton to hunt down and destroy the rebel partisan leaders and their bands. Using his own British Legion and a number of mounted Tory militia units, "Bloody Ban" went to work immediately. On August 18, he caught up with Thomas Sumter at Fishing Creek. Tarleton attacked Sumter's force of eight hundred men with 100 cavalry and 60 light infantry, freeing a number of prisoners, and killing or capturing 450 rebel partisans. The British also recaptured a number of British wagons, supplies, and cattle that Sumter had previously seized. Thomas Sumter was fortunate to escape capture.

Following his success at Fishing Creek, Tarleton focused his attention on Francis Marion. By September, Tarleton had recruited a number of Tory units to support his own legion, and developed a plan to surround and capture Marion's guerillas. He established a Tory encampment that he knew would not go unnoticed by Marion, and concealed his own legionnaires nearby in anticipation of a night attack on the camp. However, when Marion arrived to reconnoiter the Tory camp, he immediately sensed a trap, and quickly retreated. Tarleton gave chase; his hard-riding dragoons pursued Marion's horsemen for 27 hours through the backcountry before Marion and his men suddenly disappeared into the dark and gloomy Ox Swamp. Tarleton halted his men at the edge of the swamp, and according to legend exclaimed, "As for this damned old fox, the devil himself couldn't catch him."[20] From that day forward, the elusive Francis Marion was known as the "Swamp Fox."

Cornwallis recognized that Tarleton could not completely crush the backcountry rebels, but he was confident that his relentless and ruthless cavalry commander could keep them on the run, and protect the most important British outposts in the center of the state. He therefore moved into North Carolina in late September, establishing his headquarters at Charlotte. As he moved north, Cornwallis became increasingly concerned with the Carolina highlands on his western flank. Intelligence reports and his own instincts led him to believe that Loyalist support was much weaker in the highlands. The mountain folk and frontiersmen who inhabited the Blue Ridge and beyond were not inclined toward allegiance to the British Crown. Most had immigrated to America to escape the poverty of British-ruled Ireland. Known in America as the Scotch-Irish, these settlers were fiercely independent, and valued their personal freedom, wishing to live their lives as they saw fit. Other groups on the frontier included French Huguenots and Germans, who had been persecuted in their homelands by their own monarchs, and were not inclined to become loyal subjects to George III.

After the surrender of Charleston in May 1780, General Clinton appointed 36-year-old British Major Patrick Ferguson as "inspector of militia" with the responsibility of recruiting and training Loyalist militia throughout the state. Ferguson departed Charleston on May 26, 1780. The following month, he raised a regiment of 240 Loyalists at Orangeburg, and spent the next several weeks recruiting militia in the area around the British post at Ninety Six. The Loyalists flocked to the charismatic Scotsman with the nickname the "Bulldog."

Patrick Ferguson was born in June 1744, on his father's estate in Aberdeenshire, Scotland. One of six children, Ferguson was tutored in the classics and mathematics, and enjoyed riding spirited horses and fox hunting with hounds. At the age of 15, Ferguson's family purchased a commission for him as a cornet in the Royal North British Dragoons (Scots Greys), but he did not join his regiment immediately. Instead he was sent to study at the Royal Military Academy at Woolwich for two years. In the spring of 1761, the young Ferguson embarked for Germany for service in the Seven Years' War. He served in Flanders and Germany and fought at the Battle of Minden. However, his wartime service was cut short when he became seriously ill, and he was sent home in 1762. He remained in Scotland and England for the next five years, on garrison and policing duty.[21] During that period, he became involved in the debate over whether English militia laws ought to be extended to Scotland; knowledge he would put to good use when he arrived in the Carolinas.[22]

In 1768, Ferguson was promoted to captain, and sailed to the West Indies with his regiment to perform garrison duty on islands ceded by the French in 1763. Three years later, troubled by an arthritic leg, Ferguson returned to Britain. Once his leg had improved, Captain Ferguson was sent to a training camp for light infantry organized by General Sir William Howe, who had established light infantry companies in the British Army as early as 1771. Howe took note of Ferguson's intelligence and aptitude for light infantry tactics.

Before the American War for Independence broke out, Captain Ferguson designed a breech-loading rifle, later called the Ferguson Rifle. After manufacturing trial models, he field-tested the prototypes in front of several generals and government officials, and received permission to manufacture one hundred of the rifles for military use.

The Ferguson rifle was a very different weapon from the British infantry's standard firearm, the Brown Bess musket. Weighing only 7.5 pounds—3 pounds lighter than the Brown Bess—the Ferguson rifle had a maximum effective range of 200–300 yards, while the Brown Bess was accurate only at ranges between 50 and 100 yards. Perhaps even more significant was the fact that the rifle could be loaded through the breech rather than the muzzle, enabling the soldier to fire and reload from a prone position. Additionally, a well-trained soldier could fire between six to ten rounds a minute with a Ferguson rifle, while a soldier armed with the Brown Bess was expected to fire three or four rounds per minute. At first glance, the Ferguson rifle seemed to be an ideal weapon for light infantry forces fighting in the forested terrain of North America. However, the Ferguson rifle was expensive to produce, and Ferguson found only four gunsmiths in Britain who were willing to manufacture the rifle. Ferguson knew that the British Army would never adopt the rifle as part of its inventory until it was field-tested under battle conditions. He therefore petitioned the king for permission to organize and command an experimental rifle corps in the American colonies.[23] General Howe strongly supported Ferguson's proposal, and George III gave his approval.

In March 1777, Ferguson and his one-hundred-man corps of riflemen sailed to New York, arriving in May. When General Howe sailed south to the Chesapeake to launch his campaign to capture Philadelphia, Ferguson's experimental rifle corps accompanied the expedition. At the battle of Brandywine in September 1777, Ferguson, who was then reputed to be one of the best rifle marksmen in the British Army, had a clear shot at an obviously high-ranking rebel officer within killing range, but decided not to take the shot. The mounted officer wheeled his horse around exposing his back, and Ferguson thought that it was dishonorable to shoot him in the back. That rebel officer may well have been General Washington, who was reconnoitering the lines in the same area of the battlefield. Later, after being told of the officer's possible identity, Ferguson wrote, "I am not Sorry that I did not know all the time who it was."[24]

Later in the same battle, a musket ball shattered Ferguson's right elbow, permanently crippling his arm. During his painful recuperation, Ferguson taught himself to write, fence, and shoot left-handed. After occupying Philadelphia, General Howe decided to disband the experimental corps of riflemen, and store the remaining rifles. Although the Ferguson rifle was extremely accurate, it had a weak wooden stock that tended to break under combat conditions. In addition, the firing mechanism would foul up and require cleaning after firing three or four shots.

After his recuperation and rehabilitation Ferguson returned to duty, without the use of his right arm. He commanded a mixed force of British light infantry, and Loyalists. His unit fought at the battle of Monmouth, and conducted daring raids against American privateers based at Chestnut Neck and Little Egg Harbor in New Jersey. The first raid, conducted on October 6, 1778, was only marginally successful as bad weather hampered the landings and gave Pulaski's Legion time to react. Ferguson's second raid targeted a privateer base at Little Egg Harbor, guarded by a 50-man detachment from Pulaski's Legion. On October 15, Ferguson loaded 250 of his men on boats, and under the cover of darkness they rowed 10 miles before unloading on Osborne Island. He then marched his raiding party two miles and surrounded the rebel outpost. At dawn, Ferguson led a bayonet attack on the rebels. Only five of the 50 Americans manning the outpost survived the attack. The Americans called it a massacre.

In December 1779, Ferguson and his men sailed south with General Clinton's army, and participated in the siege and capture of Charleston. Ferguson was wounded again in a skirmish outside Charleston when a rebel thrust his bayonet through his left arm. Three weeks later he was fully recovered, and still had full use of his left arm.

On May 23, 1780, one week after his victory at Camden, Lord Cornwallis summoned Major Ferguson to his headquarters. The relationship between the two officers was strained. General Clinton, Cornwallis's superior, held Ferguson in high esteem, and Cornwallis's relationship with Clinton was increasingly frayed. Cornwallis preferred to make his own appointees to key positions, and General Clinton had appointed Ferguson as inspector of militia. Ferguson also carried a grudge against Lord Cornwallis, whom he believed favored Lieutenant Colonel Tarleton, and Lord Rawdon, both of whom were younger and less experienced than Ferguson—who was only five years younger than General Cornwallis. Finally, the two had followed completely different career paths in the British Army. Lord Cornwallis was always a conventional soldier adhering to the doctrine, tactics, and traditions of the British Army. On the other hand, Ferguson often used unconventional tactics, and strongly believed that properly trained Loyalist militia could fight just as well as British troops. Cornwallis lacked confidence in the Carolina Loyalist militia. Regardless of their differences, both officers knew that they had to cooperate.

Cornwallis's instructions to Ferguson were that he was to protect the left, or western flank, of the main body of the army using Loyalist militia forces. He also ordered Ferguson to continue recruiting and training Loyalist militia, and to suppress and punish the rebel partisans in the western regions of the Carolinas. Since his operational area was some distance from the British supply bases, Ferguson knew that his militia would have to rely on foraging to obtain food and supplies. Rebel farms and settlements were their main sources of food, forage, and other supplies. Cornwallis also made it clear to Ferguson that in addition to his duties as inspector general of militia, he would also exercise overall command of all Loyalist militia in the far western portions of the Carolinas. Ferguson's mission was fraught with danger and risk, and both men knew it. Ferguson's operational area was remote, and he was unlikely to receive reinforcements. Moreover, trouble was brewing on the western side of the Appalachian Mountains. The settlers and frontiersmen west of the mountains were fiercely independent and anti-British. A shadow army of partisans had mobilized under the leadership of Benjamin Cleveland, Isaac Shelby, William Campbell, and John Sevier. Initially organized to defend their settlements against British-led Indian attacks, the "over mountain men," were now prepared to take the offensive in support of the Patriot cause. The frontiersmen had a long history of launching preemptive strikes against their enemies when threatened. They had used such tactics during the Indian wars, often marching long distances to attack and burn the villages of hostile Indian tribes. If threatened by the possibility of a British invasion across the mountains, they were prepared to pick up their hunting rifles and cross the Blue Ridge to come to the aid of their "kith and kin" on the eastern side of the mountains. Major Ferguson probably did not fully realize that his actions would soon ignite a firestorm on Cornwallis's left flank.

BATTLE AT KINGS MOUNTAIN

During the long, hot southern summer of 1780, Major Ferguson worked tirelessly to recruit and train Loyalist militiamen. He formed a provisional corps of between 150 to two hundred men, and marched across the Piedmont, recruiting as he went. By summer's end he had recruited around four thousand men for the militia, and mobilized one thousand Loyalists for active service. As Ferguson's men pushed westward toward the mountains, recruitment became more difficult. Ferguson's foraging parties indiscriminately burned barns and homesteads, and confiscated livestock owned by Loyalists and rebels alike. As a result, the Patriots became even more determined to resist the British, and convinced some Loyalists to switch sides. Nevertheless, the boyishly handsome and charismatic Scotsman continued to attract followers and admirers of both sexes. As his ranks swelled with volunteers, so did the number of camp followers. As a lifelong bachelor, Ferguson had no reservations about bringing two women along on the march as his own personal servants. Both women, whom Ferguson's men nicknamed "Virginia Paul and Virginia Sal," cooked for the major, washed his uniforms and voluntarily looked after his other needs. It proved to be a fatal attraction for one of the women.

Even when on the march, Ferguson took time to train, and instill discipline in the militia ranks. Knowing how difficult it was to issue orders in the noise, smoke and confusion of battle, Ferguson used a silver whistle to signal his men to execute various movements and maneuvers on the battlefield. He also wore an easily recognizable red and white checkered shirt, rather than his regular British officer's uniform. Ferguson's flair for drama, urbane manner, and Scottish brogue set him apart from his fellow British officers, many of who exhibited an aristocratic arrogance and superior attitude toward their Loyalist allies.

Major Ferguson's attitude toward his armed opponents and civilians was far different from that of his contemporary, Lieutenant Colonel Tarleton. Although most historians agree that the two rivals had a cordial relationship, their personalities and tactics were very different. Tarleton exerted little effort in restraining his dragoons from wanton plundering and butchering their opponents, even after they surrendered. He also had little tolerance for civilians who were sympathetic to the rebels, or those who stayed neutral in the conflict. Tarleton had no reservations about seizing or destroying their property. In summary, Tarleton's tactics were meant to instill fear and terror, while Ferguson's goal was to defeat the rebels, and pacify the population. Lyman Draper, a 19th-century American historian and author, wrote that Ferguson spent hours talking with backcountry people and his own men, trying to convince them of the evil consequences of supporting local disloyal leaders in their communities.[25]

––––––––

On September 1, 1780, Major Ferguson arrived at Gilbert Town (modern-day Rutherfordton), North Carolina, located about 70 miles due west of Charlotte. He established a camp on a ridge, from where he had an excellent view of the eastern slopes of the Blue Ridge Mountains. From Gilbert Town, Ferguson and his men scoured the foothills searching for and skirmishing with rebels, and plundering their farms and settlements. On one such expedition, Ferguson marched deep into the mountain foothills, halting just 50 miles from the Holston Valley, a rebel stronghold across the mountains in eastern Tennessee and southwest Virginia. When he learned from his spies that rebel frontiersmen, or so-called "overmountain men," were gathering in significant numbers in the valleys across the mountains, Ferguson paroled a rebel prisoner and sent him across the mountains with a message for the rebel leaders. Ferguson's message was succinct and threatening. He warned the overmountain men that, "If they do not desist from their opposition to British arms, I will march my army over the mountains, hang their leaders, and lay waste to their country with fire and sword."[26] Ferguson's message had momentous unintended consequences.

Ferguson underestimated the resolve of the rebel opposition across the mountains. His opponents were not an undisciplined and disorganized mob of backwoodsmen, who knew little or nothing about warfare. The overmountain men were a highly mobile and well-armed force of hard, merciless men, hardened by years of Indian warfare. Their chosen leaders all possessed personal courage, charisma, and ambition. Moreover, partisan leaders on the frontier knew how to convince their men to temporarily surrender their individuality and independence for their common survival. Ferguson's ultimatum was first delivered to one of those leaders.

Isaac Shelby, a tall muscular 29-year-old frontiersman and surveyor, had risen rapidly through the Virginia militia ranks. When he received Ferguson's threatening proclamation, he saddled his horse and rode 40 miles to confer with his friend John Sevier, leader of the Washington County militia. Thirty-five-year-old Lieutenant Colonel Sevier had arrived in the Holston River valley in the 1760s, and earned a reputation as a fearless, courageous Indian fighter during the Cherokee War. Sevier was short and stocky and an extrovert, who claimed he could outshoot, outfight, and out-curse most of his men. He enjoyed wild rowdy frontier celebrations, and could drink most of his men under the table. He was given the nickname "Chucky Jack" by his followers.

Colonels Shelby and Sevier made plans to cross the mountains and launch surprise attacks against Ferguson and his Loyalists. They also sent their best men into the hills and valleys to spread the word of Ferguson's proclamation, and communicated with other frontier leaders. Sevier and Shelby also solicited the support of Colonel William Campbell of the Virginia settlements on the Clinch River, and from Colonel McDowell from North Carolina's Burke County.

William Campbell was a 35-year-old first-generation Virginian of Scotch-Irish ancestry. He was raised on the frontier of southwest Virginia during the French and Indian War. As an only son, he had received a superior education for that period acquiring a "correct knowledge of the English language, ancient and modern history and mathematics."[27] After his father's death in 1767, Campbell moved his mother and sisters to a remote section of the Holston valley, settling in an area near present-day

Abington, where he was appointed captain of the local militia company. During the Indian War of 1774, Campbell led his men on an expedition from southwest Virginia to the Ohio country, arriving just as a peace treaty was concluded with the Indian tribes. When the war with the British broke out in 1775, Campbell marched his company of riflemen to Williamsburg, where they were assigned to the 1st Virginia Regiment commanded by the fiery Patriot Patrick Henry. When war broke out with the Cherokees in 1776, he rushed home to the Holston Valley to defend the settlements. In April 1780, Campbell was promoted to the rank of colonel in the militia when another colonel's residence was determined to be in North Carolina not Virginia. Campbell, who stood well over six feet tall, was quick-tempered and aggressive. He relentlessly hunted down Loyalists, and gave them harsh treatment. At first, he was hesitant about leaving his home state of Virginia to join Shelby and Sevier, but he soon relented, and agreed to march south to the rendezvous with Shelby and Sevier at Sycamore Shoals.

Colonel Charles McDowell, another senior Patriot leader in the region, was already encamped at Sycamore Shoals. Thirty-seven-year-old McDowell led militia troops from Burke County, North Carolina. He excelled as an organizer of militia units, and was also a brilliant planner. It was McDowell who conceived and planned the successful expedition against the Loyalist garrison at Fort Thicketty, and also the attack on the Loyalist encampment at Musgrove Mill. McDowell did not lead those expeditions himself, but he did select two of the most competent colonels in the region, Colonels Shelby and Elijah Clarke, to lead the attacks.

By late August, groups of armed frontiersmen began to arrive at the well-known rendezvous points at Sycamore Shoals and Quaker Meadows. Sycamore Shoals was located on the swift-flowing Watauga River near Elizabethtown, Tennessee, and Quaker Meadows was located several miles west of Hickory, North Carolina. When companies of frontiersmen arrived at the rendezvous points, they were then organized into battalions, and battalions were then assigned to regiments commanded by senior militia colonels. In addition to the officers previously mentioned, other well-known leaders also arrived to join the expedition against Ferguson. Among them were Benjamin Cleveland, a Virginian with a solid reputation as an Indian fighter; William Chronicle, a veteran of many skirmishes

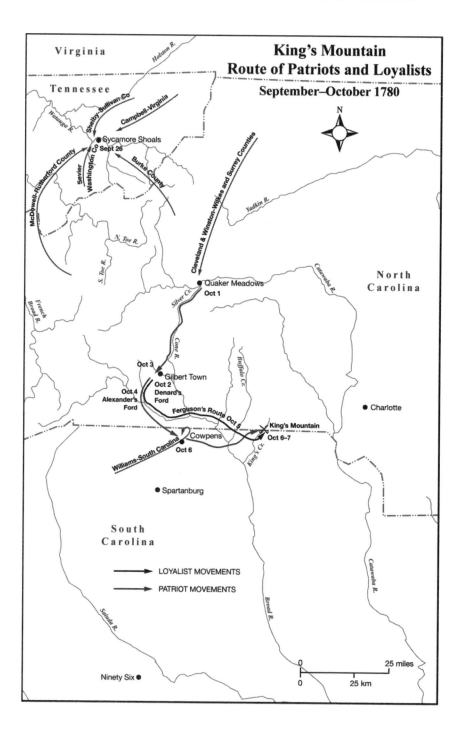

with the Loyalists; and Joseph Winston, a rough and tumble frontiersman and Indian fighter, who began fighting Indians at the age of 17.

As more and more frontiersmen flocked to the rendezvous points, the colonels concluded that, based on the size of the force, it should be commanded by a general.

Colonel McDowell was dispatched with a written request to General Gates imploring him to appoint a general officer to command the militia forces. Generals were in short supply in the southern army, so Gates never bothered to respond to the request. The senior militia colonels, putting seniority aside, selected Colonel William Campbell as overall commander of their forces. Without question, Campbell was the best educated, and most imposing figure among the group of colonels.

As their leaders hurried to finalize their plans, their men made final preparations for their long trek over the mountains. Many had brought their wives and children to the rendezvous points, and arrangements had to be made for their safety after the men departed. In the southern highlands fall comes early, and by late September the leaves had already turned on the heavily forested mountains, carpeting them with bright red, yellow and orange. Temperatures were comfortably warm by midday, but could plunge to near freezing at night and in the early morning. In the evenings the men and their families huddled around hundreds of campfires to hear exhortations from their leaders, and preachers. One such preacher was Presbyterian minister Reverend Samuel Doak, a Princeton graduate, who delivered a fiery sermon condemning Ferguson and his Loyalists, and calling upon the frontier militiamen to be "the sword of the Lord and of Gideon."[28] During the final days before their departure, the frontiersmen cleaned their long-barreled flintlock rifles, poured molten lead into molds to form rifle balls, and sharpened their hunting knives and tomahawks, while their wives and mothers filled the men's saddlebags with parched corn and maple sugar.

At dawn on the chilly autumn morning of September 26, 1780, the frontiersmen saddled their horses, and said sad goodbyes to their wives and families. Officers and sergeants shouted orders, and the men picked up their rifles, mounted their horses and formed a long column that snaked along Gap Creek headed for Shelving Rock, the first day's destination. It was a long 20-mile march.

Meanwhile Ferguson, having learned of the large force of rebel frontiersmen preparing to cross the mountains, decided to leave Gilbert Town on September 27, one day after the Patriots began their long march across the Blue Ridge. Ferguson was faced with a conundrum. He could have marched 70 miles east to Charlotte, where the major portion of Cornwallis's army was posted, but if he did so, he would have failed to protect the British army's exposed left flank. General Cornwallis certainly would have looked with disfavor on such a move. On the other hand, if he chose to stand and fight at Gilbert Town, his outnumbered force would in all likelihood lose. Ferguson was well aware that the rebels had assembled a force of over one thousand men at Sycamore Shoals, and would likely link up with a 350-man force at Quaker Meadows. Ferguson had under his command a force of some 950 men, a mixed force of battle-hardened Loyalists from New York and New Jersey, and local Loyalist militia, many of whom were recent and untrained recruits. His New York and New Jersey Loyalists numbered around 150 men. Ferguson knew he could not remain at Gilbert Town and fight the Patriots, nor could he retreat to Charlotte and face dishonor. He therefore selected another course of action. He would neither retreat, nor make his stand at Gilbert Town. Instead he decided to maneuver south of Charlotte in foothills along the North Carolina–South Carolina border. Ferguson also knew that by moving to the border area he would be within an easy two-day ride of the British outpost at Ninety Six in South Carolina, a potential source of supplies and reinforcements.

After his arrival in the border area, Ferguson attempted to spread the word among the local residents of the approach of the barbarous mountain men hoping they would rally to join his force. He issued a proclamation, and had it read widely in the settlements throughout the region. The proclamation characterized the overmountain men as barbarians and ruffians, and described their intentions for the area east of the mountains: "If you want to be pinioned, robbed, and murdered and see your wives and daughters abused by the dregs of mankind . . . If you choose to be pissed upon these mongrels say so at once."[29] Few among the uncommitted population were convinced to side with the British.

While Ferguson moved south toward the South Carolina border, Campbell's overmountain men continued their march. When their cattle herd began to slow their progress, the Patriots butchered part of the herd for a fresh supply of meat, and left the remainder of the herd behind. The next day, the Patriot column waded across the Toe River and began its ascent up Roan Mountain. When the column reached the 4,500-foot summit it began to snow. The lightly clad horsemen shivered from the cold as their horses picked their way through the rocky windswept Yellow Mountain Gap. The column halted at dusk to gather firewood and build campfires that would keep them from freezing during the night.

The following morning Colonel Campbell decided to split the column to increase the speed of their march, and lessen the chance that they would be intercepted and ambushed. Campbell led the Virginians down one trail, while Shelby and Sevier followed a second trail. Both trails led to the second rendezvous point, McDowell's plantation at Quaker Meadow, near Morganton, North Carolina. Both columns reached the rendezvous point by August 31. After linking up with the North and South Carolina troops already encamped at Quaker Meadow, the Patriot force numbered around 1,400 men. Wasting no time, the small army of Patriots set off the next morning in search of Ferguson and his men.

Marching down Silver Creek toward Gilbert Town, Colonel Campbell was forced to halt his column after a half-day's march. A light drizzle soon turned into a torrential downpour that flooded the streams, and turned the trail into a muddy morass. The chilling rains continued through the night soaking the men and their equipment. Men wrapped their rifles in blankets and hunting shirts to keep them dry, and munched handfuls of wet parched corn. The rains continued through the night and the following morning. Ignoring the rain, Campbell and his men resumed their march after daybreak. After a long wet march, they halted at dusk, still about 16 miles short of Gilbert Town. Unaware that Ferguson and his Loyalists had departed Gilbert Town, the expedition's colonels addressed their men the following morning to give them final instructions for the upcoming battle. After giving any man an opportunity to back out, the fiery Patriot Colonel Isaac Shelby summarized his orders as follows, "When we encounter the enemy, don't wait for the word of command. Let each one of you be your own officer, and do the very best you can, taking every care you can of yourselves, and availing yourselves of every advantage that chance may throw your way."[30]

When the overmountain men reached Gilbert Town on October 2, they were surprised to learn that Ferguson and his Loyalists had departed five days earlier. That same evening Campbell convened a council of war with his commanders. The colonels were in agreement that they would pursue Ferguson's force the following morning. They also agreed that the weakest horses and foot soldiers would be left behind to follow as fast as they could. The trimmed-down force rode out of camp at first light. In all, there were 950 well-mounted and well-armed men in the column.

After departing Gilbert Town, Major Ferguson followed a slow and meandering course south toward the South Carolina border. Ferguson had two objectives in mind when he marched south toward South Carolina. First, he hoped to intercept Colonel Elijah Clarke and his Georgia rebels, who were marching toward the Cowpens where they hoped to link up with Campbell's larger force.[31] Second, Ferguson hoped that he would receive reinforcements from the British outpost at Ninety Six. Ferguson wrote to Colonel Cruger, the commander at Ninety Six on September 30, requesting a large militia reinforcement. But his hopes were in vain, for Cruger's garrison consisted of less than half the number of troops requested by Ferguson.[32]

The Loyalist column continued slowly southward fording rain-swollen rivers and creeks. Encumbered with supply wagons, Ferguson's column covered only a few miles each day. On October 3, Ferguson and his Loyalists reached Tate's plantation, located one mile from Buffalo Creek near the border between North Carolina and South Carolina. Ferguson spent two full days at the plantation waiting for his wagons to catch up. He used the time to determine the location of his pursuers. On October 5, Loyalist spies reported to Ferguson that Campbell's force had reached the Cowpens, where they were reinforced by hundreds of South Carolina and Georgia militiamen. That intelligence was accurate, Campbell's force had been joined by four hundred militiamen from Georgia and South Carolina. Cowpens was less than 25 miles from Tate's Plantation.

Ferguson knew that he was running out of options. He therefore decided to move closer to Charlotte. On the evening of October 5, as Ferguson's men prepared for an early morning march, the British commander hastily wrote a dispatch addressed to General Cornwallis in Charlotte,

My Lord:—A doubt does not remain with regard to the intelligence I sent your Lordship. They are since joined by Clarke and Sumter—of course are become an object of some consequence. Happily their leaders are obliged to feed their followers with such hopes, and so to flatter with accounts of our weaknesses and fear, that, if necessary, I should hope for success against them myself; but numbers compared, that must be doubtful.

I am on my march towards you, by a road leading from Cherokee Ford, north of Kings' Mountain. Three or four hundred good soldiers, part dragoons, would finish the business. Something must be done soon. This is their last push in this quarter, etc.

Patrick Ferguson.[33]

What Patrick Ferguson did not know was that Lord Cornwallis's army was in no shape to render assistance. Cornwallis's army had reached Charlotte during late September, but the arduous march from Camden had taken its toll. The march through the Sand Hills and Piedmont regions of the Carolinas in mid-ninety-degree temperatures had exhausted Cornwallis's troops. Many of were suffering with fevers even before they departed Camden. Cornwallis himself came down with debilitating fever when he reached Charlotte. Moreover, both Lieutenant Colonel Tarleton and his deputy commander, George Hanger, were down with fever and unfit for duty. Making matters worse, British supply lines were stretched to breaking point. Partisan and militia forces led by Marion, Sumter, and others were attacking resupply trains moving north toward Charlotte on a daily basis. Tarleton's deputy, George Hanger, had brought most of Tarleton's Legion to Charlotte before he fell ill, but Cornwallis was unwilling to reinforce Ferguson with the Legion under an untested commander. He was also concerned about the security of his own headquarters at Charlotte.

Ferguson knew that he still had a chance to reach Charlotte, if he moved quickly. Lieutenant Anthony Allaire, a New York Loyalist serving in Ferguson's corps wrote on October 6, that the Loyalist troops, "Got in motion at four-o'clock in the morning," on Friday, October 6.[34] After departing Tate's plantation, Ferguson marched his men and wagons north along Cherokee Road that ran between Buffalo and Kings Creeks. He then crossed a branch of Kings Creek, and continued north until he reached a trail that led east toward Kings Mountain. Ferguson's column was only some 35 miles from Charlotte, when they reached Kings Mountain late in the day.

Kings Mountain is located at the southern extremity of Crowders Mountain. The two mountains and the saddle that connects them are oriented in a northeast to southwest direction, and their slopes face east and west. Both mountains are remnants of an ancient mountain chain that towered thousands of feet above sea level when first formed more than four hundred million years ago. During the American Revolution, both mountains were covered with old-growth forests.

When Ferguson's column reached the southern tip of Kings Mountain, the Scottish highlander scanned the terrain and ordered his men to climb the wooded slopes to reach a rock-covered ridgeline. As evening approached, Ferguson's men established a camp atop the ridge. The lower end of the oblong ridgeline was open and extended a few hundred yards before dropping into a saddle before rising again toward the higher elevations of the mountain. The width of the open area atop the ridgeline was 60 to 120 yards across, and the side slopes were covered with boulders, and ancient hardwood trees that measured six or more feet in diameter, and towered hundreds of feet in the air.

Instead of marching to Charlotte, Ferguson decided to make a stand at Kings Mountain. According to legend, Ferguson declared to his men that, ". . . he was on King's Mountain, that he was king of that mountain, and God Almighty could not drive him from it."[35]

That evening, Ferguson wrote his final letter to General Cornwallis:

Kings Mountain, Oct 6, 1780—I have arrived today at Kings Mountain and I have taken a post where I do not think I can be forced by a stronger enemy than that against us. I have wrote for the militia assembling under Colonel Floyd to join me tomorrow evening if not destined for another service. I understand that we have little or no reinforcement to expect from Col Cruger or his militia immediately. Good soldiers as reserve behind our riflemen and a few real dragoons to second with effect and support the flank of our horse militia upon the enemy flanks would enable us to act decisively and vigorously as it is with Colonel Floyd. We do not think ourselves inferior to the enemy, if you are pleased to, order us forward. But help so near at hand, it appeared to me improper of myself to commit anything to hazard.

s// Major Patrick Ferguson.[36]

As Ferguson's troops established their camp at Kings Mountain, Campbell's men prepared for a night march. Spies reported that Ferguson's force halted for their noon meal just short of Kings Mountain, and planned to march up the ridge, and establish a fortified encampment later that day.[37] Campbell and his colonels had also received intelligence that Lieutenant Tarleton's Legion would reinforce Ferguson within two days. Therefore, they were convinced that they had to move quickly to attack Ferguson the following day. Around 9 p.m., the lead column of the Campbell's force departed the Cowpens. More than nine hundred men, mounted on the strongest and fleetest horses, rode out of camp. An equal number of dismounted men, and the horses that were in weaker condition, were ordered to follow the forward column.[38]

The night march along rough muddy country roads was long and difficult. It soon began to rain. The men wrapped up the flintlocks of their rifles to keep them dry. Just after sunrise, the lead elements of the column forded the rain-swollen Broad River, and proceeded at a slow gait along a winding path that led toward a looming mountain ridgeline. The lead elements of the column were less than 10 miles from Kings Mountain, but the Virginians had taken a wrong turn and were struggling to catch up with forward units.[39] The morning drizzle soon turned to rain. The men and horses were weary and hungry after their night-long ride, but their commanders refused to halt for a breakfast meal. During short halts, the men munched on hard dry kernels of Indian corn, sharing some with their near-starving horses. Around noon the weather cleared, and a cool breeze swept across the hills.

When the head of the column reached a meetinghouse, the column was ordered to halt for a short rest. During the break, a Patriot named George Watkins approached the officers. Watkins, who had been taken prisoner by the Loyalists, was on his way home on parole. Watkins informed the officers that they were within a mile of the enemy. He also warned the officers that Ferguson had placed a picket force on the road ahead. After receiving Watkins' information, Campbell and his colonels met to plan their attack on Ferguson's encampment. According to the official report of the battle that was sent to Congress, ". . . the colonels agreed that Colonel Shelby's regiment would form a column in the center, with Colonel Campbell's regiment and part of Cleveland's regiment on the left, and the other part of Colonel Cleveland's regiment and Colonel Sevier's regiment on the right.[39] Once Ferguson's position on the ridge was completely encircled, the attack would begin.

Three columns of Patriots rode forward at a slow trot. Colonel Shelby's men from the center column surprised Ferguson's picket guard, and captured them without firing a shot.[40] Moments later, the Americans captured a boy who had just come from Ferguson's camp. When some of the men asked the boy how they could recognize Ferguson, he responded saying that he was wearing a checked shirt, and possibly a duster.[41]

Around 3:00 p.m., the Patriot force began to move silently into their final attack positions around the base of Kings Mountain, where they dismounted, fastened their loose equipment to their saddles, and tied their horses to trees before forming around their mounted officers to receive their final instructions.

James Collins, a member of Major Chronicle's regiment, which attacked up the steep northeast slope of the ridge, later wrote,

> Each leader made a short speech in his own way to his men, desiring every coward to be off immediately. Here I confess I would have been excused, for my feelings were not that pleasant. They may be attributed to my youth, not being quite seventeen... but I could not quite swallow the appellation of a coward . . . We were soon set in motion, every man throwing four or five balls in his mouth to prevent thirst, also to be in readiness to reload quick.[42]

Another 16-year-old, Private Young of Colonel Williams South Carolina regiment that attacked up the north slope, wrote, "The orders were at the firing of the first gun for every man to raise a whoop, rush forward, and fight his way as he best could."[43] Having lost his shoes, Young had to make the attack barefoot, armed with a large old musket and two musket balls.

Surprise was lost when a picket post fired upon Colonel Shelby's Kentucky riflemen as they approached the southeastern end of the ridge. Captain Alexander Chesney, a Loyalist officer, had just returned from checking on the picket posts when he heard the firing. He later wrote, "So rapid was the attack that I was in the act of dismounting . . . when we heard their (pickets) firing . . . I immediately paraded the men and posted the officers."[44] Colonel Shelby ordered his men to hold their fire until they began to ascend the slope of the ridge. Meanwhile, Colonel Campbell, hearing the firing on the opposite side of the ridge, ordered his Virginians to begin their assault up the slope. He ordered the Virginians to "shout like hell and fight like devils."[45] The whooping and hollering was soon taken up by Shelby's Kentuckians followed by Patriot troops all around the mountain.

Atop the ridge, Ferguson and his deputy, Captain Abraham DePeyster, tried to restore order among the surprised Loyalist troops. He mounted his horse and rode along the top of the ridge, blowing his silver whistle to signal his troops to assemble in volley-firing formations along the crest of the ridge. By that time, the attackers were swarming up the slopes on both sides of the ridge. The most immediate threat was on the narrow southeastern tip of the ridge, where Shelby and Campbell's men were attacking up opposite slopes. The frontiersmen were attacking Indian fashion, dodging up the slope and firing their rifles from the cover provided by the huge trees and rocks on the slope. Their rifle fire was deadly accurate, dropping Loyalist after Loyalist. Ferguson's men were answering with trained volley fire from atop the ridge. Leonard Hise, who attacked up the slope with Campbell's Virginians, managed to fire three shots before he was shot twice in the left arm. His comrades assisted him in reloading as he continued up the slope. He then took a bullet in the left leg, and a few steps later he was wounded again, this time in the right thigh. After falling to the ground, another musket ball struck his chest before he was carried off the field. He later wrote that he fired a total of 16 shots before he was carried off the mountain. Somehow he survived, receiving a pension from the government at the age of 77.[46]

Meanwhile Major Ferguson observed that the volley fire was not halting the rebel advance up the slopes, and ordered a bayonet charge down the slope in Colonel Campbell's sector. The downhill bayonet charge took Campbell's men by surprise, and they fell back down the slope pursued by their enemies. Some never made it. John Fields, one of Campbell's Virginians, received three bayonet wounds, one in the thigh, one in the hip, and one in his breast—he too survived.[47] Lieutenant Allaire led the bayonet charge on horseback. As he rode down the slope, he spotted one of Colonel Campbell's officers, and felled him with a saber blow. Bayonet charges were also made down the steep slopes off the northeastern side of the ridge in Major Chronicle's sector. Chronicle was shot and killed as he attempted to rally his men, as was William Raab, standing a few feet away from Chronicle. Enraged by the loss of two of their best officers, Chronicle's men counterattacked and drove the Loyalists back up the slope. As they neared the crest, Ferguson's men launched another bayonet assault. Robert Henry, one of Chronicle's men, was cocking his rifle when an enemy soldier stabbed him in the hand and thigh knocking him to the ground. More bayonet-wielding Loyalists moved in for the kill. By that time, Henry's comrades had reloaded their rifles, and opened fire into their ranks, driving them back up the ridge.[48] William Griffis of North Carolina, and Frederick Fisher of Virginia also received painful bayonet wounds in the counterattacks.[49]

South Carolinian Thomas Young participated in the attack in Colonel Williams's sector. In his detailed description of the battle, he wrote,

> . . . Ben Hollingsworth and I took right up the side of the mountain, and fought our way, from tree to tree, up to the summit. I recollect I stood behind one tree, and fired until the bark was nearly all knocked off, and my eyes were filled with it. One fellow shaved me pretty close, for his bullet took a piece of my gunstock. Before I was aware of it, I found myself between my own regiment and the enemy . . .[50]

The battle had reached a critical point. Everything was at stake for the Patriots and the Loyalists. It is at such moments that leadership in battle counts the most. The situation in Colonel Campbell's area was most critical. The Virginians were driven back down the slope, across a ravine, and partway up another slope. Colonel Campbell rode after his men, and convinced them to return to the fight. After reloading their rifles, the Virginians turned and charged back up the slope, driving the enemy before them. After almost reaching the top of the ridge, the Virginians were once again driven back. On their third attempt, Campbell's and Shelby's men finally gained a foothold atop the ridge. Although the bayonet charges met with some success, most of the Loyalist musket fire passed over the heads of the Patriots. Ferguson's men had forgotten that when firing downhill, you must aim low to hit your target. Conversely, the Patriot rifle fire was extremely accurate, killing and wounding dozens of Loyalists.

All around the mountain, the Patriots continued to gain ground on the slopes. Atop the ridgeline, the situation was chaotic. Flame and smoke covered the slopes and top of the ridge, and clamor of battle and the rattle of musketry reverberated around the surrounding hills. Ferguson and his officers attempted to shift their forces to meet the most threatened areas of their perimeter. Ferguson ordered his reserves to the southwest side of the perimeter to repel assaults by Campbell, Shelby, and Sevier's men. At the same time, colonels Williams, Cleveland and McDowell were gaining ground on northeastern side of Ferguson's perimeter. Ferguson again shifted his reserves to meet the new threat. That was a fatal mistake, since it enabled Campbell's, Shelby's, and Sevier's riflemen to gain a toehold on the southeastern tip of the ridge. Once atop the ridge, the frontiersmen began driving the Ferguson's Loyalists down into a narrower area atop the ridgeline, where the tents and the headquarters were set up.

The slopes on the northeastern portion of the ridgeline were more precipitous than those climbed by Campbell's and Shelby's men, and the attacks on that portion of the ridgeline by Williams's South Carolinians, and Cleveland's North Carolina mountain men got off to a slow start. Swampy ground at the base of the ridge slowed their approach. Nevertheless, the Carolina Patriots slowly fought their way up the slope. When Colonel William's horse was struck with a ball, he sprang from the animal and rushed forward on foot. Just as his men gained the top of the ridgeline, Williams fell mortally wounded, but his men held on atop the ridgeline. On the opposite slope, Colonel McDowell's and Major Joseph Winston's North Carolina men were also gaining ground, sealing off every possible escape route on the northeastern side of the ridgeline. The noose around Ferguson's Loyalists tightened.

Despite the calamity, Ferguson refused to yield. He moved from one group of Loyalists to another, blowing his silver whistle and encouraging his men to continue the fight and resist the Patriot assaults. When several of his officers including his second-in-command, Captain DePeyster, suggested that further resistance was useless, he told them that he would never yield "to such a damned banditti."[51]

Confusion and panic soon broke out in the Loyalist ranks. Campbell's, Shelby's and Sevier's men finally broke the ranks of the elite New York and New Jersey Loyalist troops, and the survivors fled in disorder down into the saddle between the two ends of the ridgeline where their camp and wagons stood. Other Loyalist militiamen cowered among the wagons, putting up little resistance. Some waved bits of white cloth begging for quarter. Sensing that all was lost, Ferguson, still mounted on his dapple-gray stallion, made a desperate attempt to break through the rebel cordon and escape. Joined by several horsemen, Ferguson and his party galloped past his headquarters tents in the saddle, and then wheeled right and headed for a path that led down the mountain. When Ferguson's party reached the path, they ran into a group of Patriot riflemen deployed on both sides of the trail. Two officers were immediately shot from their saddles, and Ferguson was hit in the arm, hip, and chest, but remained in the saddle. Seconds later he was shot in the forehead by a ball that knocked him from the saddle, but his foot was caught in a stirrup. Patriot marksmen continued to fire at Ferguson's lifeless body as it was dragged along the ground. A group of Loyalists finally managed to grab the reins of Ferguson's horse and loosened his foot. Afterwards, his men hid his body behind some large rocks.

After Ferguson was killed, Captain DePeyster assumed command of the Loyalists. His tenure as commander was short. The overmountain men, and Piedmont militiamen tightened their cordon, pushing the Loyalists into an area about 50 square yards. DePeyster ordered his men to raise white flags and his troops began shouting "Quarter, Quarter." Many of the Patriots continued to fire into the compact group of Loyalists shouting, "Buford's Play," referring to Tarleton's massacre of Buford's troops at the Wax-

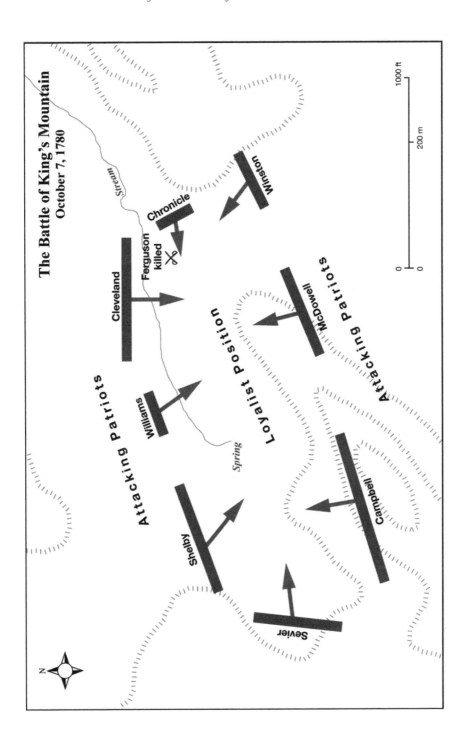

The Battle of King's Mountain
October 7, 1780

haws. Colonel Campbell, with the assistance of several other officers, attempted to regain control of their men and stop the slaughter. Campbell shouted to the Loyalists to ground their muskets and sit on the ground. He then interposed himself between his men and the terrified Loyalists. The firing dwindled then stopped, and a resounding cheer rose from the top of the ridgeline. The battle had lasted a total of one hour and five minutes.

James P. Collins, a young Patriot, surveyed the scene atop the ridge, and later wrote that, ". . . the dead lay in heaps on all sides, while the groans of the wounded were heard in every direction . . . I could not refrain from shedding tears." Nevertheless, Collins felt compelled to have a look at Ferguson's corpse. He later wrote that, "almost fifty rifles must have been leveled at him at the same time; seven rifle balls had passed through his body, both of his arms were broken, and his hat and clothing were literally shot to pieces."[52]

Once the guns grew silent, the Patriot commanders began to attend to the needs of the wounded, and tally up their losses and those of the enemy. There were no physicians in the Patriot ranks. The frontiersmen were used to looking after themselves and their comrades. On the Loyalist side, there was at least one surgeon, Uzal Johnson of New Jersey, who had travelled to South Carolina with the American Volunteers, a Loyalist unit serving in Ferguson's command. Johnson treated wounded Loyalists and Patriots alike.[53] As darkness fell on the mountain, a large number of dead and wounded still lay where they had fallen on the wooded slopes of the ridge.

Patriot partisan forces achieved a decisive victory over the Loyalists at Kings Mountain. Patriot and Loyalist casualty reports indicate that it was, in fact, a lopsided victory. Ferguson's force numbered some 1,125 men at the start of the battle, while the Patriot forces actually participating in the battle, numbered only around 940 men. American doctrine states that an attacking force should have a 3:1 advantage over the defenders to insure success.

American losses in the official report of the battle under Campbell's, Shelby's, and Cleveland's signature, were 28 killed, and 62 wounded. A breakdown of the losses was also included in the report as follows: one colonel (Williams), one major, one captain, two lieutenants, four ensigns, and 19 privates were killed, and one major, three captains, three lieutenants and 55 privates were wounded.[54] Losses for the Loyalist Regulars, and the Loyalist militia were 206 killed, 128 wounded, and 48 officers and six hundred privates taken prisoner.[55] In addition, the Patriots captured some 1,500 stand of arms, and 17 of Ferguson's baggage wagons.

Many reasons have been cited for the Patriot victory at Kings Mountain, and some of the lessons learned are applicable to all special operations forces. First, the overmountain men were better armed than their enemies. They were armed for the most part with a variety of long-range hunting rifles that were accurate at distances of up to 300 yards. Most of the frontiersmen were experienced subsistence hunters and Indian fighters, capable of hitting their targets at those ranges. Most of Ferguson's men were armed with the British Brown Bess muskets that were only effective at ranges less than 100 yards. Only a few of Ferguson's men were armed with rifles.

Secondly, the terrain at Kings Mountain was ideally suited for the tactics used by the Patriots. Using fire and movement, individuals and small groups of riflemen advanced up the slopes taking advantage of the natural cover provided by large trees and rocks. On the other hand, Ferguson's troops attempted to use volley fire, and bayonet charges to defend their positions atop the ridge. Most of the volleys of musket passed well over the heads of the Patriots, or lodged harmlessly in the huge tree trunks. The bayonet charges met with only temporary success, and Patriot marksmen shot many of the bayonet-wielding Loyalists as they attempted to withdraw back up the slopes.

Additionally, the Patriot forces were highly mobile, and capable of covering great distances in a short amount of time, even in the roughest terrain. They were not encumbered with supply and baggage wagons, and never hesitated to leave their dismounted men and weaker horses behind when speed was of the essence. On the other hand, Ferguson used wagons to carry his supplies, baggage, and plunder, slowing his progress through the backcountry. Finally, as a result of their difficult lives on the frontier, the overmountain men possessed the endurance, stamina, conditioning, and self-reliance to carry the day at Kings Mountain.

The Patriot army did not linger at Kings Mountain after the victory. At dawn on the following day, the troops arose, and made preparations to march. Food was in short supply, and many believed that Loyalist reinforcements were on their way to the area. A burial detail of Virginians and Loyalist prisoners was left behind, under Colonel Campbell's personal supervision, to bury the dead. Some corpses were buried in hastily dug pits, while others were laid in shallow depressions and trenches, and then covered with rocks, dirt, and brush. The Loyalist prisoners interred Major Ferguson's body. The corpse was cleaned and wrapped in an animal hide before it was buried alongside his loyal female servant, Virginia Sal, who was also shot and killed during the battle. In keeping with the highland tradition, a mound of stones or cairn was built over their graves. After the burial parties departed the area, many of the corpses were dug up and devoured by wolves, foxes, and wild hogs.[56]

Before departing Ferguson's camp, the Patriots burned the wagons, and rigged slings between pairs of horses to carry the non-ambulatory wounded of both sides. The Loyalist prisoners were then lined up for their march to captivity in North Carolina, carrying their own disabled weapons and those of their fallen comrades. The march commenced around 10:00 a.m. on October 8. The march was slow and painful for the wounded, and the column did not reach Gilbert Town in North Carolina until October 14, one week after the battle. After establishing a camp 10 miles north of the town, the Patriot colonels convened courts-martial to try the most notorious of the Loyalist prisoners on charges ranging from treason and desertion from Patriot militia, to murder and incitement of Indian attacks. Thirty-six Loyalist prisoners were convicted, and sentenced to hang, but only nine were executed. The others received last-minute reprieves. The executions were carried out on the evening of October 14, and the Patriots broke camp at 2:00 a.m. the following day. The overmountain men first marched north to Quaker Meadows before dispersing to return to their homes over the mountains. The remaining prisoners were turned over to Colonel Cleveland for disposition.

The rise of partisan warfare in the southern theater during 1780 thwarted Cornwallis's plan to extend British control into the backcountry of South Carolina. Moreover, it made his first incursion into North Carolina a short one. The American victory at Kings Mountain was a devastating blow to Loyalist morale in the Carolinas, and it spurred many neutral citizens to actively oppose the British and their Loyalist allies throughout the South. The American victory also left the British army's western flank exposed, and partisan attacks continued to disrupt the British supply route to Charleston. As a consequence, Cornwallis decided to withdraw from North Carolina, and move 60 miles south to Winnsboro, South Carolina. The march over the muddy red clay country roads was a nightmare. The most seriously ill soldiers, including Lord Cornwallis, filled the wagons that followed the marching column.

The American victory at Kings Mountain also led to more partisan attacks against isolated British and Loyalist outposts in the backcountry of South Carolina, and the main British army at Winnsboro was soon threatened on both of its flanks. Partisan leader Colonel Francis Marion operated between the Santee and Pee Dee Rivers, and from that locale he was able to threaten supply and communication lines between the British post at Camden and the main army at Winnsboro. On the British left flank, Brigadier General Thomas Sumter's forces operated west of the Broad River, threatening the strategically important outpost at Ninety Six. Both Francis Marion and Thomas Sumter continued to make life in the backcountry as miserable and dangerous as possible for the British.

The partisan victories of 1780 gave Major General Nathaniel Greene, the southern Continental Army's new commander, time to rebuild and reorganize his forces following General Gates' disastrous defeat at Camden in August of 1780. Unlike his predecessor, General Nathaniel Greene demonstrated that militia and partisan forces could augment Continental troops in major battles with British Regulars. During the year 1781, militia and partisan troops fought side by side with Continental troops at the Cowpens, Guilford Courthouse, Eutaw Springs, and conducted a number of other attacks on isolated British forts and outposts in the Carolinas and Georgia.

8

THE WHALEBOAT WARS

TO LIEUTENANT-COLONEL DAVID HUMPHREYS
INSTRUCTIONS
Sir,
You will take command of such of the Detachments of Water Guards, now on the River, as you may think necessary, and with them attempt to surprise and bring off Genl. Kyphausen from Morris's House on York Island, or Sir Henry Clinton from Kennedy's in the City, if, from the Tide Weather, and other Circumstances, you shall judge the Enterprise to be practical. In the execution of it, you will be guided by your own discretion; and I have only to suggest, that secrecy, rapidity, and prudence in making good your retreat, will be indispensably necessary to insure success. Given at Head-Quarters, 23d of December, 1780.
—*George Washington to David Humphreys*[1]

AFTER GENERAL WILLIAM HOWE MARCHED HIS VICTORIOUS BRITish army into New York in September 1776, British naval and ground forces stationed in Manhattan, Staten Island, Long Island, and on the surrounding waters soon found themselves targets of Patriot raiding parties. The raiders crossed the rivers, the Lower Bay, and Long Island Sound in whaleboats and other small craft to reach their targets. The raids were carefully planned based on timely intelligence, and were often approved by the highest echelons of the Continental Army. The targets of the raids were varied, and included attacks on British naval vessels and merchant ships, raids on British outposts and garrisons, raids on supply depots to

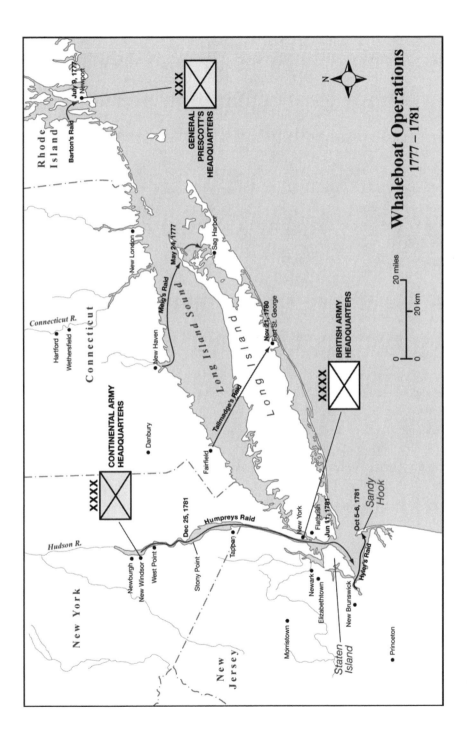

capture badly needed supplies, and raids on British headquarters. In the latter case, the raiders' mission was to capture high-ranking officers who could later be exchanged for high-ranking American prisoners. The raiders demonstrated a high degree of expertise in infiltration and exfiltration on their raids into hostile territory. They also were experts in small-boat handling, and other specialized skills. The men who led these raids also demonstrated remarkable adaptability, improvisation, and innovation. Not all the raids were carried out using Continental or militia troops. Privateers often carried out attacks on British navy ships and merchantmen. While some raids ended in failure, a remarkable number were successful. Since the raids occurred on a frequent basis, many were not described in detail in official reports, journals, and other correspondence. This chapter will describe a few.

Most of the raids conducted in New Jersey, New York, Connecticut, and Rhode Island involved the use of whaleboats to infiltrate and exfiltrate the target areas. A whaleboat is a narrow open boat that is pointed at the stern and bow, which enables it to move forwards or backwards equally well. Most of the whaleboats used by the raiders were 36 feet in length or longer, and some had mounted swivel guns. Swivel guns of that era were small cannon mounted on a swiveling stand or fork allowing for a wide arc of movement. Most of the guns were capable of firing both grapeshot and small-caliber round shot. Typically, whaleboats were oared in pairs, and could be moved swiftly and silently by the oarsmen. Some of the boats also had dismountable masts and sails. Whaleboats were also relatively light, and could be beached and carried to hiding places when not in use. In short, the whaleboat was an ideal watercraft for carrying out raids in hostile territory.

COLONEL MEIGS'S RAID ON SAG HARBOR

On May 24, 1777, a force of Continental troops under the command of Colonel Return Jonathan Meigs conducted a raid on Sag Harbor, Long Island. The raid was partially in response to a successful British raid on Danbury, Connecticut one month earlier. Meigs was chosen to lead the raid by Brigadier General Samuel Holden Parsons of the Connecticut Line. Parsons conceived and organized the raid after receiving intelligence indicating that the British were collecting forage on the east end of Long

Island to supply their army in New York. Sergeant Nathan Jennings of the 1st Connecticut Regiment had grown up in Sag Harbor, and probably provided that intelligence. Jennings later wrote, "I volunteered myself to Colonel Meigs, stating the situation of Sag Harbor and the strength of the British guard and how easy they might be taken, and that I would pilot him and a detachment of troops across the sound to Long Island . . . The colonel was highly pleased with my plan . . ."[2]

General Parsons and Colonel Meigs carefully selected men from several Connecticut regiments for the raiding party. Fourteen officers including one major, four captains, and nine subalterns were selected, along with 220 enlisted men. The raiders' mission was three-fold. First, they were to attack British outposts in the vicinity of Sag Harbor. Secondly, they were ordered to destroy the forage that had been collected, and finally they were to capture or destroy any British ships in the harbor. It was a difficult mission fraught with hazards.

The raiders had to row across Long Island Sound from Connecticut, and enter Gardiners Bay on the northwest tip of Long Island. The raiders then had to land in the vicinity of Sag Harbor to surprise and destroy British outposts, locate and destroy the forage collected by the British, and capture or destroy British ships anchored in the harbor. Finally, they had to make their way back to their whaleboats, and row back across Long Island Sound to Connecticut. The average width of Long Island Sound is about 21 miles. The course set by the raiders was much longer. Fog, squalls, tidal currents, high winds and rough seas make any crossing in small boats hazardous. Moreover, British navy ships prowled the sound on a daily basis in search of American shipping. Meigs was fully aware of the hazards, and selected his whaleboat crews from the most experienced seamen living along the Connecticut coasts; men who had made their living fishing and trading along Long Island Sound prior to the war.

Colonel Meigs was born in Middletown, Connecticut in 1740. When war broke out in April 1775, Meigs led a light infantry company to Boston. There he was promoted to major in the 2d Connecticut Regiment of the Continental Army. Later that year, he served as a battalion commander in Colonel Benedict Arnold's expedition that marched 350 miles through Maine's uncharted wilderness to attack Quebec. During the failed assault on Quebec City, Meigs was captured and imprisoned. He was formally exchanged in January 1777, and subsequently joined the 3d Connecticut Regiment of the Connecticut Line. On May 12 of the same year, he was promoted to lieutenant colonel, and assumed command of the 6th Connecticut Regiment, when its commander became ill. Based on his previous military experience, Meigs was well qualified to lead the raid on Sag Harbor.

Colonel Meigs's raiders boarded 13 whaleboats, and departed New Haven, Connecticut on May 21, 1777. They proceeded some 14 miles along the coast of Connecticut before they were forced to land at Guilford due to high winds and rough seas. The weather grew worse the following day, and the raiders were delayed until the afternoon of May 23.

Departing Guilford around 1:00 p.m., Meigs's convoy of whaleboats, escorted by two armed sloops and one unarmed sloop, set off across the Sound. After five hours of hard rowing the convoy arrived off Southold on the northern fork of Long Island around 6:00 p.m. Meigs knew from intelligence reports that British troops had departed the northern fork of Long Island two days earlier. He also knew that 60 enemy troops were stationed at Sag Harbor some 15 miles away.

After landing on a rocky beach near Southold, the raiders carried their whaleboats across the beach to a wooded area. Meigs then selected 130 men, who were to march overland to Gardiners Bay. At nightfall, the raiders set off for Gardiners Bay carrying 11 of the whaleboats. After reaching the bay, the raiders boarded the whaleboats and rowed south to a landing point about four miles from Sag Harbor. They beached their boats at the landing point around midnight. After concealing the boats in a wooded area and posting a guard, Meigs split his raiding party into separate detachments. Each detachment was assigned to attack a specific set of targets. The targets included guard posts and barracks, shipping in the harbor, and buildings where forage was stored.

The detachments moved out in the order in which the targets were to be attacked. Leading the march were the detachments assigned to attack and silence the guard posts. The raiders marched off in the darkness with fixed bayonets, determined not to fire a shot unless absolutely necessary. Captain Troop followed the lead detachments. His mission was to secure the vessels in the harbor, and the buildings on the wharf where the forage was stored.

After a four-mile march in the dark, the raiders silenced the British sentry posts, and then slipped quietly into the harbor town. All went according to plan until a crewman on a 12-gun schooner spotted the raiders moving along the wharf. The alarm was given, and the schooner opened fire on the raiders with grape and round shot.[3] The raiders returned fire, and a 45-minute firefight ensued. The schooner was anchored only 50 yards offshore, within easy range of Meigs' marksmen. While the American marksmen kept the crew of the schooner pinned down, other raiders set fire to ships and the forage storage buildings. With the town and ships ablaze, the raiders hunted down the remaining British soldiers in the town. They soon succeeded in killing or capturing all but six of the enemy soldiers and sailors.

The raid was a huge success. Twelve brigs and sloops were set afire, along with the armed schooner. In addition, some 120 tons of pressed hay, oats, corn and other forage were destroyed. The fires along the wharf also consumed 10 hogsheads of rum, and a large quantity of other supplies. Having accomplished the mission, Colonel Meigs ordered his raiders to withdraw to their whaleboats with the ninety prisoners taken during the raid. The raiders reached Southold safely, and by 2:00 p.m. on May 24, Meig's raiders had crossed Long Island Sound and arrived at Gilford, Connecticut with their prisoners without suffering any casualties.

The raid on Sag Harbor was an amazing success even by today's standards. In less than 25 hours, the raiding party traveled nearly nintey miles on water and land to reach and destroy their targets, and then returned safely with ninety prisoners. The success of the raid was the result of sound planning, accurate intelligence support, and carefully selected troops, who possessed incredible stamina and courage.

THE CAPTURE OF GENERAL PRESCOTT

On December 7, 1776, two months after British troops occupied New York City, a British fleet entered Narragansett Bay and captured the town of Newport, Rhode Island. The British navy planned to use Newport and its large sheltered harbor as a major base of operations on the New England coastline. During the first few months of the occupation, Newport was relatively peaceful, although the citizens were resentful that the British insisted on quartering their soldiers in private residences. However, the situation grew even worse after British General Hugh Percy resigned his command, and departed Newport in May 1777. His successor, Brigadier General Richard Prescott allowed his troops to chop down most of the town's trees for use as firewood. His men also used the town's wooden sidewalks, wooden grave markers, and fences for the same purpose. Making matters worse, the 52-year-old brigadier had a pompous and arrogant demeanor that aggravated the town's citizens and their leaders. Having spent 10 months as a prisoner of the Americans after the fall of Montreal in November 1775, Prescott had nothing but distain for Americans, and treated them accordingly. His treatment of American prisoners was particularly harsh and cruel, and would not be forgotten.

After assuming command at Newport in the spring of 1777, Prescott relocated his headquarters from Newport to Overing (Prescott) farm located about five miles out of town. Locating his headquarters in a somewhat isolated location was not, as it turned out, a wise decision. On June 20, an American prisoner named Coffin escaped from the British in Newport, and entered the American lines. He was taken to the headquarters of Major William Barton, the commander of Rhode Island troops stationed in the area. Coffin provided Barton with detailed information on the disposition of British forces at Newport, including the location of General Prescott's headquarters. He was able to describe in minute detail the layout of the house in which Prescott resided, and the security arrangements at the headquarters.[4] Coffin's information was corroborated a few days later by a British deserter.[5] Barton was determined to exploit the new intelligence.

William Barton was born in Warren in Bristol County, Rhode Island in 1748. When war broke out in 1775, Barton joined Rhode Island State troops as a corporal. He marched to Boston with the Rhode Island troops, and fought in the Battle of Bunker (Breed's) Hill. By the summer of 1777, he had risen through the ranks to major in the Continental Army's Rhode Island Line. Barton's headquarters was at Tiverton, Rhode Island, 15 miles north of Newport on the eastern shore of Narragansett Bay. From that location, Barton was able to monitor British troop and naval dispositions on and around Aquidneck Island where the town of Newport is located.

After learning the location of General Prescott's headquarters outside Newport, Barton devised a bold, but risky plan to capture the British general. He then met with his immediate superior, Colonel Joseph Stanton, to seek his approval. The colonel gave Barton wide authority "to attack the enemy when and where he pleased."[6] Barton then began to organize the raid. He approached five of his most reliable and experienced officers and, without going into any detail, asked if they would volunteer for an important and hazardous mission that could cost them their lives. All five immediately volunteered.

Major Barton's immediate concern was the procurement of the necessary number of whaleboats to carry out the mission. There were only two available for his immediate use, but within a few days he procured a total of five whaleboats, and equipped them for the raid. Barton delayed the selection of enlisted men for the raid until the last possible moment. He was concerned that any flurry of activity within the American lines might alert the British. When he was ready to select his raiders, Barton ordered the entire regiment of Rhode Island Continentals to assemble for parade. He then announced that he was looking for brave men who would be willing to participate in a very dangerous mission without giving any details. Barton then asked that anyone, who wished to volunteer, to take two steps forward. Then according to Barton, "Without *one exception*, or a *moment's hesitation* the whole regiment advanced."[7]

Barton then walked through the ranks speaking to each man to determine his qualifications and experience. In particular, Barton wanted highly disciplined men with combat experience particularly those who had experience in handling of small boats. He eventually selected 36 men with the requisite qualifications. Several free African-American Rhode Islanders were among those selected.

Major Barton selected July 4, 1777 as the date to launch the raid. It is likely that he chose that date, not because it was the first anniversary of the nation's independence, but rather because the moon was at very end of its last quarter on that date. After the raiders departed Tiverton and began crossing Mount Hope Bay to Bristol, a severe thunderstorm separated the boats. Major Barton's boat and one other landed at Bristol just after midnight. After landing, Barton made his way to the headquarters of the local American commander, where he received updated intelligence. A British deserter who had just crossed over to the American lines reported that there had not been any recent changes in British troop dispositions or headquarters on the island.

The following morning the three boats that were blown off course during the storm arrived at Bristol. Barton and his officers then rowed to Hog Island on a reconnaissance mission. From Hog Island, the party had a better view of British ships operating in the northern portion of Narragansett Bay, and the British troop dispositions ashore. During their reconnaissance, Barton revealed the details of the mission to his officers, and their assignments during the raid. Barton's plan called for raiders to row west across the bay from Bristol to Warwick Neck on the mainland. From Warwick Neck, the raiders would follow a course that would take them between Patience and Prudence islands before landing at Coddington Cove about five miles north of Newport. After landing, Barton planned to move overland to Prescott's headquarters at Overing farm. After briefing his officers on the details of his plan, and stressing the need for absolute secrecy, Major Barton and his officers returned to Bristol to complete final preparations for the raid.

On the evening of July 6, Major Barton and his raiders rowed across Narragansett Bay to Warwick Neck. On the following day, a weather front passed through the area, and severe storms forced a two-day weather delay. On July 9, the weather cleared, and Barton decided to launch the raid that same night. About 9:00 p.m., Barton assembled his men, and disclosed the purpose and plans for the raid. The raiders were then broken down into squads. Each squad was led by an officer, and assigned a specific mission. The boats were numbered, and each squad was assigned to a numbered boat. After the briefing, the raiders proceeded directly to the whaleboats waiting on the shoreline.

Major Barton was a meticulous planner, who attempted to plan for all possible contingencies. His main concern was that his boats would be spotted as they crossed the bay. With that in mind, he directed the commanding officer at Warwick Neck that if he heard three musket shots, he was to send all available boats to rescue the raiders.

At nightfall, the raiders pushed off in their whaleboats and using muffled oars they began rowing across the bay. Major Barton was in the lead boat holding a ten-foot pole with a handkerchief attached for the other boats to follow. As the boats slipped silently past the north end of Prudence Island, the raiders heard sentinels on nearby British ships shouting the cry, "All's Well!" When the boats were rowed into Coddington Cove north of Newport, some raiders thought they heard the sound of running horses, but Barton ordered his men to keep rowing toward the beach. After landing unopposed on the beach, the raiders hid their boats and left one man behind to guard each boat.

General Prescott's headquarters lay about one mile from the shoreline. Five raider squads marched silently through the darkness; each one had a specific mission. The house that served as General Prescott's headquarters had three entrances; one each on the south, east, and west sides of the house. The first squad was assigned to block the south door, second squad the west, and third the east. The fourth squad was assigned to guard the road that led to the house, while the fifth squad remained in reserve to react to any unforeseen events. As they approached the farm, the raiders slipped silently past an outbuilding that served as a guardhouse, and bypassed a house that was used as quarters for a cavalry troop. Continuing on, Barton and his men slowly advanced toward the house where the general slept. As the raiders neared the front yard gate of the house, they were challenged by a sentry. Most of the raiders were still concealed by a row of trees. The sentry repeated the challenge. Major Barton then walked forward toward the sentry exclaiming, "Damn you, we have no counter-sign, have you seen any rebels tonight?" When he was within arm's length of the nervous sentry, Barton grabbed the soldier's musket, and told him that he was a prisoner, and that if he resisted, or gave any further alarm, he would be killed on the spot. Barton then asked the terrified sentry whether the general was in the house. When the sentry confirmed that he was, Major Barton deployed his squads around the house. Major Barton accompanied the squad that was assigned to cover the south door. At Barton's direction, the squad burst into the house, while the other squads blocked the other doors to prevent anyone from escaping. In the ensuing confusion inside the house, an off-duty British soldier managed to escape in his sleepwear. The terrified soldier ran to the house that quartered the cavalry troop, and awakened the troop commander. The officer listened to the soldier's story, but concluded that the hysterical young soldier had had a nightmare, and ordered him to return to his post. Had the entire guard force turned out to investigate the soldier's claim, Major Barton's raid would have ended as a disastrous failure.

Meanwhile, Major Barton was questioning a civilian taken prisoner on the first floor of the house. Under duress, the man told Barton that the general was sleeping in a bedroom on the second floor of the house. Accompanied by four of his raiders including Jack Sisson, a powerful African American soldier, Barton climbed the stairs to the second floor, and burst into General Prescott's sleeping quarters. Alarmed and half asleep, the general realized that he was about to be taken prisoner, and asked if he could dress, but Barton refused, and he was escorted out of the house in his nightshirt. Prescott's aide, who was asleep in another bedroom, was aroused by the commotion and attempted to escape by jumping through a window, but was quickly apprehended in the yard of the house.

With the chance of discovery increasing by the minute, Barton ordered his squads to return to their boats. The raiders and their two prisoners—General Prescott and his aide—rushed through the darkness, and arrived safely at their boats. The general was placed in Major Barton's boat, and his aide in another, and the small flotilla of whaleboats shoved off. When the boats were a few hundred yards from shore, they heard a cannon discharge, and saw three sky rockets ascend into the still dark sky. The deck watchmen on the British ships anchored in the bay saw the flares, but did not recognize the cause for the alarm onshore, and did not alert their captains. Barton ordered his men manning the oars to quicken the pace. The raiders reached the safety of Warwick Neck shortly after daybreak. The duration of the raid from the time the raiders departed Warwick to the time they returned was six and one-half hours.

After landing at Warwick, Major Barton ordered a coach and took General Prescott and his aide to Providence, Rhode Island where he turned them over to Major General Joseph Spencer, commander of Rhode Island Continental troops. General Prescott was eventually sent to Philadelphia to await exchange, and was eventually exchanged for Major General Charles Lee on the orders of General Washington and the Continental Congress. General Prescott earned the dubious distinction of being the only British general captured twice during America's War of Independence.

Major Barton's successful raid on General Prescott's headquarters demonstrated several principles that still apply to present-day special operations. First, the operation was based on timely and accurate intelligence on the British dispositions in Newport and the surrounding area. Capturing an enemy high-ranking officer in hostile territory, and returning him to safely to friendly territory is one of the most difficult tasks a special operations force can undertake. Major Barton also had a keen awareness of the critical importance of secrecy and security prior to the execution phase of the raid. Speed is always critical during a raid of this type, and the short duration of this raid was remarkable. It took only six and one-half hours to complete the mission. The waterborne infiltration and exfiltration phases were conducted flawlessly without alerting the enemy. Additionally, the tactics used by Major Barton to isolate and secure the enemy headquarters and its surroundings closely resemble tactics that are still used today by special operations forces. Finally, the selection process used by Major Barton insured that his 36 volunteers had the requisite qualifications required for the raid.

BENJAMIN TALLMADGE'S RAID ON FORT ST. GEORGE, LONG ISLAND

By the summer of 1780, the war in the north was approaching a stalemate. British troops still occupied New York City, but a large number of British troops were sent south to capture Charleston, South Carolina as part of British new southern strategy to retain the Carolinas, Georgia, and Virginia for the Crown. However, the British troops based in New York were far from passive. In June, Hessian General Wilhelm von Knyphausen led an attack on the Continental Army encampment at Morristown. Knyphausen's advance met stiff resistance from New Jersey militia at Connecticut Farms on June 7, 1780, and he was forced to withdraw to New York City. Undeterred, the British made a second attempt to reach Morristown. On June 23, General Knyphausen's six-thousand-man force met an American force led by Major General Nathaniel Greene at Springfield, New Jersey. Knyphausen and his troops were repulsed by a mixed force of Continentals and militia, and withdrew to Staten Island.

The arrival of French troops at Newport, Rhode Island on July 11,

1780, bolstered the American cause, virtually ending any possibility of a British victory in the Northern Theater. Nevertheless, the British remained determined to hold New York City and most of Long Island. General Washington knew that he could not attack and retake New York City without the full cooperation and support of the French corps based at Newport and the French navy, and the French were adamantly opposed to an attack on the city. Nevertheless, Washington continued to keep the pressure on the British garrison in New York City by attacking their sources of food, forage and other supplies.

By the summer of 1780, foraging operations in New Jersey were difficult and costly for the British. The reorganized New Jersey militia, aided by local partisans, attacked almost every foraging party sent into New Jersey's northern counties. Therefore, the British had to increasingly rely on Long Island as a source of food, and forage for their horses.

Long Island extends 118 miles eastward from New York Harbor to Montauk Point, and has a land area of 1,401 square miles. During the Revolutionary War, Long Island was largely rural and agricultural with widely scattered settlements, farms, and estates. In 1771, the combined population of Kings, Nassau, and Suffolk counties numbered around eighteen thousand, including a significant number of African-American slaves. Many of Long Island's villages and towns had large Loyalist populations.[8] Many Connecticut Loyalists escaped persecution by crossing the Sound to Long Island, after the British occupied New York City and Long Island. A similar Loyalist migration occurred when the French took control of Newport, Rhode Island in July 1780. Although many New York Patriots fled to Connecticut when the British took control of New York City, a significant number remained in the city and on Long Island. Some of those who remained behind British lines provided valuable intelligence to the Continental Army and Congress. In 1778, several Patriots who resided in the city or on Long Island joined the highly secretive Culper Spy Ring organized by Benjamin Tallmadge. The ring was intended to gather intelligence on the British army's troop movements, positions, fortifications and plans in the New York area including Long Island. The spies used elaborate codes, invisible ink, and dead drops to prepare and transport their reports to Washington's headquarters.

Benjamin Tallmage was born in 1754 at his father's Presbyterian parsonage in Brookhaven in Suffolk, Long Island.[9] After spending his youth on Long Island, Tallmadge was accepted to Yale College, graduating in 1773. While attending classes at Yale, Tallmadge became close friends with Nathan Hale and several other Patriots who would later join the ranks of the Continental Army. After graduation, Tallmadge was hired as a teacher in Wethersfield, Connecticut. In June 1776, he was commissioned as a lieutenant in a Connecticut regiment. Tallmadge's regiment fought in the battle of Long Island in August 1776. In December of the same year, he was promoted to captain of the 1st Troop of Colonel Elisha Sheldon's 2d Continental Dragoons. Tallmadge later assumed command of one of the Dragoons' squadrons. When he was promoted to the rank of major in April 1777, Tallmadge assumed duties as a field officer in the Connecticut Line.[10]

Major Tallmadge soon gained the attention of General Washington, who had a passion for intelligence gathering. The commander-in-chief recruited some of his best and brightest officers in the Continental Army for intelligence duties. Although General Charles Scott was nominally in charge of intelligence operations, he was also in charge of the army's light infantry units, and Washington was aware that Scott devoted little attention to recruiting and training spy networks. Consequently, Washington assigned Tallmadge to Scott's staff to assist in those efforts. From the start, there was a mutual enmity between the two officers. Tallmadge attempted to accommodate his superior in every way, but Scott resented the fact that Tallmadge had Washington's confidence. He thought Tallmadge's efforts to organize and train a permanent spy network were unnecessary, and preferred traditional intelligence-gathering methods such as military reconnaissance using his own military assets. Scott also insisted that intelligence reports pass through formal channels before reaching the desk of the commander-in-chief. As a result, the reports were of little value by the time they reached Washington. By late 1780, Washington concluded that the traditional method of gathering and processing intelligence was failing, and that a new approach was needed. He therefore bypassed Scott, and instructed Tallmadge to form a civilian spy network in New York and Long Island, and pass intelligence reports in a timely manner directly to him.[11]

In 1778, Tallmadge opened a "private correspondence with some persons in New York (for Gen. Washington), which lasted through the war."[12] Tallmadge never revealed in detail his role in recruiting, organizing, and training the agents who formed the Culper Spy Ring, but it is clear that he was the spy master of the network. During the campaigns of 1778 and 1779, Tallmadge, in addition to his regular duties as a Dragoon field officer, was deeply involved in intelligence operations in New York and all parts of Long Island.

In early 1780, Tallmadge conceived a plan to disrupt British control of Long Island using a special force of dismounted dragoons. General Washington approved Tallmadge's plan, and gave him a special command of dismounted dragoons and a body of horse. After organizing his dragoons into two companies of light infantry, Tallmadge moved his command to North Stamford, Connecticut. From that location, Tallmadge was able to monitor British troop movements both on the mainland and on Long Island.

After British Major John Andre was captured on September 20, 1780, foiling Benedict Arnold's plot to turn the key fortress at West Point over to the British, Washington assigned Tallmadge to serve as Andre's escort during his trial. Since Andre and Tallmadge were both in the spy business, Washington probably hoped that Andre would reveal additional details of Benedict Arnold's plot to Tallmadge before his execution. Tallmadge never completely broke his self-imposed silence on his role in the spy business during the war, but late in life he defended Andre's memory as an honorable man.[13]

When Tallmadge returned to his command, he began to refine his plans for a raid on British fortifications on Long Island. He was informed by one of his agents on Long Island that the British had occupied the St. George Manor House on Mastic Neck in Suffolk County. The house was owned by Judge William Smith, an ardent Patriot. After occupying the property, British and Loyalist troops began fortifying the property around the manor, erecting a 12-foot high triangular stockade. The fort was surrounded by a deep ditch, and was encircled with an abatis of sharpened pickets. A strongly barricaded house stood inside the stockade.[14] According to Tallmadge, Fort St. George was the "most easterly point of defense," for the British on Long Island.[15]

Tallmadge's agents kept him informed on the progress of the work on Fort St. George. When the work was nearing completion, Tallmadge presented his plan to Washington. The plan called for Tallmadge's dismounted dragoons to cross Long Island Sound in whaleboats, and land on Long Island's western shore. They would then march across the island to Mastic Neck on the eastern shore where they would attack and destroy Fort St. George. Washington thought the plan too risky, and at first refused to approve the mission. However, Tallmadge did not abandon the project. He continued to press his agents for more information about British troop dispositions in Suffolk County and the fort itself.

Around the end of October, or the beginning of November, Tallmadge decided to conduct his own personal reconnaissance. He crossed Long Island Sound and reconnoitered possible landing beaches, and then crossed the island to get a close-up look at Fort St. George. By that time, work on the fort had been completed, and a store of supplies and arms had been moved inside the enclosure. Tallmadge also learned that a large quantity of hay and other forage had been collected by the British and was stored at Coram, located in the center of Long Island, about 14 miles from Fort St. George. After completing his personal reconnaissance, Tallmadge re-crossed the sound and returned to his headquarters. He then provided General Washington with the details of his reconnaissance, and sought permission to launch the raid. On November 11, Washington replied to Tallmadge by letter giving his approval for the raid.[16] By November 21, all preparations for the raid were completed, and the raid commenced about 4:00 p.m. the same day.

Major Tallmadge's two companies of dismounted dragoons departed Fairfield, Connecticut in eight whaleboats and rowed across Long Island Sound. The raiders completed the 12-mile crossing in about five hours landing at a place called Old Man's Harbor (present-day Mount Sinai) at around 9:00 pm. Tallmadge selected Old Man's Harbor because of its remoteness. The nearest British force was stationed more than 30 miles away, at Huntington. After concealing his boats, and posting a detachment to guard them, Tallmadge and his raiders began a 20-mile night march across the island. After marching about four or five hours, heavy winds swept across the island, followed by a heavy downpour. Tallmadge decided to return to his boats to wait out the storm. After returning to the harbor, the men took shelter under the overturned whaleboats, and tried to get some sleep. It continued to rain heavily throughout the night, and most of the following day. By the evening of November 22, the rains finally began to abate, and Tallmadge ordered his men to set out again across the island. By 4:00 a.m., the raiders were within two miles of Fort St. George. Tallmadge called a halt to make the final arrangements for the attack, and allow his men time to rest and eat their rations.

Tallmadge planned to lead the main column directly through the main gate of the fort, while two smaller detachments cut their way through the abatis, and assaulted the ramparts on both sides of the triangular fort. The detachments were ordered not to begin their assaults until the British fired on the main column. The attack got underway at dawn. The pioneers, who moved ahead of the main column, got within 40 yards of the stockade before the enemy discovered them. A sentry stationed outside the main gate challenged the lead elements, and then fired his musket to alarm the garrison inside the fort. This was the signal for the assault to begin. Tallmadge's sergeant rushed forward and bayonetted the sentry, and all detachments rushed forward, each vying for the honor of being the first to enter the fort. Tallmadge led a bayonet charge through the main gate toward the fort's parade ground, where the British troops were beginning to assemble. Simultaneously, the two smaller dragoon detachments carried the ramparts on the other two sides of the fort shouting, "Washington and glory."[17] The British struck their colors signaling the fort's surrender. The Americans thought they had captured the fort without firing a shot. Suddenly, musket fire erupted from the windows of the barricaded house within the fort. Tallmadge ordered his men to load and return fire on the house. When the British hold-outs refused to surrender, Tallmadge led a charge on the house. After the pioneers cut their way through the barricades and doors of the house, the raiders rushed inside to clear the rooms of enemy snipers. Snipers hiding on the upper floor of the house were bayonetted, and thrown out the windows to the ground. Tallmadge and his officers had to intervene to prevent a full-scale massacre of the captives.

Meanwhile, British ships anchored near the fort were preparing to get underway. Tallmadge had the fort's cannon turned on the ships, and fired several warning shots in their direction. The ships then returned to their berths, and were secured by the raiders. Once all the prisoners were disarmed and placed under guard, the raiders began to demolish the fortifications. The raiders also destroyed the supplies stored inside the fort, and burned the ships and their cargoes. Once the destruction of the fort was complete, the raiders and their prisoners began their long march back across the island.

Tallmadge had one more task to complete before he departed Long Island. He wanted to destroy the large quantity of forage stored at Coram. He ordered his second-in- command, Captain Edgar, to continue marching toward Old Man's Harbor with the main body and prisoners. Then he selected a dozen raiders, mounted them on horses captured at Fort St. George, and rode off to destroy the stores at Coram. After a grueling 14-mile ride, Tallmadge's detachment galloped into Coram, charged the guards, and set the storage buildings on fire. Tallmadge's dragoons then rode to the prearranged rendezvous point, and rejoined the main column. After allowing time for his men to rest, Tallmadge ordered his men to continue their march to the boats. The entire raiding party and their prisoners reached their boats around 4:00 p.m. and by sundown, the whaleboats were loaded and the raiders set off across the Sound. The boats were separated during the night crossing, but all eight whaleboats arrived safely at Fairfield by 1:00 a.m. the following day.

In the aftermath of the raid, Tallmadge received the thanks of his commander-in-chief, General Washington and the Congress.[18] Fort St. George, the strongest fortification in Suffolk County, was destroyed along with a large quantity of supplies and ammunition. The forage collected by the British in Suffolk County and stored at Coram was also destroyed. With winter coming on, this was a serious setback for the British mounted units, artillery, and supply trains. Additionally, the Americans captured some 50 prisoners, including a colonel, a captain, a lieutenant and a surgeon, all of whom could be exchanged for American officers of commensurate rank. During the raid, Tallmadge had one man seriously wounded, while the British and the Loyalist allies lost a total of seven killed and wounded.[19]

One of Tallmadge's raiders, 25-year-old Sergeant Elijah Churchill, was awarded the Badge of Military Merit for his actions during the raid. General Washington established the award for soldiers who demonstrated unusual gallantry in battle, and Churchill is one of only three known recipients. His citation reads in part,

> That Sergeant Elijah Churchill of the 2d Regiment of Light Dragoons, in the several enterprises against Fort George and Fort Slongo on Long Island, acted in a very conspicuous and singularly meritorious part; that at the head of each body of attack he not only acquitted himself with great gallantry, firmness and address; but that surprise in one instance, and the success of the attack in the other, proceeded in a considerable degree from his conduct and management.[20]

Tallmadge's raid on Fort George demonstrates the importance of Special Reconnaissance (SR) in planning and executing any direct action mission. A modern definition of SR reads in part, "SR entails reconnaissance and surveillance actions conduced as SO [Special Operations] in hostile, denied, or diplomatically sensitive environments to collect or verify information of strategic or operational significance, employing military capabilities not normally found in CF [Conventional Forces]."[21] While planning the raid on Fort George, Tallmadge continued to receive updated intelligence from agents of the Culper Ring operating on Long Island. Fort George was under constant surveillance by Tallmadge's agents before the raid. A large detachment of British troops stationed near Huntington was also kept under surveillance, since those troops could reinforce Fort George, or cut off Tallmadge's raiders as they withdrew across the Island. Tallmadge also took the precaution of conducting his own special reconnaissance of the target, routes of infiltration and exfiltration, and potential landing points on Long Island Sound.

Another factor contributing to the success of the raid was the facts that Tallmadge was able to personally select and train his men. The raiders were on detached service from the 2d Dragoons for several months prior to the raid, during which time they performed other missions behind British lines. Finally, the versatility and skills of the raiders is worthy of mention. They were skilled and experienced in both mounted and dismounted combat, and were skilled in small-boat handling. They also had the stamina required to cover great distances to reach and attack targets behind enemy lines, and then safely exfiltrate back to friendly territory.

LIEUTENANT COLONEL DAVID HUMPHREYS' CLANDESTINE MISSION

Both the British and the Americans attempted to capture prominent general officers during the War for Independence. Abduction of general officers disrupted campaign planning and execution, and created a need for special-security units such as Washington's elite Life Guards, to provide for the personal security and protection of high-ranking officers. In December 1780, Washington tasked Lieutenant Colonel David Humphreys, one of his most trusted aides, to undertake one such clandestine abduction mission.

Twenty-nine-year-old David Humphreys was a Yale graduate and aspiring poet. He was the youngest of five children of a Connecticut Congregational parson. As a youth, he demonstrated a keen interest in books of varied subjects. He entered Yale College when he was 15 years old, and graduated with distinguished honors four years later. After graduation, Humphreys became principal at a public school in Wethersfield, Connecticut. Two years later he was hired as a private tutor for a prominent Tory family in Yonkers, New York, during which time he became committed to the revolutionary cause. In July 1776, he enlisted in the Continental Army, accepting the post of adjutant in the 2d Connecticut Regiment, where he made the acquaintance of Colonel Meigs. During the spring of 1777, Humphreys accompanied Colonel Meigs on his successful raid on Sag Harbor. A year later, Humphreys led his own 30-man raid on Long Island during which his men destroyed three British ships without losing a man. After the raid, he was promoted to captain, and soon thereafter to the rank of major. On June 23, 1780, Humphreys assumed duties as one of the aides-de-camp on General Washington's personal staff. He demonstrated his skills as a staff officer, and quickly gained Washington's special trust and confidence.

Washington had a keen interest and appreciation for covert operations including spying, gunrunning, defections, and kidnappings. Moreover, he often involved himself in the planning of those operations, and personally selected the men who would lead them. In December 1780, Washington conceived a plan to kidnap Hessian General Knyphausen from his head-quarters at Morris House on Staten Island, or General Sir Henry Clinton from his headquarters in New York City, whichever was found to be most practical. He selected David Humphries to lead the covert operation, and gave him wide latitude in carrying out his mission.

Lieutenant Colonel Humphreys' hand-selected detachment of 27 men set out by barge and whaleboats from Dobbs Ferry on the Hudson River during the bone-chilling evening of Christmas Day 1780. The river was nearly frozen over, and clogged with huge pieces of ice, making any boat trip extremely hazardous, particularly at night. As the boats slipped into the channel under a new moon, only the groaning, creaking, and cracking of the river's ice broke the stillness of the night. Humphreys hoped to cover the 25 miles to New York City around midnight, but nature did not favor the plan. As the boats approached the city, strong northwest winds scattered the boats, and swept them past the lower end of Manhattan. One boat landed at Sandy Hook, New Jersey, and another put in on a remote beach on Staten Island miles away from General Knyphausen's headquarters. Over the next few days, Humphreys located all of his boats and their half-frozen crews, but his men were in no condition to carry out their mission. Humphreys decided to abort the mission. The detachment then made its way to Brunswick, New Jersey, where it reentered American lines. Humphrey was able to reach Washington's New Windsor headquarters on January 1, 1781, to report the failure of the operation.[22]

The failure of Humphrey's mission can be attributed to several factors, not all of which were under his control. Joint Publication 3-05 stresses the importance of using environmental data in the decision-making process for special operations, from initial planning to execution. Such meterological data is available and easily accessible today, but during the Revolutionary War, such data was very limited. Weather forecasts were based primarily on speculation. Some hydrography data and tidal infor-mation was available to planners, but that too was limited, and often wrong. Planners were aware of the moon's phases, and the use of stars for navigation. It is noteworthy that the infiltration and exfiltration phases of the special operations covered in this chapter were almost always conducted at night during the first few days of a new moon.

Lieutenant Colonel David Humphreys was an extremely intelligent and capable officer, well qualified to undertake the kidnap mission. Whether he had the detailed intelligence necessary to accomplish his mission is unknown. The spy network operating in New York City and on Staten Island may have provided intelligence on headquarters layouts and security measures. Agent reports arrived at Washington's headquarters on a regular basis, and it is likely that Humphreys would have read them. The fact that Humphrey was able to reassemble his widely scattered detachments, and return safely to American lines with all his men is a tribute to his leadership and determination.

WHALEBOAT PARTISANS AND PRIVATEERS

From the arrival of the first British fleet in New York Harbor in June and July 1776, the waters surrounding New York were teeming with British warships and merchantmen. Soon after the British captured New York City, large convoys of merchantmen escorted by Royal Navy ships sailed back and forth across the Atlantic carrying supplies for the British Army. In addition, the normal lucrative trade between the West Indies and New York continued. Schooners and sloops from the West Indies unloaded their cargos of sugar, salt, molasses, and rum on New York's wharves on a daily basis. There were also more than 150 sloops, schooners and barges plying the waters around Manhattan carrying foodstuffs from Tory farms in New Jersey, Staten Island and Long Island to Manhattan.[23] Despite the protection of British guns, the shipping was under constant risk of attacks and seizure by a fleet of American privateers lurking along various rivers, creeks, and coastal inlets along the Jersey shore, and the western shore of Long Island Sound. Between late June 1778 and September 1783, there were 108 engagements on New Jersey's rivers and off the immediate coast of New Jersey.[24] Many of those engagements involved privateer attacks on British shipping sailing in and out of New York. Those attacks drove up maritime insurance rates for British merchant ships, and the captured supplies were an important contribution to the Patriot war effort. The British characterized the whaleboat attacks as acts of piracy, and did not recognize the Letters of Marque issued by the Continental Congress.

Privateer attacks on British merchant ships were most often conducted using armed whaleboats and other small craft, which could slip out of small inlets under the cover of darkness and come alongside a much larger vessel. Armed with boarding pikes, pistols, and cutlasses, the privateers would then board the merchantman, and swarm across the decks to capture the surprised, and often sleeping crewmembers.

When possible, the privateers would attempt to capture the vessel intact, and sail it as a prize to a friendly harbor. If pursued by British navy ships, the whaleboat raiders would seek safety in one of the numerous winding channels and creeks where the heavier draft warships could not follow. If it became apparent that escape with their prize was not possible, the raiders would unload as much booty as their whaleboats could carry, and then set fire to the captured ship.

American Patriots also used whaleboats in raids to capture prominent Loyalists living beyond their normal reach in British-controlled territory. After capture, the Loyalists faced trial and punishment, or were exchanged for Patriots held captive by the British. From 1777 until the end of the war in 1783, no prominent Loyalist living in New York City or on Long Island was completely safe, and immune from capture by American raiders.

Two of the most prominent and active leaders of the whaleboat privateers were William Marriner and Adam Hyler. Both men lived in New Brunswick, New Jersey, and both were deeply involved in the partisan war in northern New Jersey. William Marriner served as a private in Lord Sterling's New Jersey Regiment early in the war. After his service, he operated a tavern on the banks of the Raritan River just outside the town of New Brunswick. The tavern soon became a gathering place for members of his old regiment, whaleboat owners and crewmen, partisans, and local militiamen. Among the latter was a Captain John Schenck of the New Jersey militia. Schenck's family had migrated from Long Island to New Jersey long before the revolution, but they still maintained contact with family and friends living in the Dutch communities around the New Utrecht and Flatbush areas of Long Island.[25] Marriner, Schenck and other Patriots from the New Brunswick area were incensed by British raids on the homes of prominent Patriot leaders in northern New Jersey. Local Loyalists played a key role in planning and conducting the raids, identifying the Patriot leaders and guiding the British to their homes. After capture, the Patriots were often imprisoned on the infamous British prison ships anchored off Manhattan with little hope of survival or exchange. In June 1777, Marriner and Schenck conceived a bold plan to redress the situation.

Marriner and Schenck's plan called for a raiding force to cross the lower bay to the Long Island shore, and make their way to the country homes of prominent Loyalists in the Flatbush area. A list of the prominent Loyalists was soon drawn up. At the top of the list was the Tory mayor of New York, David Matthews; followed by Miles Sherbrook, a personal enemy of Marriner; Jacob Suydam, a wealthy Loyalist; Colonel Axtell, who was commissioned by General Howe to raise a Loyalist regiment on Long Island; and Theophylact Bache, president of the New York Chamber of Commerce.

On the night of June 11, 1777, the raiding force of 26 hand-picked whaleboat men departed the southwest shore of Raritan Bay in two whaleboats. After crossing the choppy bay, the raiders rowed north hugging the shoreline of Staten Island before crossing the Narrows and landing on a beach near New Utrecht. After hiding their whaleboats in a wooded area and posting guards on the boats, Marriner and Schenck organized their men into four squads, each with a specific target. After moving to the homes of their Loyalist targets, the four squads were to strike simultaneously at the appointed hour, breaking into the homes of their intended prisoners to take them captive, then reuniting with the other squads at a designated rally point before returning to the boats.

Moving silently through the darkness, each squad succeeded in reaching their target undetected. After entering the homes of the four Loyalists, two of the squads were surprised to learn that Mayor Matthews and Colonel Axtell were not in residence, but were spending the night in Manhattan. However, the other two squads enjoyed better luck. Although Jacob Suydam was not at his home, the raiders did liberate Captain Alexander Gradon, a Continental officer who was staying with the Suydams while awaiting exchange. Bache was found asleep in his home and taken captive. Marriner had difficulties in tracking down his old enemy, Miles Sherbrook, but finally found him hiding in a neighbor's home. Marinner then withdrew quickly to the rally point at a local church with his captive.

After all the squads reassembled at the rally point, the raiders moved swiftly to their whaleboats, and rowed across the bay landing safely at Matawan by 6:00 a.m.

Although Marriner's first raid did not net the number of prisoners intended, Marriner considered it a success, and was encouraged to launch similar missions on several occasions over the next several months. All of the captives taken in these raids were, "taken back to New Jersey and subsequently exchanged for Patriot leaders or officers of the Continental Army."[26]

Marriner also led attacks against British ships in the waters surrounding New York. On the night of April 8–9, 1780, Marriner and nine whaleboat men rowed down the Raritan River from New Brunswick to Raritan Bay. After crossing the bay, Marriner and his men rowed east to Sandy Hook Bay, where two British ships were at anchorage in a cove inside the tip of the hook. One of the British ships was the powerful guardship HMS *Volcano*, and the other was the brig *Blacksnake*, a Rhode Island privateer that had been taken as a prize by the British. Marriner planned to recapture the *Blacksnake* from under the nose of the *Volcano*, and sail it off to a friendly port as a prize.[27]

Marriner's whaleboat entered the cove in darkness, and approached the stern of the *Blacksnake*. Still undetected, the raiders nudged their boat alongside the *Blacksnake*, and began to board the brig. The captain and the 20-man crew of the *Blacksnake* were asleep in their quarters as Marriner and his men swarmed aboard and silenced the lone deck watchman before he could sound the alarm. The raiders then locked the hatches that led below deck, and posted a guard at the door of the captain's cabin. Marriner ordered his men to cut the anchor cable, and raised enough sail to catch the breeze allowing the brig to slip slowly out of the cove. The deck watch on the *Volcano* never detected the movement of the brig.

By daylight, Marinner's whaleboat and their prize were in the shipping lanes off the coast of New Jersey. Around 6:00 a.m., Marriner and his men spotted the lightly armed schooner *Morning Star* as she made her way up the coastline. With his men manning the *Blacksnake*'s 8-pounders, Merriman sailed alongside the *Morning Star* and demanded her surrender. The captain acceded to the demand, but when he saw the small size of Marriner's prize crew who were boarding his ship, he ordered his crew to resist. It was too late. Marriner's men quickly cut down the captain and his loyal crewmembers, as the others passively looked on in silence. After securing the *Morning Star*, Marriner and his raiders sailed down the New Jersey coast to Toms River, New Jersey. Marriner's daring maritime raid was his last successful operation. He was captured a few weeks later on Long Island. After months of captivity he was paroled, and returned to New Brunswick to resume his career as a tavern owner. By that time, an even more daring privateer had emerged from the New Brunswick area.

Adam Hyler was born in Germany, and may have been impressed for service in the Royal Navy for a time. He arrived in the New Brunswick area before the outbreak of the Revolutionary War, and operated a small fleet of sloops and trading vessels that sailed between New Jersey and New York. When war broke out in 1775, Hyler supported American independence from Great Britain, and became a leader of whaleboat privateers in the New Brunswick area. He may have served under Marriner in the early years of the war, but he soon became an independent captain of the privateers. He came to public attention in New York and New Jersey newspapers in the fall of 1780, after capturing the sloop *Susannah* off Staten Island. Following in Marriner's footsteps, Hyler conducted his own prisoner-hunting raid on Long Island in August 1781. He captured a Loyalist militia officer and a ship's captain, and then returned safely with his captives to New Brunswick.[28] Two months later, Hyler reached the apex of his career as privateer when he led a raid on Sandy Hook against seemingly insurmountable odds.

On the night of October 5–6, 1781, Adam Hyler departed New Brunswick aboard the sloop *Revenge,* with two whaleboats in tow. The privateers arrived at South Amboy at the mouth of the Raritan River at daybreak. Hyler decided to wait for nightfall before crossing Raritan Bay to reach the Sandy Hook anchorage. As darkness descended the *Revenge* set sail across the bay toward the enemy anchorage. A British guard ship stood watch over five smaller ships in the anchorage including three merchantmen and two armed sloops. Both of the sloops mounted more guns than the *Revenge*, and all of the ships were under the cover of the guns of a shore redoubt.

Hyler had the *Revenge* lay off the entrance of the anchorage, and sent one of his whaleboats in to reconnoiter the British ships. Rowing with leather-wrapped oars, the whaleboat men slipped silently into the harbor, and approached each of the smaller craft to determine their alertness. After completing their reconnaissance, the whaleboat men rowed back to the *Revenge* to report their findings to Hyler.

Hyler's men reported that the three merchantmen appeared almost deserted with only a few crewmembers remaining aboard. There were crewmen aboard the armed sloops, but their security was lacking as the whaleboat went unchallenged as it nudged close to each one. Although the whaleboat did not approach the British guard ship, it too appeared to have no one on watch. After listening to the reports, Hyler decided on his plan of action. He assigned one of his whaleboat crews to board the three undermanned merchantmen, while the second whaleboat attacked the smaller of the armed sloops. Meanwhile, the *Revenge* would attack and capture the larger armed sloop.

Having received their orders from Hyler, the two whaleboats set off toward their targets. After giving his whaleboats time to get in close to their targets, Hyler edged the *Revenge* slowly into the anchorage. Once his sloop was abreast of its target, and no more than a few feet apart, Hyler's men tossed their grappling hooks across the enemy ship's bulwarks, and pulled the two vessels together. When the two sloops were inches apart, Hyler and his men leaped over to the enemy deck. The slumbering deck watch was quickly overcome, and the boarders raced to the forecastle where the surprised enemy crew were arming themselves to repel the boarders. Several of those who made it on deck were cut down, while others retreated to the aft deck, dove overboard and swam toward the shore. All resistance ended within minutes, and the *Revenge* crew had control of their prize.

Hyler's two whaleboats met with equal success. The smaller enemy sloop and the three merchantmen were surprised and captured intact without any alarm that would alert the huge guard ship. However, Hyler realized that time was not on his side. Once the enemy crewmembers swam to shore and reached the shore redoubt, a general alarm would be raised. The heavily armed guard ship would then blow the raiders' small flotilla to pieces. Racing against time, Hyler ordered his men to load the cargo, swivel guns, and other plunder from the captured merchantmen and sloops onto the *Revenge* and the two whaleboats. The raiders then set fire to the enemy sloops and two of the merchantmen, sparing another that had a woman and her children aboard. As the raiders reboarded the *Revenge*, the shore battery opened fire, but the redoubt's small cannon lacked the range to reach the ships, and the balls splashed harmlessly into the water. Nonetheless, the cannon fire alerted the crew of the British guard ship, and her crew sprang into action, opening her gun ports and loading her cannon.

Hyler's crewmembers quickly raised the *Revenge*'s sails, and with the whaleboats in tow, the sloop soon exited the harbor. Flames from the burning ships illuminated the dark sky over the anchorage, and the heavy cannon of guard ship roared breaking the silence of the night. Soon the entire anchorage was blanketed in smoke. Off the aft end of the *Revenge*, the waters spouted then frothed as the round shot from the guard ship's cannon tried to reach their fleeing target. Moments later the *Revenge* quickly slipped away into the darkness of the outer bay. There was no pursuit.

The *Revenge*, and the two whaleboats laden with prisoners and booty, reached New Brunswick safely the following day. In addition to destroying four British ships, the whaleboat men had returned with a number of prisoners, sails and cordage stripped from the enemy ships. The plunder also included 250 bushels of wheat, several swivel guns, a cask of gunpowder, and a quantity of dry goods.[29] Following several more successful raids, Adam Hyler died quietly in bed in 1782, at the age of 47.

Despite the fact that many of the privateers who fought the whaleboat wars were motivated as much by profit as patriotism, they made a significant contribution to the war effort. The fledgling Continental Navy was far too small to seriously disrupt the flow of supplies from Great Britain to North America, and interdict the Loyalist commerce in American waters. Congress issued around 1,700 Letters of Marque to some eight hundred armed privateers on a per voyage basis. Without doubt many others sailed without proper authorization. In all, privateers, including whaleboat crews, were credited with capturing or destroying about six hundred British ships. Those losses helped drain the British treasury particularly in the latter stages of the war, and disrupted the entire British economy. Moreover, the captured supplies, weapons, and goods helped supply the needs of the Continental Army.

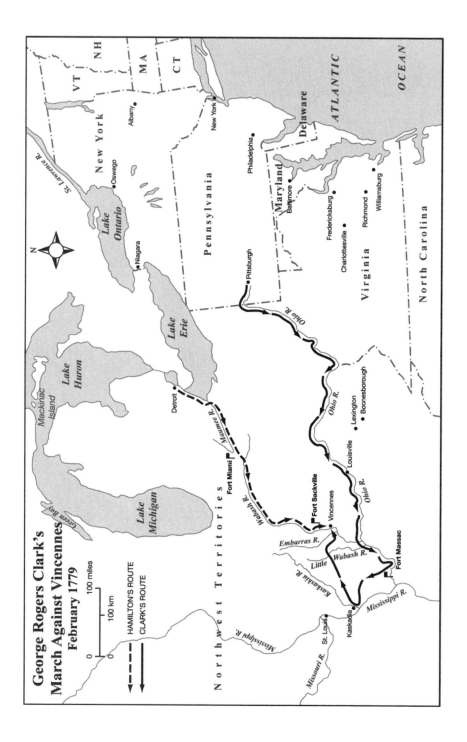

**George Rogers Clark's
March Against Vincennes
February 1779**

HAMILTON'S ROUTE
CLARK'S ROUTE

9

GEORGE ROGERS CLARK'S MARCH TO VINCENNES

February 17, 1779, Marched early crossed Several Rivers very deep sent Mr Kennedy (our commissary) with three Men to cross the River Embara (Embarras) to endeavor to cross if possible and proceed to a plantation (opposite) post Vincent in order to steal Boats or canoes to ferry us across the Wabash—About One hour before sunset We got Near the River Embara found the country all overflown, we strove to find the Wabash traveld till 8 O Clock in mud and water but could find no place encamp on still kept marching on but after some time Mr Kennedy and his party return'd found it impossible to cross the Embara River we found the Water fallen from a small spot of Ground staid there the remainder of the Night drisly and dark Weather.

— From the Journal of Joseph Bowman

WHEN THE REVOLUTIONARY WAR BEGAN IN APRIL 1775, IT HAD little immediate impact on the frontier settlements in Kentucky. Hunters, trappers, land speculators, and other adventurers roamed the region prior to the Revolution, but it was not until Daniel Boone led a team that cleared the "Wilderness Road" through the wilderness from Virginia to central Kentucky that permanent settlers began to arrive in the region. The early settlers were initially more preoccupied with matters important to their survival than the events occurring nearly one thousand miles away in Massachusetts.

The biggest threat to the survival of the settlers was that posed by the Indian tribes that roamed the Kentucky area. During the early months of the Revolution, the British did not incite the Indians to attack the newly arrived settlers in Kentucky probably because their numbers were so few.[1] It was not until 1777 that the British actively began to encourage Indian raids against the American frontier settlements in Virginia and Pennsylvania. Most of the tribes needed little encouragement to launch attacks on those who had recently settled on their hunting grounds. The man most responsible for implementing the new British policy was Henry Hamilton, who was serving as Canada's lieutenant governor at Fort Detroit. Hamilton was born in Ireland, the son of an Irish Member of Parliament. He began his career as a British officer during the French and Indian War, and fought at the battles of Louisbourg and Quebec. After his promotion to brigade major, Hamilton left the British Army to accept a position as lieutenant governor and superintendent of Indian Affairs at Fort Detroit, Michigan. Arriving at his new post in 1775, Hamilton soon managed to establish good relations with Native American tribal leaders in the region.

When the tribes began raiding the settlements in 1777, Hamilton assigned British officers and Canadian militia units to accompany the Indian war parties, ostensibly to prevent the slaughter of noncombatants, but they did little good. The raids were carried out with such zeal that Hamilton soon earned the sobriquet, "the Hair Buyer." While there is no evidence that Hamilton actually paid for scalps, he did shower the Indians with gifts to encourage them to launch raids.

Defense of Virginia's western frontier was a complicated matter. The Virginia Colony's original Royal Charter was vague on Virginia's western boundaries, and one interpretation was that the colony could claim lands all the way west to the Pacific. However, it remained unclear during the Revolution whether Virginia would attempt to exercise claims to the western lands once independence was won, or whether the new national government would assume responsibility for the relatively unsettled western lands beyond the Atlantic seaboard. Complicating matters further, land speculation companies had negotiated with some of the Native American tribes and purchased vast tracts of lands west of the Alleghenies. Nonetheless, Virginia generally assumed responsibility for the defense of the newly opened settlements in the area of present-day Kentucky. At the national level, the Continental Congress and General Washington were concerned about the defense of the area west of the Alleghenies, but the Continental Army simply lacked the resources to mount a successful campaign in the lands beyond the mountains. Kentucky, in particular, was not a high priority for the Congress and the Continental Army. Therefore the Kentucky settlements had to organize their own defense, and seek support from the state of Virginia.

The various settlements in Kentucky were widely scattered, and the inhabitants were for the most part farmers and subsistence hunters. They were willing to take up arms to defend their families and neighbors, but local militiamen and their leaders were initially reluctant to leave their homes and farms to aid other settlements, or carry the war into enemy territory. However, after the Indian raids in the summer of 1777, it was clear that the local militia's defensive strategy was no longer effective, and new centralized leadership was needed. Kentucky needed a strong leader with a broader strategic vision, and the rank and authority to manage the local resources, and petition the Virginia government authorities for additional assistance. The region soon found their man in the person of 23-year-old George Rogers Clark.

George Rogers Clark was born in November of 1752, in Albemarle County, Virginia near Charlottesville. He was the second-born of 10 children, and one of five siblings who served as officers during the Revolutionary War. William Clark, the youngest son, was too young to fight in the Revolution, but with Meriwether Lewis he would lead the Lewis and Clark Expedition (1804–06) to explore the lands west of the Mississippi. The Clark family lived near a plantation owned by Thomas Jefferson's father, but later moved to a plantation in in Caroline County. Clark led the life of typical planter's son. He was tutored at home, and received his common education at local private school, where James Madison was one of his classmates. While away at school, Clark lived with his grandfather, who taught him how to survey land, a necessary skill for any planter who wanted to expand his land holdings.

In 1772, 20-year-old George Rogers Clark made his first trip into the wilderness of western Virginia. Clark was a tall and slender, yet powerful, young man with reddish hair and a fair complexion.[2] Departing Pittsburgh by boat, Clark's party followed the Ohio River as far as the mouth of the Great Kanawha River. After exploring the region; he traveled through the mountains to his home in Virginia. Clark returned to the same area two months later, and surveyed and claimed a plot of land below Wheeling. He also surveyed land for other newly arrived settlers. For the next two years, Clark shuttled back and forth between his father's plantation in Virginia, and his own land along the Ohio River. In 1773, Clark made his first trip to the newly opened Kentucky region. He was impressed with the fertile land and natural resources of the area and wanted to further explore the region, but would be unable to return until 1775. In the interim, Clark had his first wartime experience.

In 1774, war broke out between the Colony of Virginia and the Shawnee and Mingo Indian nations who inhabited the upper Ohio River Valley. The conflict resulted from a long period of escalating violence between white settlers—who were exploring and moving into lands south of the Ohio River (modern-day West Virginia and Kentucky)—and the Indian tribes who held treaty rights to hunt there. Lord Dunmore, Virginia's royal governor, asked Virginia's House of Burgesses to declare war on the hostile Indian nations and to order up an elite volunteer militia force for the campaign. Clark served as a captain of the Virginia militia in this short war, but he saw little, if any, fighting. Nonetheless, he acquired valuable knowledge of the strengths and weaknesses of the militia, as well as the Indian methods of waging war. Clark also learned how to organize a military force, and equip it for a wilderness campaign. He also met a number of militia leaders whose support he would require in future years. More importantly, Clark discovered that he possessed the requisite leadership qualities to be a successful military commander.

After the war, Clark made his first trip to central Kentucky. He was employed by the Ohio Company as a surveyor. His terms of employment allowed him to carve his own lands out of the wilderness as well as the company's. As a landowner himself, Clark soon became embroiled in conflicting land claims in the region. He became convinced that the best solution would be to have the Virginia government clarify the status of the region. He also suggested to the settlers that they should elect delegates to the Virginia General Assembly to represent Kentucky. Following this advice, the settlers elected Clark and a young lawyer from the region to represent them in the Virginia General Assembly. The pair made the long dangerous journey to eastern Virginia carrying petitions that supported the formation of a new Virginia county in Kentucky. Unfortunately, by the time Clark and his companion reached Williamsburg in November, the assembly had already adjourned for the year, and would not reconvene until the following October. Nevertheless, Clark decided to remain in eastern Virginia to advance the interests of the Kentucky settlements.

Clark first visited Virginia's governor, Patrick Henry. The governor was sympathetic to the needs of the Kentucky settlements, which included an urgent request for gunpowder to defend the settlements. He indorsed Clark's request for 500 pounds of powder, and forwarded it to Virginia's Executive Council. At first, the councillors ruled that they could not grant the request, since Kentucky might not be a part of Virginia, but they eventually agreed to lend the powder to "Friends in Distress." The councillors further specified that Clark had to arrange for the safe delivery of the powder, and assume personal responsibility for repayment, if the assembly refused to extend Virginia's jurisdiction over the area. Clark refused to accept the offer on those terms, and cleverly turned up the heat on the council, pointing out that the settlers might be destroyed for want of "this small supply." Clark realized that there was more at stake than the gunpowder. He knew that if his original request was approved, Virginia's government was accepting responsibility for defense of the region, and thereby assuming its jurisdiction over the region. In the end, the council reconsidered Clark's proposal, and informed him that 500 pounds of gunpowder would be sent to Fort Pitt for delivery to George Rogers Clark, for the use of the inhabitants of Kentucky.[3]

When the Virginia General Assembly convened in October 1776, Clark and his fellow delegate argued passionately for the formal recognition of Kentucky as one of the state's counties. With strong support from several influential members of the assembly including Thomas Jefferson, Kentucky County was finally granted recognition in early December 1776. When the new county's government was formed during the summer of 1777, George Rogers Clark was commissioned as a major in the county's militia, making him the senior ranking commander in the huge county.

Clark's appointment as senior officer of militia came just in time. British Governor Henry Hamilton was moving ahead with his plans to launch Indian and Loyalist militia raids against the frontier settlements in Kentucky. Clark had long since concluded that the best strategy for defending Kentucky's settlement was take the offensive, and carry the war to enemy territory. His first priority was to drive the British out of their forward outposts north of the Ohio River, and to defeat their Indian allies that inhabited the region. Clark also wanted to capture Detroit, but that would have to wait.

Before launching the offensive, Clark needed current intelligence on the region of present-day southern Illinois and Indiana. He dispatched agents to the area to determine the status of enemy preparations for raids, the alertness of garrisons occupying forward outposts, and the attitudes of the French inhabitants of the area toward the war. He also sent agents to Spanish-held St. Louis to determine if the Spanish authorities were sympathetic to the American cause. Based on the intelligence collected by his agents, Clark knew that most of the Indian tribes north of the Ohio River had joined the British, but the French inhabitants preferred to remain neutral, or give their tacit support to the American cause. Clark concluded that the British really did not expect the Americans to challenge their control of the region, and decided to launch a phased campaign to eliminate the threat to Kentucky.

Clark chose the town of Kaskaskia as his first objective. The town of some one thousand inhabitants is located 75 miles south of St. Louis on the Mississippi River. Kaskaskia was key to controlling the Mississippi River south of St. Louis, an important supply and trade route between the Spanish settlements and Kentucky. The river was also a convenient avenue of approach for Indian war parties moving south to raid western Kentucky. Clark planned to use Kaskaskia as a forward operating base from which he could launch an overland offensive against the British post at Vincennes.

Clark knew that he lacked the authority to conduct military operations outside his own county, and therefore had to solicit approval for his plans from the Virginia's state government. He also wanted the state government to provide the resources to support his plans. So in October 1777, Clark departed Kentucky, arriving in Williamsburg on December 10. He briefed Governor Patrick Henry and his advisors on his plan, and they agreed to support it, but legislative approval was still necessary. The Executive Council received the governor's recommendations in early January 1778, and authorized the expenditure of £1,200 to finance the campaign. In addition, Clark was formally placed in command of the expedition, with the rank of lieutenant colonel in the Virginia militia. Virginia's General Assembly subsequently passed an act that authorized the governor to mount an expedition to attack any of Virginia's "western enemies."[4]

Governor Henry's instructions to Clark were carefully crafted and vague to prevent compromise of the details of the plan. In short, Clark was authorized to enlist seven companies of 50 men each from any county in Virginia for three months' service in the Kentucky region under his command. Clark was also given wide discretion on how to best employ his troops. A second set of secret instructions gave Clark authority to proceed to the enemy's settlements beyond Kaskaskia, including Vincennes and Detroit.[5]

Over the next several weeks, Clark selected his second-in-command and company commanders, and began recruiting troops in Virginia's eastern counties. Additional troops were recruited in the northern Holston settlements in southwestern Virginia.

Clark had planned to launch his campaign by early spring 1778, but he was unable to enlist the numbers of troops authorized by the Virginia assembly in time to mount a spring expedition, and was to delay until early summer. Even though he was still only able to assemble a small force of 175 men, Clark decided to launch his expedition on June 24. Clark's expedition departed Corn Island in the Ohio River just north of Louisville. His men pulled their boats upstream for nearly a mile to get into the right channel for shooting the rapids. Clark had decided not to travel all the way to Kaskaskia by boat, since the British carefully monitored the river traffic at the junction of the Ohio and Mississippi Rivers. Instead he followed the Ohio only as far as its junction with the Tennessee River. From that location, he planned to march overland some 120 miles to Kaskaskia.

After reaching the abandoned Fort Massac near the mouth of the Tennessee River, Clark's men hid their boats, and departed for Kaskaskia on June 29. Clark's column moved swiftly in single file, taking with them only what they could carry. His main concern was that Indian scouts might pick up their trail, and the element of surprise would be lost before they reached their objective. By the fourth day of the march, Clark's men were out of food, and he would not risk sending out hunting parties fearing they would alarm the enemy. Despite a shortage of rations, Clark continued to press his men hard, and by the evening of July 4, his exhausted men reached a farmhouse less than a mile from Kaskaskia. Thus far, the Kentuckians' presence was undetected by the townspeople and the garrison of the fort.

After searching the area near the farmhouse, Clark's men found boats to cross the river. He then split his force into two detachments; one would occupy the town, while Clark would lead the second detachment to seize the fort under the cover of darkness. Clark's detachment broke into the fort meeting no resistance, and quickly captured the entire garrison including the fort's commander. The Americans also captured a collection of documents and correspondence between the fort's commander and his superior, Governor Henry Hamilton. Meanwhile, the other detachment raced into the town of some one thousand people, shouting in French that the fort had been taken, and warning the citizens to stay in their houses. Once the raiders secured all the roads leading in and out of the town, the citizens were ordered to turn in all of their arms, or face execution. The terrified citizens promptly complied. Interrogation of the town's leading citizens then began. Clark's intention was to determine what level of support and sympathy for the British existed among the town's citizens. After daybreak on July 5, Clark allowed the citizens to emerge from their homes, but Clark kept the townspeople off balance by ordering the arrest of the town's militia leaders. When the town elders approached Clark, he informed them that the citizens could go about their business, but no one could leave town. It soon became apparent to Clark that the French population of the town had little knowledge of the American Revolution, and had just followed the orders of their pro-British commandants at the fort.

Once Kaskaskia was secured, Clark turned his attention to the other Illinois settlements that were administered by the British lieutenant governor at Detroit.

Clark sent his second-in-command, Captain Joseph Bowman, with 30 mounted men to seize the town of Cahokia located about 50 miles north of Kaskaskia. Bowman forced the surrender of the town, and then succeeded in getting the majority of its citizens to sign an oath that they would not longer give their support to the British cause.

Having established his operating base at Kaskaskia, Clark began preparations to capture the British Fort Sackville located at Vincennes, a town almost as large as Kaskaskia. The fort and town of Vincennes were located almost two hundred miles east of Kaskaskia on the Wabash River. It was a strategically important location for the Americans. If the Americans could seize the British post, they would be able to threaten the Indian tribes that posed the greatest danger to the Kentucky settlements. Moreover, once Vincennes was in American hands, it could be used as a staging area for an attack on Detroit.

Soon after he seized Kaskaskia, Clark sent his scouts to the Vincennes area to determine the status of its defenses. The scouts reported that the British officer in command at Vincennes had already departed for Detroit, and the French-speaking citizens in the area would not oppose an American takeover of the area. Clark quickly dispatched Captain Leonard Helm to take command of the fort. With Vincennes and Kaskaskia in American hands, most of the Indians inhabiting the Illinois country were neutralized. During late August 1778, Clark met with the leaders of a number of tribes, and succeeded in convincing most of them to cooperate with the Americans. This was the most important achievement of Clark's 1778 campaign, since the British strategy in the northwest depended almost completely on the military power of their Indian allies.[6]

Having accomplished the military objectives of his 1778 campaign, Clark soon realized the weaknesses in his strategy of forward defense. By fall, the number of troops at his disposal became a serious problem. The six-month enlistments of his militia troops were about to expire. Clark had managed to convince some one hundred men to extend their enlistments for eight months, but an almost equal number refused to do so. As a consequence, he was forced to drastically reduce the size of the garrisons in the towns and forts that he had captured. To disguise how small his army had become, Clark ordered his commanders to avoid assembling their men for parades or other gatherings where British scouts could count their numbers. Clark's other major problem was supplying his troops. He received little support from Virginia and the Kentucky settlements, so he was forced to depend on the Illinois country and Spanish-occupied St. Louis to supply his needs. Since the Continental and Virginia governments had failed to honor the bills forwarded by Clark, he was forced to pledge his own property and credit to purchase supplies. It was soon apparent that Clark was isolated in the Illinois region with too few resources to sustain his forward defense strategy. The British were also aware of Clark's weaknesses, and were determined to recapture Fort Sackville and the town of Vincennes before winter set in.

On October 7, 1778, British Governor Hamilton set out from Detroit with a small force of British officers, Canadian militia and Indians to recapture Fort Sackville. Gathering more Indian allies as he traveled south, Hamilton completed the arduous six-hundred-mile journey in 71 days, arriving in the Vincennes area on December 17. He had little difficulty in seizing the fort, and succeeded in capturing its commander, Captain Leonard Helm. Hamilton immediately put his men to work improving the fortifications, while he sought to regain the allegiance of the French-speaking citizens, and Indian tribes in the region. His efforts met with little success, since the news that France had entered the war on the side of the Americans had reached the frontier, and the Indians around Vincennes still feared that Clark would return to the area. Nevertheless, Hamilton decided to remain at Vincennes for the winter, and then resume his campaign to regain control of the Illinois country in the spring. It was a decision he would soon regret.

Governor Hamilton assumed that George Rogers Clark lacked the resources and manpower to recapture Vincennes, particularly during the winter months. His agents reported that Clark had only a few widely scattered troops, and that his men were worn out, and their morale and discipline were at low ebb. Furthermore, the weather was unfavorable for a winter campaign. Although the months of December, January, and February were warmer than normal, they were also exceedingly wet. Most of the Illinois country was flooded making river travel hazardous, and overland movement almost impossible. Confident that the Americans would not make an attempt to recapture Vincennes that winter, Hamilton was not concerned when most of his Indian allies, and many of the French-speaking militia, returned to their homes for the winter. By mid-December, Hamilton's force of six hundred men had dwindled to fewer than one hundred.[7]

Clark was quite aware of the enemy situation at Vincennes and Fort Sackville, but he was frustrated that he had not received any intelligence, support, or guidance from Virginia's government. In early February 1779, Clark wrote to Virginia's governor, Patrick Henry, complaining that, ". . . it is now near twelve months since I have had the least intelligence from you, I almost despair of any relief sent me."[8] In the same letter, Clark described in detail Hamilton's efforts to improve the fortifications at Fort Sackville, and his efforts to recruit local tribes for a spring offensive writing, "They are very busy in repairing the fort, which will shortly be very strong; one brass 6-pounder, two iron 4-pounders and all kinds of warlike stores, making preparation for the reduction of the Illinois."[9] After describing his situation and that of the enemy, Clark boldly wrote that he intended to "risqué the whole on a single battle."[10] Clark was taking a huge risk, and he knew it. If he failed to capture Fort Sackville his career would be over, and it would possibly cost him his life and those of his men. More importantly, it would leave the Kentucky settlements at the mercy of the "Hair Buyer" and his Indian allies.

Two days after he penned what could have been his last letter to the Virginia authorities, Clark launched his expedition to recapture Vincennes. Preparations had been underway for more than a month. Realizing that he could expect no support from across the mountains, Clark was forced to rely on the inhabitants of the Illinois country to provide provisions, stores, and necessary winter clothing for the long winter march. He also needed volunteers to fill his depleted ranks. According to Clark, "The whole country took fire at the alarm and every order was executed with cheerfulness by every description of the inhabitants—preparing provisions, encouraging volunteers, etc.—and, as we had plenty of stores, every man was completely rigged with what he could desire to withstand the coldest weather."[11]

Clark's plan to retake Vincennes depended on the speed, surprise, and stamina of his troops, and was heavily influenced by environmental conditions in the Illinois area. He planned to march his troops east from Kaskaskia over two hundred miles of prairies and lowlands to reach Vincennes on the Wabash River. Most of the supplies, stores, and artillery would be moved by a "large Mississippi boat" that Clark had purchased and had converted into an armed row-galley mounting two 4-pounders, and four large swivel guns. With a crew of 46 men, the galley would depart on February 4, and proceed up the Ohio River to the mouth of the Wabash River. The galley would then force its way up the Wabash to the mouth of the White River, where it would remain hidden awaiting Clark's approach by land. The galley would also be able to block any British attempt to escape the Vincennes area by moving down the Wabash. It was a risky plan. Clark knew full well that the rivers in the region had passed the flood stage, and most of the country he had to traverse was under at least several inches of water. Fortunately, the temperatures in the region were unseasonably mild. Nevertheless, it was a high-risk military operation.

On February 4 and 5, Clark's force was reinforced by the arrival of two volunteer companies composed mostly of French-speaking inhabitants of the Illinois region. With the reinforcements, Clark's force numbered around 170 men.[12] After receiving a blessing from a Catholic priest, Clark's troops crossed the Kaskaskia River at midafternoon on February 5, and began their long march across the muddy prairies and flooded lowlands. Clark was well aware of the trials that lay ahead during the march, and put a high priority on maintaining his men's morale. He later wrote,

> My object now was to keep the men in spirits. I suffered them to shoot game on all occasions and feast on them, like Indians' war dances, each company by turns inviting the other for their feasts, which was the case everynight . . . Myself and principal officers hailing on the woodsmen, shouting now and then, and running as much through the mud and waster as any of them.[13]

The weather was awful from the start. The daytime temperatures were relatively mild for the season, but most of the marches were made in daylong drizzly rains. The few roads that existed were covered with mud and water. Traveling without tents, Clark's men gathered around huge bonfires at night to dry their soaked clothing. When Clark's column reached the relatively flat level plains of south central Illinois, they found the entire area under several inches of water due to poor drainage.[14] Small rivers and streams had become formidable obstacles, and in some cases, trees were felled to enable the men to cross the flooded waterways.[15]

On February 13, Clark's men reached two branches of the Little Wabash River. A distance of nearly three miles normally separated the two waterways, but both branches had overflowed their banks, becoming a single obstacle to cross. The water depth ranged between 3 and 4 feet, and the distance to the nearest high ground on the opposite hills was nearly five miles. Even though the men had gorged themselves on buffalo meat the day before, they were exhausted.[15] Clark called a halt, and set his men to work on building a canoe to ferry his supplies and the sick and exhausted men across the obstacle. Work on the canoe was completed by 4:00 p.m. on the following day. It took the remainder of that day, and the following two days to cross the two branches of the Wabash, and the flooded area between them. The first men across built a platform above water on the opposite shore. Supplies were ferried across using the canoe, and piled on the scaffold. Then with Clark in the lead, the remainder of the men waded through the chest-deep water to reach the far shore.

When Clark's force encamped on the hills beyond the branches, he ordered his men not to fire their guns unless they were attacked. On February 16, Clark ordered his men to resume their march. It continued to rain throughout that day. Provisions were in short supply, since firearms could no longer be used for hunting. On the following day, Clark's column reached the flooded terrain near the Embara River. Clark's men continued marching through the mud and water until 8:00 p.m., searching for a piece of dry ground to spend the night. They finally found a piece of high ground barely large enough to accommodate all of the men. That same night a scouting party that had been sent ahead to locate and steal boats to cross the Embara River reported back to Clark with the bad news. They had found no boats, and were unable to cross the flooded Embara.

After spending a wet cold night, Clark's men were awakened by the firing of the morning reveille gun at Fort Sackville. Instead of attempting to cross the Embara, Clark decided to march his men downstream. About 2:00 p.m. on February 18, they reached the banks of the Wabash River about nine miles south of Vincennes, where they established camp. So far, Clark's force had not been detected by the British.

Clark's immediate challenge was to find a means of crossing the Wabash to attack Fort Sackville on the opposite shore. It was only a matter of time before the enemy detected Clark's force, and he could not afford to lose the element of surprise. He ordered four men across the river on a raft to steal canoes to facilitate a crossing. The men were unable to make landfall on the opposite bank, and returned to the shoreline. Clark then tried again using a small canoe. The canoe also failed to make the crossing, and returned quickly after spotting an enemy camp on the opposite shore. Clark was running out of options. He therefore dispatched the same canoe downriver to locate the armed galley that he supposed had arrived on the Wabash. The men were ordered to "proceed day and night," until they found the galley. In the interim, Clark set his men to work building a small fleet of canoes for the crossing. Clark noted that many of his French-speaking volunteers, "began, for the first time, to despair."[16] Many of the volunteers were disillusioned, and wanted to return to their homes. Clark and his officers continued to display an air of confidence and optimism, assuring their men that the mission would soon be successfully completed.

Around noon on February 20, a boat carrying five French-speaking citizens from Vincennes landed at Clark's riverside camp. They informed Clark that the garrison at Fort Sackville was unaware of their presence, and the citizens of the town were "well disposed" toward the Americans. They also reported that a brother of one of Clark's officers held prisoner at the fort had escaped, and set two canoes adrift on the river above the camp. Clark immediately sent one of his officers with a few men to locate the canoes. They located one of canoes and returned to camp. Clark realized that they could not delay any further.

At daybreak on February 21, Clark began ferrying his men across the river using two canoes. Two men in a canoe were spotted observing the crossings, but the men evaded capture by Clark's men. Once all of his men were across the Wabash, Clark wanted to march to Vincennes during the night of February 21–22, but his men were too exhausted after the river crossing. He therefore established a camp on a small hill where his men attempted to rest and recuperate. It rained throughout the night, and by morning the land around the hillside campsite was completely under water.

Once again, Clark led the way, stepping off into the waist-deep water. He hoped to reach a half-acre piece of high ground called the Sugar Camp by sundown. Those who were too weak and famished were transported across the flood plain in the two canoes. The two Frenchmen who had joined Clark's column told him that it was impossible to reach the town by foot before the water level fell. They also offered to return to Vincennes using Clark's two canoes and gather provisions, but Clark distrusted the men, and refused their offer. After a hard day's march across the flooded plain, the Americans reached the Sugar Camp at dusk.

The night of February 22–23 was the coldest night of the entire march. There was a hard freeze, and by dawn the ice was more than a half an inch thick near the shores of the river and across the flood plain. The rain had stopped, and Clark assembled his men in the bright morning sunlight for some final words of encouragement. He told them all they had to do was cross the plain, and enter the woods on the far side where they would have a full view of Vincennes and Fort Sackville. He then stepped off into the water to lead the march across the plain. After giving a loud huzza for their leader, the men formed a column and followed. Clark's officers organized the column, putting the strongest men to the front, and instructing them to keep passing the word back that the water was getting more shallow, and when they neared the woods to shout "land" to encourage their comrades. Clark had also assigned his deputy, Major Bowman, to march with a party of 25 hand-picked men at the rear of the long column to discourage stragglers from leaving the column. The weakest and extremely sick men were transported in the canoes.

At first the water was only knee deep, but by the time Clark passed the middle of the plain the water began to get deeper. By the time Clark neared the woods—where he had expected to find dry land—the water was up to his shoulders. The strongest and tallest men reached dry land first, and built fires, while the rest struggled to complete the march. The two canoes shuttled back and forth across the plain to pick up the weaker men and get them to dry land. Others clung to trees and floating logs until the canoes took them off. Amazingly, not a single man was lost crossing the flooded plain.

The men were exhausted by the time they reached dry land, but most recovered quickly after resting under a warming sun. Then by a stroke of good fortune, Clark's men spotted an Indian canoe filled with squaws and children crossing the plain that they had just crossed. Clark sent his two canoes to intercept the Indians. The Indian canoe was loaded with a hindquarter of buffalo, some corn, and cooking kettles. Broth was immediately made and served to the most sick and famished men. All others received a small portion of the meat.

After a short rest, Clark pushed on, ferrying his men across a long narrow lake in three canoes, and then marching a short distance to a copse of timber called Warriors Island about two miles from Vincennes, where they had a full view of the town and the fort. Moments later, Clark's men captured a man who was hunting ducks. The prisoner revealed that wall of the fort was recently completed and there were a large number of Indians in town. Clark estimated that there were upwards of six hundred inhabitants, Indians, and troops at Vincennes. Clark still had no idea of the location of his armed galley with 50 men and artillery onboard, but he could not afford to wait for its arrival. He knew that he had to move quickly to capture Fort Sackville before the British discovered his presence.

Clark knew that he had to neutralize the inhabitants of the town before launching an attack on the fort. He therefore had a placard made addressed to the inhabitants of Vincennes, alerting them that he intended to capture the fort that very night, and that they should remain in their houses. The placard also warned that if anyone attempted to warn the fort's garrison, they would be dealt with severely. He then sent the placard into town with the captive duck hunter. The man walked into town, and the town's citizens gathered in the town's square to read Clark's message. The residents were well aware of Clark's reputation and took his threats seriously. No one attempted to warn Fort Sackville's garrison.

In late afternoon, Clark marched his men slowly out of the woods toward the town. He selected a route across the plain that was in full view of onlookers in the town, but was not visible from the fort. To disguise his relatively small numbers, he marched and countermarched formations of men in and out of the trees with different colors displayed on long poles. The plain he had to cross to reach the town was partially flooded and not entirely flat. Clark took advantage of the terrain. Instead of marching straight into town, he marched his companies obliquely when he reached the low ground so they could not be easily counted by on-lookers in the town. He also mounted some of his officers on horseback, and had them ride back and forth between the formations shouting orders. By dusk, Clark's force had advanced halfway to the town. As dark-ness enveloped the plain, he altered his direction of march, and swept around the town. By 8:00 p.m. his men had gained the heights behind the town. There was still no indication that the garrison at Fort Sackville was on alert.

In fact, Lieutenant Governor Hamilton had received some informa-tion that indicated an enemy force might be in close proximity to Vin-cennes. On the afternoon of February 22, a patrol that had been pursuing deserters returned to Fort Sackville. The patrol leader, Captain Francis Maisonville, informed Hamilton that he had seen 14 campfires on the east side of the Wabash, "about four leagues below the fort, and he con-cluded that they must be Virginians."[17] Hamilton immediately sent out a 20-man patrol led by two trusted officers to confirm "who these people might be."[18] As a precaution, Hamilton moved ammunition from the magazine to the fort's blockhouses. The garrison also erected scaffolding on the north and south walls of the fort to serve as firing platforms. As a further precaution, Hamilton ordered the town's militia commander to take up arms, and ordered a recently purchased quantity of Indian corn and rum moved to the fort. Otherwise, Hamilton made no other prepa-rations for the fort's defense, and the garrison went on with their daily activities. At least one of the town's militia commanders conspired with Clark—Captain Bosseron offered his militia company's services to Clark, and provided him with a store of powder that he had secreted in town.

After gaining the rear of the town, Clark ordered Lieutenant Bailey and 20 men to move into a position where they could begin firing on the fort. Meanwhile, he moved his main body into the "strongest part of the town."[19] Lieutenant Bailey's men opened fire on the fort just after the garrison's evening roll call ended. At first, Hamilton thought the gunfire was from some drunken revelers in the town, and was not unduly con-cerned. When the firing continued, he walked from his quarters to the parade ground where he found out otherwise. One sergeant had been wounded in the first burst of rifle fire, and his troops were running for cover. He quickly ordered his men to take up arms, and man the blockhouses and firing platforms. As darkness descended, the firing increased in intensity. Clark sent reinforcements from the town to fire on the fort from three different sides.

Meanwhile, Clark was busy reconnoitering the town and the fort's defenses. He discovered that the cannon mounted in the blockhouses had only limited fields of fire, and could not be depressed sufficiently to fire on attackers who were close to the walls of the fort. He quickly ordered construction of breastworks close to the fort. Clark had only one or two men wounded, but his expert riflemen were exacting a toll on the fort's defenders. At least four of Hamilton's men were wounded and unable to continue the fight. Although, the number wounded at this point was not large, Hamilton was concerned since his garrison numbered fewer than 80 men. Due to the severe cold, the defenders were forced to light fires, which gave Clark's riflemen another advantage. Since the log pickets of the stockade were not properly aligned or closely spaced, the riflemen could see their enemies moving about inside the fort.

Clark was not concerned with the militia that remained in town, but he remained concerned about the Indians camped around Vincennes. One local chief offered to join the fight, but Clark refused the offer. In principle, he did not believe in using Indians to attack his enemies. When Hamilton's 25-man reconnoitering party heard the firing at the fort, they doubled back, and all but two of the men slipped back into the fort during a lull in the firing. Captain Bowman wrote in his journal that Clark sent a party to intercept them, but missed them. Clark preferred to have them inside the fort rather than outside where they could organize the Indians who wanted to stay loyal to the British.

Around 4:00 a.m. the firing slackened, then resumed again at sunrise. The cannon located in the blockhouses opened fire on the houses closest to the fort, but Clark's riflemen poured fire through the blockhouse loopholes, silencing the guns and wounding two of the artillerymen. Another man was wounded while walking across the fort's parade ground. Clark's men had excellent cover, and fired on the fort from two breastworks constructed during the night. One large breastwork was located 200 yards from the fort's walls, and another smaller breastwork was within 30 yards.[20]

Clark and his deputy commander, Bowman, decided not to launch an all-out assault on the fort that day. He only had 170 men, and his reinforcements were aboard the armed galley *Willing*. The *Willing* also carried his artillery, and he had no expectation that it would arrive that day. Major Clark and Captain Bowman agreed that the proper course of action was to persuade Hamilton to surrender the fort without delay. At 11:00 a.m. on February 24, Clark sent an emissary under a flag of truce to demand the fort's surrender. Clark understood psychology and framed his demands in the harshest terms writing as follows:

> Sir In order to save yourself from the Impending Storm that now Threatens you I order you to Immediately surrender yourself up with all your Garrison Stores &c. &c. for if I am obliged to storm, you may depend upon such Treatment justly due to a Murderer beware of destroying Stores of any kind or any papers or letters that is in your possession or hurting one house in the Town for by heavens if you do there shall be no Mercy shewn you.[21]

Hamilton's response was curt and precise without a hint of any accommodation to Clark's demands. "Lieutenant Governor Hamilton acquaints Colonel Clarke, that neither he or his garrison are to be prevailed on by threats to act in a manner unbecoming of the character of British Subjects."[22]

After receiving Hamilton's reply, Clark ordered his men to resume firing on the fort. The rifle fire was extremely accurate, and Hamilton's men hesitated to expose themselves to fire a shot. After several minutes, Hamilton began to have doubts about the reliability of the local militia troops inside the fort. He had read Clark's surrender demand to his men, and his reply. The English-speaking defenders stood by Hamilton to a man promising that they would stick to him "as the shirt on his back," but the French-speaking militiamen, including their sergeants, "hung their heads," muttering that it was hard to fight against their friends and family members who had joined forces with the Americans. Hamilton decided that he had no other recourse but surrender, since half of Fort Sackville's garrison could not be counted on in a fight to the finish.

About noon, firing from the fort ceased, and an officer emerged under a flag of truce. Clark ordered his men to hold their fire. Hamilton's proposal stated that he would surrender the fort, provided that he and his men were granted honorable terms. He also requested that Clark to come to the fort to confer with him. Clark rejected Hamilton's proposal, demanding the fort's immediate surrender. He also rejected Hamilton's proposal that he enter the fort to confer personally with him. Clark gave Hamilton 30 minutes to surrender, indicating that he could no longer restrain his men. Before the time expired, Hamilton sent Clark another message that proposed a three-day truce during which neither side could construct any further works, while final surrender terms were negotiated. Clark rejected that proposal as well, but agreed to meet Hamilton near Saint Xavier's Catholic Church.

Clark viewed the meeting with Hamilton as an opportunity to intimidate his adversary, and convince his Indian allies that their British allies could do nothing to protect them. Unbeknownst to Hamilton, Clark's men had ambushed a small party of French and Indians returning from a raid on the Kentucky settlements. In a short fight, Clark's men had killed three Indians, and captured the rest. Clark summarily ordered the execution of the prisoners by tomahawk. Two Frenchmen were spared after their relatives appealed to Clark, and one Indian was also spared since his father had once befriended one of Clark's officers. The other four Indians were tomahawked in full view of the townspeople and the fort, and their bodies were unceremoniously tossed in the river, while Hamilton waited at the church to meet Clark.

Hamilton was shocked when Clark and his deputy arrived at the meeting place covered in blood and sweat. Clark's and Hamilton's accounts of the meeting vary, but both reveal that Clark was waging psychological warfare against his adversary by exaggerating the size of his force (claiming he had eight hundred men), and demonstrating that he had detailed knowledge of conditions at the fort including the discontent among the French members of the garrison. He also implied that his troops were impatient, and wanted to storm the fort immediately to exact revenge on the defenders. Clark also got personal with the Governor, and accused him of having the innocent blood of American women and children on his hands. Hamilton tried to shift the blame to his superiors for ordering him to incite the Indians to raid the Kentucky settlements. Clark was in no mood for further negotiations, and advised Hamilton to return to the fort and prepare for battle. Before Hamilton reached the fort, Captain Bowman intercepted him. Bowman told Hamilton that Clark would send him final surrender terms, and would allow him only 30 minutes to respond.

Colonel Clark's terms included five articles as follows:

1st Lt. Gov. Hamilton engages to deliver up to Col. Clark Fort Sackville as it is at present with all stores, ammunition, provisions, &

2nd. The Garrison will deliver themselves up as Pris. Of War to march out with their arms accouterments, Knapsacks &

3d. The Garrison to be delivered up tomorrow morning at 10 o'clock.

4th. Three days to be allowed to the Garrison to settle their accounts with the traders of this place and inhabitant.

5th. The officers of the Garrison to be allowed their necessary baggage &

(signed) Post Vincents 24 Feb. 1779 G. R. Clark[23]

Clark's threats and intimidation had the desired effect on Lieutenant Governor Hamilton. Even though Hamilton still had the means to resist, he decided to agree to Clark's surrender terms. His reply simply read:

Agreed to for the following reasons—remoteness from succour, the state and quantity of Provisions & the unanimity of officers and men on its expediency, the Honerable terms allowd and lastly the confidence in a generous Enemy.

(signed) H. Hamilton Lt Gov & Superintend.[24]

After receiving Hamilton's reply, Clark posted guards, and dispatched patrols to prevent anyone escaping from the fort. That night Clark's men got their best night's sleep since leaving Kaskaskia. The surrender ceremony took place the following morning, and the American flag flew once more over Fort Sackville. Two days later, the American galley *Willing* arrived at Vincennes with the artillery and reinforcements. Strong river currents on the Ohio and Wabash Rivers had detained her.

The state of Virginia treated Lieutenant Governor Hamilton as a war criminal because he had encouraged and incited Indian raids on the Kentucky settlements. He was sent to Williamsburg, Virginia where he was placed under arrest by order of Thomas Jefferson, Virginia's new governor. General Washington eventually granted him parole, and in 1781 he was exchanged, and permitted to travel to London. He later returned to Canada, and became deputy governor of Quebec.

After capturing Vincennes, George Rogers Clark planned to mount an expedition in June 1779, to seize the British fort at Detroit. He estimated that he could capture Detroit with three hundred men, but his numbers were still far below that. He therefore moved most of his troops back to the Kaskaskia area to disguise his true intentions, and to recruit additional troops. After arriving at Kaskaskia, he began making preparations for the expedition against Detroit. Virginia provided only a pittance of the money Clark requested, and he personally assumed a substantial debt by purchasing his own supplies. By late spring, his plans for launching the expedition in June began to fade, when only 150 riflemen arrived from Virginia instead of the five hundred he had been promised. Nevertheless, Clark moved his understrength force to Vincennes in June, still hoping to get underway to Detroit that summer. By mid-summer, he received disheartening news. The British garrison at Detroit had received reinforcements. Clark realized that his window of opportunity was closed, and Detroit lay beyond his grasp.

In 1781, Governor Thomas Jefferson promoted George Rogers Clark to brigadier general in the Virginia militia. Jefferson also appointed Clark as commander of all Virginia militia forces in the Kentucky and Illinois counties.

It was largely due to the efforts and courage of George Rogers Clark and his men that Britain officially ceded the lands north of the Ohio River and west of the Appalachians to the United States at the end of the Revolutionary War. On July 13, 1787, Virginia and the other Atlantic seaboard states relinquished all claims to the lands west of Pennsylvania and northwest of the Ohio River, and the area was organized as an incorporated territory of the United States commonly known as the Northwest Territory. The states of Ohio, Indiana, Illinois, Michigan, Wisconsin, and the portion of Minnesota east of the Mississippi River were later created from the Northwest Territory.

George Rogers Clark's operation to seize Vincennes and Fort Sackville was a brilliant strategic victory. More remarkable is the fact that he accomplished his mission in an austere harsh winter environment with minimal support from the state of Virginia, and without any support from the Continental Army. Without doubt, it was a high-risk operation, but the outcome of the mission justified the risk. The capture of Lieutenant Governor Hamilton was a major setback to Britain's efforts to retain control of the lands west of the Appalachians. The British strategy of using the Native American tribes to drive the American settlers from the lands west of the Appalachians was cruel, and not in the best interests of the Native American tribes. The tribes that supported the British paid a heavy price for their service, and were eventually driven from the lands east of the Mississippi.

EPILOGUE

From colonial times to present-day conflicts, special operations have been an integral part of US military operations. Over the past 234 years, special operations forces have continued to evolve and develop following experience in wars and conflict and in response to advances in technology. Unfortunately, it was not until the late 20th century that special operations forces became a permanent part of the US armed forces. Prior to that special operations forces witnessed periods of improvisation, rapid wartime buildups and subsequent post-conflict drawdowns. But fortunately, the lessons learned in earlier wars were recorded, and have now been incorporated into a doctrine for special operations.

An analysis of the special operations conducted during the Revolutionary War reveals that they all adhered to certain principles of war. In particular, they all emphasized the importance of security, simplicity, surprise, speed, and a sense of purpose. By adhering to those principles, special operations forces were able to achieve relative superiority at the pivotal moments during the operation, and accomplish their mission.

Several other fundamental truths can be learned from the special operations during the Revolutionary War. First, quality is always more important than quantity when selecting troops for participation in special operations. Special operations personnel must have extraordinary stamina, courage, commitment, and specialized skills to survive for extended periods of time behind enemy lines with limited external support. In the end people, not equipment, make the difference. Most of the special operations described in this book were conducted by volunteers personally selected by the leaders of those operations, based on their proven abilities and skills. As a result, units such as Ethan Allen's Green Mountain Boys, Knowlton's Rangers, Whitcomb's Rangers, and the Continental Marines developed exceptionally strong unit cohesion and morale, which was conducive to the success of their missions. In addition, the leadership qualities of the men who commanded the special operations described in this book contributed immeasurably to mission accomplishment. Without question, the commanders were bold, courageous, and intelligent leaders, who persevered in the face of adversity. Moreover, they all understood the importance of planning, preparation, and rapid execution as well as adherence to the principles of security, speed, simplicity and surprise during a mission.

Secondly, there must be a clear and unambiguous chain of command for each special operation. Ethan Allen's capture of Fort Ticonderoga clearly demonstrates this point. The entire mission was jeopardized when Benedict Arnold attempted to assume command of the operation hours before the attack was to commence. As the war continued, General Washington recognized the need for special operation forces and became intimately involved in planning special operation missions. As commander-in-chief of the Continental Army, he often reserved his right to personally approve such operations. As the war continued, theater commanders—such as Nathaniel Greene in the southern theater—began to exploit the capabilities of militia forces by supporting their operations with highly mobile cavalry and dragoon units from the Continental Army such as Lee's Legion and Colonel William Washington's light dragoons.

Washington also made full use of militia and partisan forces to harass and disrupt British and Loyalist operations in contested areas. Operating in small units, those forces were able to interdict enemy supply and communication lines and conduct attacks on enemy outposts. In addition, local militia and partisans provided valuable intelligence on enemy troop movements in areas that were not accessible to Continental troops, and provided forward defense for the army. The unconventional style of warfare employed by local militia and partisan forces was a prototype for future unconventional warfare operations.

An analysis of the special operations conducted during the American Revolution demonstrates that ad-hoc volunteer forces could successfully conduct special operations after the outbreak of hostilities, or even during military campaigns. However, the time required to organize, train, and equip special operations forces is the price any nation pays for not having a standing special force as part of their armed forces. Due to the unstable nature of world politics in the 21st century, and the rising threat of terrorism and asymmetric warfare, it is absolutely necessary to have standing special operations forces.

ENDNOTES

Prologue

1. Adam J. Hirsch, "The Collision of Military Cultures in Seventeenth-Century New England," in *The Journal of American History* (Vol. 74, No. 4, March 1988), pp. 1191–1192.
2. Frank E. Grizzard, D. Boyd Smith, *Jamestown Colony: A Political, Social, and Cultural History* (Santa Barbara, CA: 2007), pp. 128–132.
3. Ibid, p.133.
4. Kevin McBride, David Naumec, *Battle of Mystic Fort Documentation Plan* (Mashantucket, CT, 2009), pp. 8–12. John Mason, Paul Royster (ed.), *A Brief History of the Pequot War (1736)* (Lincoln, NE: 2007), pp. 4–21.
5. Ibid.
6. Charles H. Lincoln, *Narratives of the Indian Wars, 1675–1699* (New York: 1913), pp. 12–73.
7. Ibid, pp.104–106.
8. Joseph J. Ellis, *His Excellency George Washington* (New York: 2004), pp. 13–15, 17–18.
9. Ibid, p. 22.
10. Edward P. Hamilton, *The French and Indian Wars* (New York: 1962), p. 190.
11. Robert Rogers, *Journals of Major Robert Rogers* (Albany, NY: 1883), pp. 96–103.
12. Ibid, pp. 102–103.
13. Ibid, pp. 141–149.

CHAPTER 1: The Capture of Fort Ticonderoga

1. Justin H. Smith, *Our Struggle for the Fourteenth Colony* (New York & London: 1907), p. 115.
2. Ibid, p. 111.
3. Ibid.

4. Ibid, p. 113.

5. Ibid.

6. John Pell, "Extract of a Biography of Ethan Allen," in *Bulletin of the Fort Ticonderoga Museum* (Vol. VIII, No. 2, July 1948), pp. 46–58.

7. Edward Mott, "Journal of Captain Edward Mott of Connecticut," in Henry Commager & Richard Morris, *Spirit of Seventy-six* (New York: 1995), p. 100.

8. James Kirby Martin, *Benedict Arnold Revolutionary Hero, An American Warrior Reconsidered* (New York & London: 1997), p. 67.

9. Ibid, p. 65.

10. Ibid, p. 69.

11. Joint Publication (JP), 3-05 Joint Special Operations (18 April 2011), pp. III–1.

12. Daniel Chipman, *Memoir of Colonel Seth Warner* (Middlebury: 1848), p. 137.

13. Epaphras Bull, "Journal of Epaphras Bull," in *Bulletin of the Fort Ticonderoga Museum* (Vol. VIII, No. 2, July 1948), p. 40.

14. Benedict Arnold to Continental Congress, May 1775.

15. Hugh Moore, *Memoir of Ethan Allen* (Plattsburgh, NY: 1834), p. 93.

16. Allen French, *The Taking of Ticonderoga in 1775, A study of Captors and Captives* (Cambridge: 1928), p. 41.

17. Ibid.

18. Moore, p. 95.

19. French, p. 43.

20. Richard B. Smith, *Ethan Allen and Capture of Fort Ticonderoga: America's First Victory* (Charleston & London: April 2010), p. 85.

21. Moore, pp. 95–96.

CHAPTER 2: **The New Providence Raid**

1. Edmund C. Burnett, *Letters of Members of the Continental Congress* (Washington, 1921), pp. 284–285.

2. Charles R. Smith, *Marines in the Revolution, a History of the Continental Marines in the American Revolution 1775–1783* (Washington, DC: 1975), pp. 12–13.

3. Ibid, p. 41.

4. Ibid.

5. Edward Field, *Esek Hopkins Commander-in-Chief of The Continental Navy During the American Revolution* (Providence, RI: 1898), pp. 84–87.

6. William Fowler Jr, *Rebels Under Sail* (New York: 1976), p.48.

7. Field, p. 104.

8. Smith, p. 42.

9. Samuel E. Morison, *John Paul Jones* (Annapolis, MD: 1959), p. 66.

10. Smith, p. 46.

11. Ibid, p. 48.

12. Ibid, p. 49.

13. Edward Field, *Esek Hopkins, Commander-in-Chief of the Continental Navy* (Providence RI: 1898), p. 113.
14. "Journal of the Schooner, *St John*," in *Naval Documents of the American Revolution, Volume 4, 1776* (Washington: 1969), p. 173.
15. Smith, p. 50.
16. Ibid, pp. 381–382.
17. Ibid, p. 325.
18. Ibid.
19. Samuel Nicholas, "Extract of a Letter From Captain Samuel Nicholas, April 1776," in Smith, *Marines in the Revolution, a History of the Continental Marines in the American Revolution 1775–1783*, pp. 381–382.
20. Smith, p. 68.
21. Nicholas, p. 381.
22. John Trevett, "Diary of John Trevett," in Smith, *Marines in the Revolution, a History of the Continental Marines in the American Revolution 1775–1783*, p. 325.
23. Esek Hopkins, *Inventory of British Stores and Arms* (March 3, 1776), in George Washington Papers at the Library of Congress, 1741–1799: Series 4. General Correspondence. 1697–1799.
24. "Commodore Esek Hopkin's Sailing Orders from New Providence" in *Naval Documents of the American Revolution, Vol 4* (Washington: 1969), p. 403.
25. "John Hancock to Esek Hopkins, June 14, 1776," in *Letters of Members of the Continental Congress* (Washington: 1921), p. 489.

CHAPTER 3: Knowlton's Rangers

1. David McCullough, *1776* (New York, London, Toronto and Sydney: 2005), p. 109.
2. Henry Woodward, *Historical Address, Statue of Colonel Thomas Knowton Ceremonies at the Unveiling* (Hartford CT: 1895), p. 32.
3. Ashbel Woodward, *Memoir of Col. Thomas Knowlton of Ashford, Connecticut* (Boston, 1861), p. 7.
4. George Scheer & Hugh Rankin, *Rebels and Rankin* (New York: 1957), p. 58.
5. Woodward, p.13.
6. Ibid.
7. Ibid.
8. McCullough, p. 180.
9. Scheer & Rankin, p. 175.
10. George Seymour, *Documentary Life of Nathan Hale* (Whitefish MT: 2010), pp. 315–318.
11. Ibid, p. 308.
12. Moses Fargo, *Orderly book and journals kept by Connecticut men* (Hartford CT: 1899), p. 193.

13. Ibid, p. 194.
14. McCullough, p. 183.
15. Ashbel, p. 14.
16. Henry Johnston, *The Campaign of 1776 around New York and Brooklyn* (New York: 1878), p. 62.
17. *Thomas Knowlton and His Rangers: The Taproot of U.S. Army Intelligence.* p. 4.
18. Joseph Martin, *A Narrative of a Revolutionary Soldier* (New York: 2001), p. 37.
19. Scheer & Rankin, p. 184.
20. Ibid.
21. Ibid, p. 185.
22. Pension Application of David Thorpe.
23. Scheer & Rankin, p. 185.
24. George Washington to the President of the Continental Congress, Sept. 18, 1776.
25. Scheer & Rankin, p. 184.
26. Johnson, pp. 87–88.
27. General Orders Headquarters, Harlem Heights, Sept. 17, 1776
28. William Phelps, *The Life and Death of America's First Spy* (New York: 2008), p. 156.
29. Ibid, p. 174.
30. Ibid, p. 192.

CHAPTER 4: Whitcomb's Rangers
1. Benjamin Whitcomb, "Journal of a Scout from Crown Point to St Johns Chamblee," in *The American Historical Record* (Philadelphia: 1872), pp. 437–438.
2. William Ketchum, *Saratoga Turning Point of America's Revolutionary War* (New York: 1997), p. 161.
3. Michael Barbieri, "Benjamin Whitcomb's Independent Corps of Rangers" in *Rutland Historical Society Quarterly* (Vol VIII No. 4, 1978), p. 29.
4. Ibid.
5. Ketchum, pp. 101–102.
6. Ibid, p. 63.
7. John Ferling, *Almost a Miracle* (Oxford & New York: 2007), p. 216.
8. Ibid, p.219.

CHAPTER 5: John Paul Jones' Raids on Britain's Coast
1. Joseph Callo, *John Paul Jones, America's First Sea Warrior* (Annapolis MD: 2006), p. 8.
2. Ibid.
3. Ibid, pp. 12–13.
4. Ibid, p. 24.
5. Samuel Morison, *John Paul Jones* (Annapolis MD: 1959), p. 65.
6. Ibid.
7. Edward Field, *Esek Hopkins, Commander-in-Chief of The Continental Navy during the*

American Revolution, 1775 to 1778 (Providence RI: 1898), p. 161.

8. Morison, pp. 117–118.

9. George Preble & Walter Green, *Diary of Ezra Green, MD* (Boston: 1875), p. 18.

10. David McCullough, *John Adams* (New York, London, Sydney, & Singapore: 2001), p. 214.

11. Callo, p. 41.

12. Reginald De Koven, *The Life and Letters of John Paul Jones* (New York: 1913), pp. 247–248.

13. Ibid.

14. Charles R. Smith, *Marines in the Revolution* (Washington DC: 1975), p. 139.

15. Ibid.

16. Ibid, p. 140.

17. Ibid.

18. Preble & Green, p. 21.

19. Ibid.

20. Smith, p. 141.

21. Preble & Green, p. 22.

22. Ibid.

23. *Cumberland Chronicle Extraordinary* (April 23, 1778).

24. Morison, p. 175.

25. Don Seitz, *Paul Jones, His Exploits in the Irish Sea during 1778–1780* (New York: 1917), pp. 9–10.

26. Morison, p. 176.

27. James Otis, *The Life of John Paul Jones* (New York: 1900), p. 93.

28. Ibid.

29. *Morning Chronicle and London Advertiser, May 9, 1778.*

30. Ibid.

31. Morison, p. 200.

32. Ibid, p. 199.

33. Smith, p. 14.

CHAPTER 6: Partisan Warfare in the Northern Theater

1. *Department of Defense Joint Publication 1-02, Department of Defense Dictionary of Military and Associated Terms* (Washington DC: 2010), p. 161.

2. Ibid.

3. *Department of Defense Joint Publication 3-05, Special Operations* (Washington DC: April 18, 2011), GL-8.

4. Henry Commager & Richard Morris, *The Spirit of Seventy-Six: The Story of the American Revolution as told by Participants* (New York: 1995), p. 424.

5. Ibid, p. 527.

6. Ibid, p. 525.

7. Ibid.
8. Mark Kwasny, *Washington's Partisan War* (Kent, OH & London: 1996), p. 112.
9. David Fischer, *Washington's Crossing* (Oxford & New York: 2004), p. 171.
10. Michael Adelberg, *The American Revolution in Monmouth County: The Theatre of Spoil and Destruction* (Charleston, SC & London: 2010), p. 17.
11. Fischer, p. 172.
12. Adelberg, p. 18.
13. George Washington to William Heath, February 14, 1777.
14. Kwasny, pp. 114–115.
15. Adrian Leiby, *The Revolutionary War in the Hackensack Valley* (New Brunswick, NJ: 1992), p. 103.
16. Ibid, p. 127.
17. John Peebles, *John Peebles' American War: the Diary of a Scottish grenadier, 1776–1782* (Mechanicsburg, PA: 1998), p. 298.
18. Ibid, p. 300.
19. Kwasny, p. 119.
20. Ibid, p. 120.
21. Barbara Mitnick, *New Jersey in the American Revolution* (New Brunswick, NJ: 2005), p. 215.
22. Fischer, p. 419.
23. Mitnick, p. 51.

CHAPTER 7: The Rise of Partisan Warfare in the Southern Theater

1. Henry Commager & Richard Morris, *The Spirit of Seventy-Six: The Story of the American Revolution as told by Participants* (New York: 1995), p. 1111.
2. Ibid.
3. Ibid.
4. Ibid.
5. Ibid.
6. Ibid.
7. George Scheer & Hugh Rankin, *Rebels and Redcoats, the American Revolution through the Eyes of those Who Fought and Lived It* (New York: 1957), p. 402.
8. Ibid.
9. James Swisher, *The Revolutionary War in the Southern Backcountry* (Gretna, LA: 2008), p. 180.
10. Commager & Morris, p. 118.
11. Swisher, p. 181.
12. Commager & Morris, p. 1119.
13. Ibid, p. 1120.
14. Swisher, p. 183.
15. Ibid, p. 189.

16. Commager & Morris, p. 1123.
17. Ibid.
18. J. B. O. Landrum, *Colonial and Revolutionary History of Upper South Carolina* (Greenville, SC: 1897), pp. 129–131.
19. Ibid.
20. Swisher, p. 201.
21. M. M. Gilchrist, *Patrick Ferguson, A Man of Some Genius* (Edinburgh: 2003), pp. 20–35.
22. Wilma Dykeman, *With Fire and Sword* (Washington, DC: 1978), p. 29.
23. Gilchrist, p. 33.
24. Ibid, p. 40.
25. Lyman Draper, *Kings Mountain and its Heroes* (Cincinnati, OH: 1881), p. 198.
26. Ibid, p. 169.
27. Ibid, p. 379.
28. Dykeman, p. 44.
29. Draper, p. 204.
30. Dykeman, p. 49.
31. Draper, p. 206.
32. Ibid, p. 203.
33. Ibid, p. 208
34. Robert Dunkerly, *The Battle of Kings Mountain, Eyewitness Accounts* (Charleston, SC: 2007), p. 123.
35. Draper, pp. 210–211.
36. Dunkerly, pp. 137–138.
37. Dykeman, p. 56.
38. A. S. Salley, *Col. William Hill's Memoirs of the Revolution* (Columbia, SC: 1921), p. 23. Dunkerly, pp. 78–79.
39. Dunkerly, p. 25.
40. Ibid, p. 79.
41. Dykeman, p. 57.
42. Scheer & Rankin, pp. 417–418.
43. Ibid, p. 418.
44. Scheer & Rankin, p. 418.
45. Dunkerly, p. 20.
46. Pension application of Leonard Hise (Hice), S8713.
47. Pension application of John Fields S8471.
48. Dunkerly, p. 48.
49. Pension application of William Griffis R4323. Pension Statement of Frederick Fisher S20364.
50. Dunkerly, p. 92.
51. Dykeman, p. 65.

52. Commager & Morrris, p. 1144.
53. Dunkerly, pp. 141–143.
54. Ibid, p. 26.
55. Ibid.
56. Ibid, pp. 32–35.

CHAPTER 8: **The Whaleboat Wars**

1. George Washington to David Humphreys, December 23, 1780.
2. John Dann, *The Revolution Remembered—Eye Witness Accounts of the War for Independence* (Chicago, IL: 1980), pp. 324–325.
3. Charles Hall, *Life and Letters of Samuel Holden Parsons* (Binghampton, NY: 1905), pp. 97–98.
4. Mary Mitford, *Our Village* (London: 2011), pp. 301–308
5. Ibid.
6. Ibid.
7. Ibid.
8. David McCullough, *1776* (New York & London: 2005), p. 119.
9. Benjamin Tallmadge, *Memoir of Col. Benjamin Tallmadge* (New York: 1858), p. 5.
10. Ibid, p. 20.
11. Alexander Rose, *Washington's Spies* (New York: 2006), pp. 76–77.
12. Tallmadge, p. 29.
13. Rose, p. 280.
14. Tallmadge, p. 39.
15. Ibid.
16. George Washington to Benjamin Tallmadge, November 16, 1780.
17. Tallmadge, p. 41.
18. George Washington to Benjamin Tallmadge, November 28, 1780.
19. Rose, p. 241.
20. Donald Moran, "Sergeant Elijah Churchill of the Second Continental Light Dragoons," in *The Liberty Tree Newsletter, Sons of the American Revolution* (April 2007).
21. Joint Publication 3-05, *Special Operations* (Washington, DC: April 2011), p. GL-13.
22. Robert Tonsetic, *1781—The Decisive Year of the Revolutionary War* (Philadelphia: 2011), pp. 3–5.
23. Fred Cook, *What Manner of Men—Forgotten Heroes of the American Revolution* (New York: 1959), p. 275.
24. Barbara Mitnick, *New Jersey in the American Revolution* (New Brunswick, NJ & London: 2005), p. 58.
25. Mark Donnelly & Daniel Diehl, *Pirates of New Jersey: Plunder and High Adventure on the Garden State Coastline* (Mechanicsburg, PA: 2010), p. 58.
26. Cook, p. 280.

27. Ibid, p. 281.
28. Ibid, pp. 283–284.
29. Ibid, p. 287.

CHAPTER 9: George Rogers Clark's March to Vincennes

1. Lowell Harrison, *George Rogers Clark and the War in the West* (Lexington, KY: 1976), p. 1.
2. Ibid, p.5.
3. Ibid, p. 9.
4. Ibid, p. 17.
5. Ibid, p. 18.
6. Ibid, p. 35.
7. Ibid, p. 44.
8. Henry Commager & Richard Morris, *The Spirit of Seventy-Six, The Story of the American Revolution as told by Participants* (New York: 1955), p. 1042.
9. Ibid.
10. Ibid, p. 1043.
11. William English, *Conquest of the Country Northwest of the Ohio River 1778–1783 and Life of Gen. George Rogers Clark, Volume 1, Journal of Joseph Bowman* (Indianapolis, IN & St Louis, MO: 1897), pp. 255–256.
12. James Alton James, *George Rogers Clark Papers 1771–1781, Volume VIII* (Springfield, IL: 1912), p. 156.
13. George Scheer & Hugh Rankin, *Rebels and Rankin* (New York: 1957), p. 347.
14. English, p. 156.
15. Ibid, p. 157.
16. Ibid, p. 299.
17. James, pp. 185–186.
18. Ibid.
19. Ibid, pp. 160–168.
20. Ibid.
21. Ibid.
22. Ibid.
23. Ibid, p.168.
24. Ibid, p. 193.

BIBLIOGRAPHY

BOOKS

Adelberg, Michael S. *The American Revolution in Monmouth County: The Theatre of Spoil and Destruction (NJ)*. Charleston, SC: The History Press, 2010.

Beck, Alverda S. *The Correspondence of Esek Hopkins: Commander In Chief of the United States Navy*. Providence, RI: Roger Williams Press, 1933.

Brands, H. W. *The First American: The Life and Times of Benjamin Franklin*. New York, NY: Doubleday, 2000.

Brandt, Clare, *The Man in the Mirror: A Life of Benedict Arnold*. New York, NY: Random House, 1994.

Burnett, Edmund C. *Letters of Members of the Continental Congress*. Washington DC: The Carnegie Institution of Washington, 1921.

Callo, Joseph, *John Paul Jones: America's First Sea Warrior*. Annapolis, MD: Naval Institute Press, 2006.

Chadwick, Bruce, *The First American Army—The Untold Story of George Washington and the Men Behind America's First Fight for Freedom*. Naperville, IL: Sourcebooks, 2005.

Clark, William B. Ed. *Naval Documents of The American Revolution*. Washington DC: U.S. Government Printing Office, 1969.

Commager, Henry S. and Morris, Richard B. *The Spirit of Seventy-Six: The Story of the American Revolution as told by Participants*. New York, NY: Da Capo Press, 1995.

Cook, Fred, *What Manner of Men: Forgotten Heroes of the American Revolution*. New York, NY: William Morrow & Company, 1959.

Dann, John, *The Revolution Remembered: Eye Witness Accounts of the War for Independence*. Chicago, IL: University of Chicago Press, 1999.

De Koven, Mrs. Reginald, *The Life and Letters of John Paul Jones*. New York, NY: Charles Scribner's Sons, 1913.

Donnelly, Mark & Diehl, Daniel, *Pirates of New Jersey: Plunder and High Adventure on the Garden State Coastline.* Mechanicsburg PA: Stackpole Books, 2010.

Draper, Lyman, *Kings Mountain and its Heroes.* Cincinnati, OH: Peter G. Thomson, 1881. Dunkerly, Robert M. *The Battle of Kings Mountain: Eyewitness Accounts.* Charleston, SC & London: The History Press, 2007.

Dykeman, Wilma, *The Battle of Kings Mountain: With Fire and Sword.* Washington, DC: National Park Service U.S. Department of the Interior, 1978.

Ellis, Joseph J. *His Excellency George Washington.* New York, NY: Alfred A. Knopf, 2004.

English, William, *Conquest of the Country Northwest of the Ohio River 1778–1783* and *Life of Gen. George Rogers Clark, Volume II.* Indianapolis, IN & Kansas City MO: The Bowen-Merrill Company, 1897.

Ferling, John, *Almost a Miracle: The American Victory in the War of Independence.* Oxford & New York: Oxford University Press, 2007.

Field, Edward, *Esek Hopkins Commander in Chief of the Continental Navy during the American Revolution.* Providence RI: The Preston & Rounds Company, 1898.

Fischer, David Hackett, *Washington's Crossing.* Oxford & New York: Oxford University Press, 2004.

Fowler, William M. *Rebels Under Sail.* New York, NY: Charles Scribner's Sons, 1976.

French, Allen, *The Taking of Ticonderoga in 1775—A Study of Captors and Captives.* Cambridge MA: Harvard University Press, 1928.

Gilchrist, M.M. *Patrick Ferguson: A Man of some Genius.* Edinburgh, SCT: NMS Publishing, 2003.

James, James A. *George Rogers Clark Papers 1771–1781, Volume V & III.* Springfield, IL: Trustees of the Illinois State Historical Library, 1912.

Johnston, Henry P. *The Campaign of 1776 around New York and Brooklyn.* New York, NY: The Long Island Historical Society, 1878.

Ketchum, Richard M. *Saratoga Turning Point of America's Revolutionary War.* New York, NY: Henry Holt and Company, Inc. 1997.

Kwasny, Mark V. *Washington's Partisan War 1775–1783.* Kent, OH & London, England: The Kent State University Press, 1996.

Landrum, John B. *Colonial and Revolutionary History of Upper South Carolina.* Greenville, SC: Shannon & Co. Printers and Binders, 1897.

Lengle, Edward G. Ed. *The Glorious Struggle—George Washington's Revolutionary War Letters.* Washington DC: Smithsonian Books, 2007.

Leiby, Adrian C. *The Revolutionary War in the Hackensack Valley—The Jersey Dutch and the Neutral Ground, 1775–1783.* New Bruswick NJ: Rutgers University Press, 1992.

Lincoln, Charles H. *Narrative of the Indian Wars, 1675–1699.* New York NY: Charles Scribners Sons, 1913.

Mackesy, Piers, *The War for America 1775–1783.* Lincoln NE & London: University of Nebraska Press, 1993.

Martin, James K. *Benedict Arnold Revolutionary Hero—An American Warrior Reconsidered.* New York NY & London: New York University Press, 1997.

McCullough, David, *1776.* New York NY & London: Simon & Shuster, 2005.

McCullough, David, *John Adams.* New York NY & London: Simon & Shuster, 2001.

McRaven, William H. *Spec Ops: Case Studies in Special Operations Warfare: Theory and Practice.* Novato CA: Presidio Press, 1996.

Mitford, Mary R. *Our Village.* London: MacMillan & Co: 1893.

Mitnick, Barbara J. *New Jersey in the American Revolution.* New Brunswick NJ: River Gate Books, 2005.

Morison, Samuel E. *John Paul Jones—A Sailors Biography.* Annapolis MD: Naval Institute Press, 1999.

Otis, James, *The Life of John Paul Jones.* New York NY: Grosset & Dunlap Publishers, 1900.

Peebles, John, *John Peebles' American War: the Diary of a Scottish Grenadier, 1776–1782.* Mechanicsburg PA: Stackpole Books, 1998.

Phelps, M. William, *The Life and Death of America's First Spy.* New York NY: Thomas Dunn Books St. Martin's Press, 2008.

Rose, Alexander, *Washington's Spies—The Story of America's First Spy Ring.* New York NY: Bantam Dell, 2006.

Scheer, George F. & Rankin, Hugh F. *Rebels and Redcoats—The American Revolution through the Eyes of those Who Fought and Lived It.* New York NY: Da Capo Press, 1957.

Seitz, Don C. *Paul Jones—His Exploits in English Seas during 1778–1780.* New York NY: E.P. Dutton and Company, 1917.

Seymour, George D. *Documentary Life of Nathan Hale,* Whitefish MT: Kessinger Publishing, LLC, 2010.

Smith, Charles R. *Marines in the Revolution—A History of the Continental Marines in the American Revolution 1775–1783.* Washington DC: U.S. Government Printing Office, 1975.

Smith, Justin H. *Our Struggle for the Fourteenth Colony.* New York NY & London: The Knickerbocker Press, 1907.

Smith, Richard B. *Ethan Allen and the Capture of Fort Ticonderoga.* Charleston SC: The History Press, 2010.

Southern, Ed, *Voices of the American Revolution in the Carolinas.* Winston Salem NC:

John F. Blair Publisher, 2009/

Swisher, James K. *The Revolutionary War in the Southern Back Country*. New Orleans LA: Pelican Publishing Company, 2008.

Tonsetic, Robert L. *1781—The Decisive Year of the Revolutionary War*. Philadelphia PA: Casemate Publishers, 2011.

Wallace, William M. *Traitorous Hero—The Life and Fortunes of Benedict Arnold*. New York NY: Harpers and Brothers Publishers, 1954.

DIARIES, JOURNALS, AND MEMOIRS

Chipman, Daniel, *Memoir of Colonel Seth Warner*. Middlebury, VT: L. W. Clark: 1848.

Martin, Joseph P. *A Narrative of a Revolutionary Soldier*. New York NY: Signet Classic, 2001.

Fargo, Moses, *Orderly Book and Jouirnals kept by Connecticut Men While taking part in the American Revolution*. Hartford, CT: Connecticut Historical Society, 1899.

Preble, George & Green, Walter, *Diary of Ezra Green, M.D., Surgeon on board the Continental Ship-of-War "Ranger."* New Haven CT: Yale University Library, 2010.

Rogers, Robert, *Journals of Major Robert Rogers*. Albany NY: Joel Munsell's Sons, 1883.

Salley, A.S. Ed. *Colonel William Hill's Memoirs of the Revolution*. Columbia SC: Historical Commission of South Carolina, 1887.

Tallmadge, Benjamin, *Memoir of Col. Benjamin Tallmadge*. New York NY: Thomas Holman and Job Printer, 1858.

Woodward, Ashbel, *Memoir of Col. Thomas Knowlton, of Ashford, Connecticut*. Charleston SC: Nabu Press, 2010.

US GOVERNMENT PUBLICATIONS

Joint Publication 1-02, *Department of Defense Dictionary of Military and Associated Terms*. Washington DC: Department of Defense, 2012

Joint Publication 3-0, *Joint Operations*. Washington DC: Department of Defense, 2011.

Joint Publication 3-05. *Special Operations*. Washington D.C: Department of Defense, 2011.

CORRESPONDENCE

The correspondence cited in the text and endnotes can be found in a number of sources including: the Library of Congress American Memory Collection, George Washington Papers at the Library of Congress, 1741–1799, Journals of the Continental Congress, Volumes 19–21, the writings of George Washington from the original manuscript sources (Electronic Text Center, University of Virginia Library). An excellent online archives of letters from primary American, French and British Revolutionary War military and civilian leaders can be found on the Family Tales website, http://www.familytales.org/

PENSION APPLICATIONS/STATEMENTS

Revolutionary War Pension Records are held at the National Archives, Washington DC. Over ten thousand transcribed pension applications and 70 rosters from the southern campaign of the Revolutionary War can be accessed online at the web site, http://southerncampaign.org/pen/index.
htm

INDEX